The Shepherd's Calendar
by James Hogg

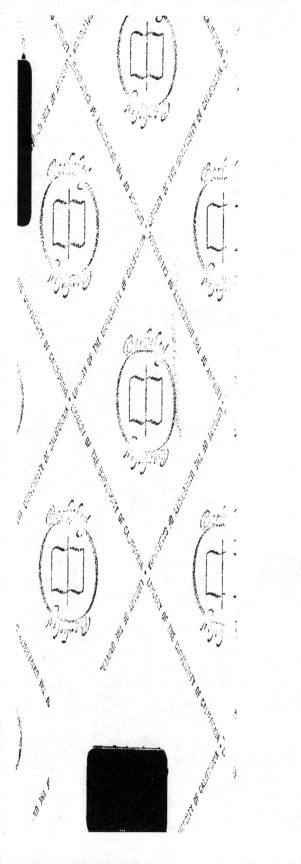

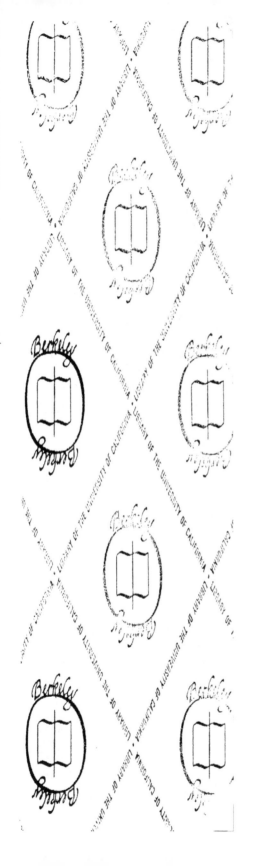

THE

SHEPHERD'S CALENDAR.

EDINBURGH : PRINTED BY BALLANTYNE AND COMPANY.

THE

SHEPHERD'S CALENDAR.

BY JAMES HOGG,

AUTHOR OF " THE QUEEN'S WAKE," &c. &c.

IN TWO VOLUMES.

VOL. I.

WILLIAM BLACKWOOD, EDINBURGH;
AND T. CADELL, LONDON.
MDCCCXXIX.

CONTENTS OF VOL I.

ADVERTISEMENT.

THE greater number of the Tales contained in these volumes appeared originally in BLACK-WOOD'S EDINBURGH MAGAZINE. They have been revised with care; and to complete the Collection, several Tales hitherto unpublished have been added.

SHEPHERD'S CALENDAR.

CHAPTER I.

ROB DODDS.

I<small>T</small> was on the 13th of February 1823, on a cold
stormy day, the snow lying from one to ten feet deep
on the hills, and nearly as hard as ice, when an extensive store-farmer in the outer limits of the county of
Peebles went up to one of his led farms, to see how
his old shepherd was coming on with his flocks. A
partial thaw had blackened some spots here and there
on the brows of the mountains, and over these the
half-starving flocks were scattered, picking up a scanty
sustenance, while all the hollow parts, and whole sides
of mountains that lay sheltered from the winds on the
preceding week, when the great drifts blew, were
heaped and over-heaped with immense loads of snow,
so that every hill appeared to the farmer to have
changed its form. There was a thick white haze on

the sky, corresponding exactly with the wan frigid
colour of the high mountains, so that in casting one's
eye up to the heights, it was not apparent where the
limits of the earth ended, and the heavens began. There
was no horizon—no blink of the sun looking through
the pale and impervious mist of heaven ; but there, in
that elevated and sequestered *hope,* the old shepherd
and his flock seemed to be left out of nature and all
its sympathies, and embosomed in one interminable
chamber of waste desolation.—So his master thought;
and any stranger beholding the scene, would have been
still more deeply impressed that the case was so in
reality.

But the old shepherd thought and felt otherwise.
He saw God in the clouds, and watched his arm in
the direction of the storm.   He perceived, or thought
he perceived, one man's flocks suffering on account of
their owner's transgression ; and though he bewailed
the hardships to which the poor harmless creatures
were reduced, he yet acknowledged in his heart the
justness of the punishment. " These temporal scourges
are laid upon sinners in mercy," said he, " and it will
be well for them if they get so away.   It will teach
them in future how to drink and carouse, and speak
profane things of the name of Him in whose hand are
the issues of life, and to regard his servants as the
dogs of their flock."

Again, he beheld from his heights, when the days were clear, the flocks of others more favourably situated, which he interpreted as a reward for their acts of charity and benevolence ; for this old man believed that all temporal benefits are sent to men as a reward for good works ; and all temporal deprivations as a scourge for evil ones.

"I hae been a herd in this hope, callant and man, for these fifty years now, Janet," said he to his old wife, "and I think I never saw the face o' the country look waur."

"Hout, gudeman, it is but a clud o' the despondency o' auld age come ower your een ; for I hae seen waur storms than this, or else my sight deceives me. This time seven and thirty years, when you and I were married, there was a deeper, and a harder snaw baith, than this. There was mony a burn dammed up wi' dead hogs that year ! And what say ye to this time nine years, gudeman ?"

"Ay, ay, Janet, these were hard times when they were present. But I think there's something in our corrupt nature that gars us aye trow the present burden is the heaviest. However, it is either my strength failing, that I canna won sae weel through the snaw, or I never saw it lying sae deep before. I canna steer the poor creatures frae ae knowe-head to another, without rowing them ower the body. And sometimes

when they wad spraughle away, then I stick firm and
fast mysell, and the mair I fight to get out, I gang aye
the deeper. This same day, nae farther gane, at ae
step up in the Gait Cleuch, I slumpit in to the neck.
Peace be wi' us, quo' I to myself, where am I now?
If my auld wife wad but look up the hill, she wad see
nae mair o' her poor man but the bannet. Ah! Janet,
Janet, I'm rather feared that our Maker has a craw to
pook wi' us even now!"

"I hope no, Andrew; we're in good hands; and if
he should e'en see meet to pook a craw wi' us, he'll
maybe fling us baith the bouk and the feathers at the
end. Ye shouldna repine, gudeman. Ye're something
ill for thrawing your mou' at Providence now and
then."

"Na, na, Janet; far be't frae me to grumble at
Providence. I ken ower weel that the warst we get
is far aboon our merits. But it's no for the season
that I'm sae feared,—that's ruled by Ane that canna
err; only, I dread that there's something rotten in the
government or the religion of the country, that lays it
under His curse. There's my fear, Janet. The scourge
of a land often fa's on its meanest creatures first, and
advances by degrees, to gie the boonmost orders o'
society warning and time to repent. There, for instance, in the saxteen and seventeen, the scourge fell
on our flocks and our herds. Then, in aughteen and

nineteen, it fell on the weavers,—they're the neist class, ye ken ; then our merchants,—they're the neist again ; and last of a' it has fallen on the farmers and the shepherds,—they're the first and maist sterling class of a country. Na, ye needna smudge and laugh, Janet ; for it's true. They *are* the boonmost, and hae aye been the boonmost sin' the days o' Abel ; and that's nae date o' yesterday. And ye'll observe, Janet, that whenever they began to fa' low, they gat aye another lift to keep up their respect. But I see our downfa' coming on us wi' rapid strides.—There's a heartlessness and apathy croppen in amang the sheep-farmers, that shows their warldly hopes to be nearly extinct. The maist o' them seem no to care a bodle whether their sheep die or live. There's our master, for instance, when times were gaun weel, I hae seen him up ilka third day at the farthest in the time of a storm, to see how the sheep were doing ; and this winter I hae never seen his face sin' it came on. He seems to hae forgotten that there are sic creatures existing in this wilderness as the sheep and me.—His presence be about us; gin there be nae the very man come by the window !"

Janet sprung to her feet, swept the hearth, set a chair on the cleanest side, and wiped it with her check apron, all ere one could well look about him.

" Come away, master ; come in by to the fire here ; lang-lookit-for comes at length."

" How are you, Janet ?—still living, I see.   It is a pity that you had not popped off before this great storm came on."

" Dear, what for, master ?"

" Because if you should take it into your head to coup the creels just now, you know it would be out of the power of man to get you to a Christian burial. We would be obliged to huddle you up in the nook of the kail-yard."

" Ah, master, what's that you're saying to my auld wife ?   Aye the auld man yet, I hear ! a great deal o' the leaven o' corrupt nature aye sprouting out now and then.   I wonder you're no fear'd to speak in that regardless manner in these judgment-looking times !"

" And you are still the old man too, Andrew ; a great deal of cant and hypocrisy sprouting out at times. But tell me, you old sinner, how has your Maker been serving you this storm ?   I have been right ter- rified about your sheep ; for I know you will have been very impertinent with him of evenings."

" Hear to that now !   There's no hope, I see !   I thought to find you humbled wi' a' thir trials and warldly losses ; but I see the heart is hardened like Pharaoh's, and you will not let the multitude of your sins go.   As to the storm, I can tell you, my sheep are just at ane mae wi't. I am waur than ony o' my neighbours, as I lie higher on the hills; but I may hae been as it chanced, for you; for ye hae never lookit near me mair than you had had no concern in the creatures."

" Indeed, Andrew, it is because neither you nor the creatures are much worth looking after now-a-days. If it hadna been the fear I was in for some mishap coming over the stock, on account of these hypocritical prayers of yours, I would not have come to look after you so soon."

" Ah, there's nae mense to be had o' you! It's a good thing I ken the heart's better than the tongue, or ane wad hae little face to pray either for you, or aught that belangs t'ye. But I hope ye hae been nae the waur o' auld Andrew's prayers as yet. An some didna pray for ye, it wad maybe be the waur for ye. I prayed for ye when ye couldna pray for yoursell, and had hopes that, when I turned auld and doited, you might say a kind word for me; but I'm fear'd that warld's wealth and warld's pleasures hae been leading you ower lang in their train, and that ye hae been trusting to that which will soon take wings and flee away."

" If you mean riches, Andrew, or warld's wealth, as you call it, you never said a truer word in your life; for the little that my forbears and I have made, is ac-

tually, under the influence of these long prayers of
yours, melting away from among my hands faster than
ever the snow did from the dike."

" It is perfectly true, what you're saying, master.
I ken the extent o' your bits o' sales weel enough, and
I ken your rents ; and weel I ken you're telling me nae
lee.   And it's e'en a hard case.   But I'll tell you what
I would do—I would throw their tacks in their teeth,
and let them mak aught o' them they likit."

" Why, that would be ruin at once, Andrew, with
a vengeance.   Don't you see that stocks of sheep are
fallen so low, that if they were put to sale, they would
not pay more than the rents, and some few arrears that
every one of us have got into ; and thus, by throwing
up our farms, we would throw ourselves out beggars?
We are all willing to put off the evil day as long as
we can, and rather trust to long prayers for a while."

" Ah! you're there again, are you ?—canna let
alane profanity !   It's hard to gar a wicked cout leave
off flinging.   But I can tell you, master mine—An
you farmers had made your hay when the sun shone,
ye might a' hae sitten independent o' your screwing
lairds, wha are maistly sair out at elbows ; and ye ken,
sir, a hungry louse bites wicked sair.   But this is but
a just judgment come on you for your behaviour.   Ye
had the gaun days o' prosperity for twenty years ! But
instead o' laying by a little for a sair leg, or making

provision for an evil day, ye gaed on like madmen.
Ye biggit houses, and ye plantit vineyards, and threw
away money as ye had been sawing sklate-stanes. Ye
drank wine, and ye drank punch ; and ye roared and
ye sang, and spake unseemly things. And did ye
never think there was an ear that heard, and an ee
that saw, a' thae things ? And did ye never think that
they wad be visited on your heads some day when ye
couldna play paw to help yoursells ? If ye didna
think sae then, ye'll think sae soon. And ye'll maybe
see the day when the like o' auld Andrew, wi' his
darned hose, and his cloutit shoon ; his braid bannet,
instead of a baiver ; his drink out o' the clear spring,
instead o' the punch bowl ; and his good steeve ait-
meal parritch and his horn spoon, instead o' the draps
o' tea, that costs sae muckle—I say, that sic a man wi'
a' thae, and his worthless prayers to boot, will maybe
keep the crown o' the causeway langer than some that
carried their heads higher."

" Hout fie, Andrew !" quoth old Janet ; " Gudeness be my help, an I dinna think shame o' you ! Our
master may weel think ye'll be impudent wi' your
Maker ; for troth you're very impudent wi' himsell.
Dinna ye see that ye hae made the douce sonsy lad
that he disna ken where to look ?"

" Ay, Janet, your husband may weel crack. He

kens he has feathered his nest off my father and me. He is independent, let the world wag as it will."

" It's a' fairly come by, master, and the maist part o't came through your ain hands. But my bairns are a' doing for themsells, in the same way that I did; and if twa or three hunder pounds can beet a mister for you in a strait, ye sanna want it, come of a' what will."

" It is weel said of you, Andrew, and I am obliged to you. There is no class of men in this kingdom so independent as you shepherds. You have your sheep, your cow, your meal and potatoes; a regular income of from sixteen to thirty pounds yearly, without a farthing of expenditure, except for shoes; for your clothes are all made at home. If you would even wish to spend it, you cannot get an opportunity, and every one of you is rich, who has not lost money by lending it. It is therefore my humble opinion, that all the farms over this country will soon change occupants; and that the shepherds must ultimately become the store-farmers."

" I hope in God I'll never live to see that, master, for the sake of them that I and mine hae won our bread frae, as weel as some others that I hae a great respect for. But that's no a thing that hasna happened afore this day. It is little mair than a hundred and forty years, sin' a' the land i' this country changed masters already; sin' every farmer in it was reduced, and the farms were a' ta'en by common people and strangers at half naething. The Welshes came here then, out o' a place they ca' Wales, in England; the Andersons came frae a place they ca' Rannoch, some gate i' the north; and your ain family came first to this country then frae some bit lairdship near Glasgow. There were a set o' MacGregors and MacDougals, said to have been great thieves, came into Yarrow then, and changed their names to Scotts; but they didna thrive; for they warna likit, and the hinderend o' them were in the Catslackburn. They ca'd them aye the Pinolys, frae the place they came frae; but I dinna ken where it was. The Ballantynes came frae Galloway; and for as flourishing folks as they are now, the first o' them came out at the Birkhill-path, riding on a haltered pony, wi' a goat-skin aneath him for a saddle. The Cunninghams, likewise, began to spread their wings at the same time; they came a' frae a little fat curate that came out o' Glencairn to Ettrick. But that's nae disparagement to ony o' thae families; for an there be merit at a' inherent in man as to warldly things, it is certainly in raising himsell frae naething to respect. There is nae very ancient name amang a' our farmers now, but the Tweedies and the Murrays; I mean of them that anciently belanged to this district. The Tweedies are very auld, and took the name frae

the water.   They were lairds o' Drummelzier hunders
o' years afore the Hays got it, and hae some o' the
best blood o' the land in their veins ; and sae also have
the Murrays ; but the maist part o' the rest are up-
starts and come-o'-wills.   Now ye see, for as far out-
bye as I live, I can tell ye some things that ye dinna
hear amang your drinking cronies."

   " It is when you begin to these old traditions that I
like to listen to you, Andrew.   Can you tell me what
was the cause of such a complete overthrow of the
farmers of that age ?"

   " Oh, I canna tell, sir—I canna tell ; some overturn
o' affairs, like the present, I fancy.   The farmers had
outher lost a' their sheep, or a' their siller, as they are
like to do now ; but I canna tell how it was ; for the
general change had ta'en place, for the maist part, afore
the Revolution.   My ain grandfather, who was the son
of a great farmer, hired himsell for a shepherd at that
time to young Tam Linton ; and mony ane was
wae for the downcome.   But, speaking o' that, of a
the downcomes that ever a country kenn'd in a farm-
ing name, there has never been ought like that o' the
Lintons.   When my grandfather was a young man,
and ane o' their herds, they had a' the principal store-
farms o' Ettrick Forest, and a part in this shire.   They
had, when the great Mr Boston came to Ettrick, the
farms o' Blackhouse, Dryhope, Henderland, Chapel-

hope, Scabcleuch, Shorthope, Midgehope, Meggatknowes, Buccleuch, and Gilmanscleuch, that I ken of, and likely as mony mae; and now there's no a man o' the name in a' the bounds aboon the rank of a cowherd. Thomas Linton rode to kirk and market, wi' a liveryman at his back; but where is a' that pride now? —a' buried in the mools wi' the bearers o't! and the last representative o' that great overgrown family, that laid house to house, and field to field, is now sair gane on a wee, wee farm o' the Duke o' Buccleuch's. The ancient curse had lighted on these men, if ever it lighted on men in this world. And yet they were reckoned good men, and kind men, in their day; for the good Mr Boston wrote an epitaph on Thomas, in metre, when he died; and though I have read it a hunder times in St Mary's kirk-yard, where it is to be seen to this day, I canna say it ower. But it says that he was eyes to the blind, and feet to the lame, and that the Lord would requite him in a day to come, or something to that purpose. Now that said a great deal for him, master, although Providence has seen meet to strip his race of a' their worldly possessions. But take an auld fool's advice, and never lay farm to farm, even though a fair opportunity should offer; for, as sure as He lives who pronounced that curse, it will take effect. I'm an auld man, and I hae seen mony a dash made that way; but I never saw ane o'

them come to good! There was first Murray of
Glenrath; why, it was untelling what land that man
possessed. Now his family has not a furr in the twa
counties. Then there was his neighbour Simpson of
Posso: I hae seen the day that Simpson had two-and-
twenty farms, the best o' the twa counties, and a'
stockit wi' good sheep. Now there's no a drap o' *his*
blood has a furr in the twa counties. Then there was
Grieve of Willenslee; ane wad hae thought that body
was gaun to take the haill kingdom. He was said to
have had ten thousand sheep, a' on good farms, at ae
time. Where are they a' now? Neither *him* nor *his*
hae a furr in the twa counties. Let me tell ye, master
—for ye're but a young man, and I wad aye fain have
ye to see things in a right light—that ye may blame
the wars; ye may blame the Government; and ye may
blame the Parliamenters: but there's a hand that rules
higher than a' these; and gin ye dinna look to that,
ye'll never look to the right source either o' your prosperity or adversity. And I sairly doubt that the pride
o' the farmers has been raised to ower great a pitch,
that Providence has been brewing a day of humiliation
for them, and that there will be a change o' hands
since mair, as there was about this time hunder and
forty years."

" Then I suppose you shepherds expect to have century about with us, or so ? Well, I don't see any thing very unfair in it."

" Ay, but I fear we will be as far aneath the right medium for a while, as ye are startit aboon it. We'll make a fine hand doing the honours o' the grand mansion-houses that ye hae biggit for us ; the cavalry exercises ; the guns and the pointers ; the wine and the punch drinking ; and the singing o' the deboshed sangs ! But we'll just come to the right set again in a generation or twa ; and then, as soon as we get ower hee, we'll get a downcome in our turn.——But, master, I say, how will you grand gentlemen tak wi' a shepherd's life ? How will ye like to be turned into reeky holes like this, where ye can hardly see your fingers afore ye, and be reduced to the parritch and the horn spoon ?"

" I cannot tell, Andrew. I suppose it will have some advantages——It will teach us to say long prayers to put off the time ; and if we should have the misfortune afterwards to pass into *the bad place* that you shepherds are all so terrified about, why, we will scarcely know any difference. I account that a great advantage in dwelling in such a place as this. We'll scarcely know the one place from the other."

" Ay, but oh what a surprise ye will get when ye step out o' ane o' your grand palaces into hell ! And gin ye dinna repent in time, ye'll maybe get a little experiment o' that sort. Ye think ye hae said a very witty thing there : but a' profane wit is sinfu' ; and whatever is sinfu' is shamefu' ; and therefore it never suits to be said either afore God or man. Ye are just a good standing sample o' the young tenantry o' Scotland at this time. Ye're ower genteel to be devout, and ye look ower high, and depend ower muckle on the arm o' flesh, to regard the rod and Him that hath appointed it. But it will fa' wi' the mair weight for that ! A blow that is seen coming may be wardit off ; but if ane's sae proud as no to regard it, it's the less scaith that he suffer."

" I see not how any man can ward off this blow, Andrew. It has gathered its overwhelming force in springs over which we have no control, and is of that nature that no industry of man can avail against it— exertion is no more than a drop in the bucket : and I greatly fear that this grievous storm is come to lay the axe to the root of the tree."

" I'm glad to hear, however, that ye hae some Scripture phrases at your tongue-roots. I never heard you use ane in a serious mode before ; and I hope there will be a reformation yet. If adversity hae that effect, I shall willingly submit to my share o' the loss if the storm should lie still for a while, and cut off a wheen o' the creatures, that ye aince made eedals o', and now dow hardly bide to see. But that's the gate wi' a things that ane sets up for warldly worship in place o'

the true object; they turn a' out curses and causes o'
shame and disgrace. As for warding off the blow,
master, I see no resource but throwing up the farms
ilk ane, and trying to save a remnant out o' the fire.
The lairds want naething better than for ye to rin in
arrears; then they will get a' your stocks for neist to
naething, and have the land stockit themsells as they
had langsyne; and you will be their keepers, or vassals,
the same as we are to you at present. As to hinging
on at the present rents, it is madness—the very extremity of madness. I hae been a herd here for fifty
years, and I ken as weel what the ground will pay at
every price of sheep as you do, and I daresay a great
deal better. When I came here first, your father paid
less than the third of the rent that you are bound to
pay; sheep of every description were dearer, lambs,
ewes, and wedders; and I ken weel he was making no
money of it, honest man, but merely working his way,
with some years a little over, and some naething. And
how is it possible that you can pay three times the rent
at lower prices of sheep? I say the very presumption
of the thing is sheer madness. And it is not only this
farm, but you may take it as an average of all the farms
in the country, that *before the French war began, the*
sheep were dearer than they are now—the farms were
not above one-third of the rents at an average, and the
farmers were not making any money. They have lost

their summer day during the French war, which will never return to them ; and the only resource they have, that I can see, is to abandon their farms in time, and try to save a remnant. Things will come to their true level presently, but not afore the auld stock o' farmers are crushed past rising again. And then I little wat what's to come o' ye.; for an we herds get the land, we *winna* employ you as our shepherds,—that you may depend on."

" Well, Andrew, these are curious facts that you tell me about the land having all changed occupiers about a certain period. I wish you could have stated the causes with certainty. Was there not a great loss on this farm once, when it was said the burn was so dammed up with dead carcasses that it changed its course ?"

" Ay, but that's quite a late story. It happened in my own day, and I believe mostly through mischance. That was the year Rob Dodds was lost in the Earney Cleuch. I remember it, but cannot tell what year it was, for I was but a little bilsh of a callant then."

" Who was Rob Dodds ? I never heard of the incident before."

" Ay, but your father remembered it weel ; for he sent a' his men mony a day to look for the corpse, but a' to nae purpose. I'll never forget it ; for it made an impression on me sae deep that I couldna get rest

i' my bed for months and days. He was a young handsome bonny lad, an honest man's only son, and was
herd wi' Tam Linton in the Birkhill. The Lintons
were sair come down then; for this Tam was a herd,
and had Rob hired as his assistant. Weel, it sae happened
that Tam's wife had occasion to cross the wild heights
atween the Birkhill and Tweedsmuir, to see her mother, or sister, on some express; and Tam sent the
young man wi' her to see her ower Donald's Cleuch
Edge. It was in the middle o' winter, and, if I mind
right, this time sixty years. At the time they set out,
the morning was calm, frosty, and threatening snaw,
but the ground clear of it. Rob had orders to set his
mistress to the height, and return home; but by the
time they had got to the height, the snaw had come on,
so the good lad went all the way through Guemshope
with her, and in sight of the water o' Fruid. He crossed
all the wildest o' the heights on his return in safety;
and on the Middle-End, west of Loch-Skene, he met
with Robin Laidlaw, that went to the Highlands and
grew a great farmer after that. Robin was gathering
the Polmoody ewes; and as they were neighbours, and
both herding to ae master, Laidlaw testified some anxiety lest the young man should not find his way hame;
for the blast had then come on very severe. Dodds
leugh at him, and said, ' he was nae mair feared for finding the gate hame, than he was for finding the gate to

his mouth when he was hungry.'——' Weel, weel,' quo'
Robin, ' keep the band o' the hill a' the way, for I hae seen
as clever a fellow waured on sic a day ; and be sure to
hund the ewes out o' the Brand Law Scores as ye gang
by.'——' Tammy charged me to bring a backfu' o' peats
wi' me,' said he ; ' but I think I'll no gang near the
peat stack the day.'——' Na,' quo' Robin, ' I think ye'll
no be sae mad !'——' But, O man,' quo' the lad, ' hae ye
ony bit bread about your pouches ; for I'm unco hungry ?
The wife was in sic a hurry that I had to come away
without getting ony breakfast, and I had sae far to gang
wi' her, that I'm grown unco toom i' the inside.'——' The
fient ae inch hae I, Robie, my man, or ye should hae
had it,' quo' Laidlaw.——' But an that be the case, gang
straight hame, and never heed the ewes, come o' them
what will.'——' O there's nae fear !' said he, ' I'll turn
the ewes, and be hame in good time too.'   And with
that he left Laidlaw, and went down the Middle-Craig-
End, jumping and playing in a frolicsome way ower his
stick.   He had a large lang nibbit staff in his hand,
which Laidlaw took particular notice of, thinking it
would be a good help for the young man in the rough
way he had to gang.

" There was never another word about the matter
till that day eight days.   The storm having increased
to a terrible drift, the snaw had grown very deep, and
the herds, wha lived about three miles sindry, hadna

met for a' that time.   But that day Tam Linton and
Robin Laidlaw met at the Tail Burn ; and after cracking a lang time thegither, Tam says to the tither, just
as it war by chance, ' Saw ye naething o' our young
dinnagood this day eight days, Robin ? He gaed awa
that morning to set our gudewife ower the height, and
has never sin' that time lookit near me, the careless
rascal !'

    " ' Tam Linton, what's that you're saying ? what's
that I hear ye saying, Tam Linton ?' quo' Robin, wha
was dung clean stupid wi' horror. ' Hae ye never
seen Rob Dodds sin' that morning he gaed away wi'
your wife ?'

    " ' Na, never,' quo' the tither.

    " ' Why then, sir, let me tell ye, you'll never see
him again in this world alive,' quo' Robin ; ' for he left
me on the Middle-End on his way hame that day at
eleven o'clock, just as the day was coming to the warst.
—But, Tam Linton, what was't ye war saying ? Ye're
telling me what canna be true—Do ye say that ye haena seen Rob Dodds sin' that day ?'

    " ' Haena I tauld ye that I hae never seen his face
sinsyne ?' quo' Linton.

    " ' Sae I hear ye saying,' quo' Robin again.   ' But
ye're telling me a downright made lee.   The thing's
no possible ; for ye hae the very staff i' your hand that
he had in his, when he left me in the drift that day.'

" ' I ken naething about sticks or staves, Robin Laidlaw,' says Tam, looking rather like ane catched in an ill turn. ' The staff wasna likely to come hame without the owner ; and I can only say, I hae seen nae mair o' Rob Dodds sin' that morning ; and I had thoughts that, as the day grew sae ill, he had hadden forrit a' the length wi' our wife, and was biding wi' her folks a' this time to bring her hame again when the storm had settled.'

" ' Na, na, Tam, ye needna get into ony o' thae lang-windit stories wi' me,' quo' Robin. ' For I tell ye, that's the staff Rob Dodds had in his hand when I last saw him ; so ye have either seen him dead or living——I'll gie my oath to that.'

" ' Ye had better take care what ye say, Robin Laid-law,' says Tam, very fiercely, ' or I'll maybe make ye blithe to eat in your words again.'

" ' What I hae said, I'll stand to, Tam Linton,' says Robin.——' And mair than that,' says he, ' if that young man has come to an untimely end, I'll see his blood required at your hand.'

" Then there was word sent away to the Hope-house to his parents, and ye may weel ken, master, what heavy news it was to them, for Rob was their only son ; they had gien him a good education, and muckle muckle they thought o' him ; but naething wad serve him but he wad be a shepherd. His father

came wi' the maist pairt o' Ettrick parish at his back ;
and mony sharp and threatening words past atween
him and Linton ; but what could they make o't ?   The
lad was lost, and nae law, nor nae revenge, could
restore him again ; sae they had naething for't, but to
spread athwart a' the hills looking for the corpse.   The
haill country rase for ten miles round, on ane or twa
good days that happened ; but the snaw was still lying,
and a' their looking was in vain.   Tam Linton wad look
nane.   He took the dorts, and never heeded the folk
mair than they hadna been there.   A' that height
atween Loch-Skene and the Birkhill was just moving
wi' folk for the space o' three weeks ; for the twa auld
folk, the lad's parents, couldna get ony rest, and folk
sympathized unco muckle wi' them.   At length the
snaw gaed maistly away, and the weather turned fine,
and I gaed out ane o' the days wi' my father to look
for the body.   But, aih wow ! I was a feared wight !
whenever I saw a bit sod, or a knowe, or a grey stane,
I stood still and trembled for fear it was the dead man,
and no ae step durst I steer farther, till my father gaed
up to a' thae things.   I gaed nae mair back to look for
the corpse ; for I'm sure if we had found the body I
wad hae gane out o' my judgment.

" At length every body tired o' looking, but the auld
man himsell.   He travelled day after day, ill weather
and good weather, without intermission.   They said

it was the waesomest thing ever was seen, to see that
auld grey-headed man gaun sae lang by himsell, looking for the corpse o' his only son ! The maist part o'
his friends advised him at length to give up the search,
as the finding o' the body seemed a thing a'thegither
hopeless. But he declared he wad look for his son till
the day o' his death ; and if he could but find his bones,
he would carry them away from the wild moors, and
lay them in the grave where he was to lie himsell. Tam
Linton was apprehended, and examined afore the Sheriff ; but nae proof could be led against him, and he
wan off. He swore that, as far as he remembered, he
got the staff standing at the mouth o' the peat stack ;
and that he conceived that either the lad or himsell had
left it there some day when bringing away a burden of
peats. The shepherds' peats had not been led home
that year, and the stack stood on a hill-head, half a
mile frae the house, and the herds were obliged to carry
them home as they needed them.

"But a mystery hung ower that lad's death that was
never cleared up, nor ever will a'thegither. Every
man was convinced, in his own mind, that Linton
knew where the body was a' the time ; and also, that
the young man had not come by his death fairly. It
was proved that the lad's dog had come hame several
times, and that Tam Linton had been seen kicking it
frae about his house ; and as the dog could be nowhere .

5

all that time, but waiting on the body, if that had no
been concealed in some more than ordinary way, the
dog would at least have been seen. At length, it was
suggested to the old man, that dead-lights always ho-
vered over a corpse by night, if the body was left exposed to the air; and it was a fact that two drowned
men had been found in a field of whins, where the water had left the bodies, by means of the dead-lights, a
very short while before. On the first calm night, therefore, the old desolate man went to the Merk-Side-Edge,
to the top of a high hill that overlooked all the ground
where there was ony likelihood that the body would
be lying. He watched there the lee-lang night, keeping his eye constantly roaming ower the broken wastes
before him; but he never noticed the least glimmer of
the dead-lights. About midnight, however, he heard
a dog barking; it likewise gae twa or three melancholy yowls, and then ceased. Robin Dodds was convinced it was his son's dog; but it was at such a distance, being about twa miles off, that he couldna be
sure where it was, or which o' the hills on the opposite side of the glen it was on. The second night he
kept watch on the Path Know, a hill which he supposed the howling o' the dog cam frae. But that hill being all surrounded to the west and north by tremendous
ravines and cataracts, he heard nothing o' the dog. In
the course of the night, however, he saw, or fancied he

saw, a momentary glimmer o' light, in the depth of the great gulf immediately below where he sat; and that at three different times, always in the same place. He now became convinced that the remains o' his son were in the bottom of the linn, a place which he conceived inaccessible to man; it being so deep from the summit where he stood, that the roar o' the waterfall only reached his ears now and then wi' a loud *whush!* as if it had been a sound wandering across the hills by itsell. But sae intent was Robín on this Willie-an-the-wisp light, that he took landmarks frae the ae summit to the other, to make sure o' the place; and as soon as daylight came, he set about finding a passage down to the bottom of the linn. He effected this by coming to the foot of the linn, and tracing its course backward, sometimes wading in water, and sometimes clambering over rocks, till at length, with a beating heart, he reached the very spot where he had seen the light; and in the grey o' the morning, he perceived something lying there that differed in colour from the iron-hued stones, and rocks, of which the linn was composed. He was in great astonishment what this could be; for, as he came closer on it, he saw it had no likeness to the dead body of a man, but rather appeared to be a heap o' bedclothes. And what think you it turned out to be? for I see ye're glowring as your een were gaun to loup out——Just neither more nor less than a strong mineral well ; or what the doctors ca' a callybit spring, a' boustered about wi' heaps o' soapy, limy kind o' stuff, that it seems had thrown out fiery vapours i' the night-time.

" However, Robin, being unable to do ony mair in the way o' searching, had now nae hope left but in finding his dead son by some kind o' supernatural means. Sae he determined to watch a third night, and that at the very identical peat stack where it had been said his son's staff was found. He did sae ; and about midnight, ere ever he wist, the dog set up a howl close beside him. He called on him by his name, and the dog came, and fawned on his old ac-quaintance, and whimpered, and whinged, and made sic a wark, as could hardly hae been trowed. Robin keepit haud o' him a' the night, and fed him wi' pieces o' bread, and then as soon as the sun rose, he let him gang ; and the poor affectionate creature went straight to his dead master, who, after all, was lying in a little green spritty hollow, not above a musket-shot from the peat stack. This rendered the whole affair more mysterious than ever ; for Robin Dodds himself, and above twenty men beside, could all have made oath that they had looked into that place again and again, so minutely, that a dead bird could not have been there without their having seen it. However, there the body of the youth was gotten, after having been lost for the

long space of ten weeks; and not in a state of great
decay neither, for it rather appeared swollen, as if it
had been lying among water.

"Conjecture was now driven to great extremities
in accounting for all these circumstances. It was manifest to every one, that the body had not been all the
time in that place.   But then, where had it been? or
what could have been the reasons for concealing it?
These were the puzzling considerations.   There were
a hunder different things suspectit; and mony o' them,
I dare say, a hunder miles frae the truth; but on the
whole, Linton was sair lookit down on, and almaist
perfectly abhorred by the country; for it was weel
kenn'd that he had been particularly churlish and severe on the young man at a' times, and seemed to have
a peculiar dislike to him.   An it hadna been the wife,
wha was a kind considerate sort of a body, if Tam had
gotten his will, it was reckoned he wad hae hungered
the lad to dead. After that, Linton left the place, and
gaed away, I watna where; and the country, I believe,
came gayan near to the truth o' the story at last:

"There was a girl in the Birkhill house at the time,
whether a daughter o' Tam's, or no, I hae forgot,
though I think otherwise.   However, she durstna for
her life tell a' she kenn'd as lang as the investigation
was gaun on; but it at last spunkit out that Rob
Dodds had got hame safe eneugh; and that Tam got

into a great rage at him, because he had not brought a
burden o' peats, there being none in the house. The
youth excused himself on the score of fatigue and
hunger ; but Tam swore at him, and said, ' The deil
be in your teeth, gin they shall break bread, till ye
gang back out to the hill-head and bring a burden o'
peats!' Dodds refused ; on which Tam struck him,
and forced him away ; and he went crying and greet-
ing out at the door, but never came back. She also
told, that after poor Rob was lost, Tam tried several
times to get at his dog to fell it with a stick ; but the
creature was terrified for him, and made its escape. It
was therefore thought, and indeed there was little
doubt, that Rob, through fatigue and hunger, and reckless of death from the way he had been guidit, went
out to the hill, and died at the peat stack, the mouth
of which was a shelter from the drift-wind ; and that
his cruel master, conscious o' the way in which he had
used him, and dreading skaith, had trailed away the
body, and sunk it in some pool in these unfathomable
linns, or otherwise concealed it, wi' the intention, that
the world might never ken whether the lad was actually dead, or had absconded. If it had not been for
the dog, from which it appears he had been unable to
conceal it, and the old man's perseverance, to whose
search there appeared to be no end, it is probable he
would never have laid the body in a place where it

could have been found.   But if he had allowed it to remain in the first place of concealment, it might have been discovered by means of the dog, and the intentional concealment of the corpse would then have been obvious ; so that Linton all that time could not be quite at his ease, and it was no wonder he attempted to fell the dog.   But where the body could have been deposited, that the faithful animal was never discovered by the searchers, during the day, for the space of ten weeks, baffled a' the conjectures that ever could be made.

" The two old people, the lad's father and mother, never got over their loss.   They never held up their heads again, nor joined in society ony mair, except in attending divine worship.   It might be truly said o' them, that they spent the few years that they survived their son in constant prayer and humiliation ; but they soon died, short while after ane anither.   As for Tam Linton, he left this part of the country, as I told you ; but it was said there was a curse hung ower him and his a' his life, and that he never mair did weel.——That was the year, master, on which our burn was dammed wi' the dead sheep ; and in fixing the date, you see, I hae been led into a lang story, and am just nae farther wi' the main point than when I began."

" I wish from my heart, Andrew, that you would try to fix a great many old dates in the same manner ;

for I confess I am more interested in your lang stories, than in either your lang prayers, or your lang sermons about repentance and amendment. But pray, you were talking of the judgments that overtook Tam Linton—Was that the same Tam Linton that was precipitated from the Brand Law by the break of a snaw-wreath, and he and all his sheep jammed into the hideous gulf, called the Grey Mare's Tail?"

" The very same, sir ; and that might be accountit ane o' the first judgments that befell him ; for there were many of his ain sheep in the flock. Tam asserted all his life, that he went into the linn along with his hirsel, but no man ever believed him ; for there was not one of the sheep came out alive, and how it was possible for the carl to have come safe out, naebody could see. It was, indeed, quite impossible ; for it had been such a break of snaw as had scarcely ever been seen. The gulf was crammed sae fu', that ane could hae gane ower it like a pendit brig ; and no a single sheep could be gotten out, either dead or living. When the thaw came, the burn wrought a passage for itself below the snaw, but the arch stood till summer. I have heard my father oft describe the appearance of that vault as he saw it on his way from Moffat fair. Ane hadna gane far into it, he said, till it turned darkish, like an ill-hued twilight ; and sic a like arch o' carnage he never saw ! There were limbs o'

sheep hinging in a' directions, the snaw was wedged
sae firm.   Some entire carcasses hung by the neck,
some by a spauld ; then there was a haill forest o' legs
sticking out in ae place, and horns in another, terribly
mangled and broken ; and it was a'thegither sic a
frightsome-looking place, that he was blithe to get
out o't again."

After looking at the sheep, tasting old Janet's best
kebbuck, and oatmeal cakes, and preeing the whisky
bottle, the young farmer again set out through the
deep snow, on his way home. But Andrew made him
promise, that if the weather did not amend, he would
come back in a few days and see how the poor sheep
were coming on ; and, as an inducement, promised to
tell him a great many old anecdotes of the shepherd's
life.

CHAPTER II.

MR ADAMSON OF LAVERHOPE.

ONE of those events that have made the deepest impression on the shepherds' minds for a century bygone, seems to have been the fate of Mr Adamson, who was tenant in Laverhope for the space of twenty-seven years. It stands in their calendar as an era from which to date summer floods, water spouts, hail and thunder-storms, &c. ; and appears from tradition to have been attended with some awful circumstances, expressive of divine vengeance. This Adamson is represented, as having been a man of an ungovernable temper—of irritability so extreme, that no person could be for a moment certain to what excesses he might be hurried. He was otherwise accounted a good and upright man, and a sincere Christian ; but in these outbreakings of temper he often committed acts of cruelty and injustice, for which any good man ought to have been ashamed. Among other qualities, he had an obliging disposition, there being few to whom a poor man would sooner have applied in a strait. Accordingly, he had been in the habit of assisting a less wealthy neighbour of his with a little credit for many years. This man's name was Irvine, and though he had a number of rich relations, he was never out of difficulties. Adamson, from some whim or caprice, sued this poor farmer for a few hundred merks, taking legal steps against him, even to the very last measures short of poinding and imprisonment. Irvine paid little attention to this, taking it for granted that his neighbour took these steps only for the purpose of inducing his debtor's friends to come forward and support him.

It happened one day about this period, that a thoughtless boy, belonging to Irvine's farm, hunted Adamson's cattle in a way that gave great offence to their owner, on which the two farmers differed, and some hard words passed between them. The next day Irvine was seized and thrown into jail ; and shortly after, his effects were poinded, and sold by auction for ready money. They were consequently thrown away, as the neighbours, not having been forewarned, were wholly unprovided with ready money, and unable to purchase at any price. Mrs Irvine came to the enraged creditor with a child in her arms, and implored him to put off the sale for a month, that she might try what could be done amongst her friends to prevent a wreck so irretrievable. He was at one time on the very point of yielding; but some bitter recollections coming over his mind at the moment, stimulated his spleen against her husband, and he resolved that the sale should go on. William Carruders of Grindiston heard the following dialogue between them; and he said that his heart almost trembled within him; for Mrs Irvine was a violent woman, and her eloquence did more harm than good.

"Are ye really gaun to act the part of a devil, the day, Mr Adamson, and turn me and thae bairns out to the bare high-road, helpless as we are? Oh, man, if your bowels binna seared in hell-fire already, take some compassion; for an ye dinna, they *will* be seared afore baith men and angels yet, till that hard and cruel heart o' yours be nealed to an izle."

"I'm gaun to act nae part of a devil, Mrs Irvine; I'm only gaun to take my ain in the only way I can get it. I'm no baith gaun to tine my siller, and hae my beasts abused into the bargain."

"Ye sall neither lose plack nor bawbee o' your siller, man, if ye will gie me but a month to make a shift for it—I swear to you, ye sall neither lose, nor rue the deed. But if ye winna grant me that wee wee while, when the bread of a haill family depends on it, ye're waur than ony deil that's yammering and cursing i' the bottomless pit."

" Keep your ravings to yoursell, Mrs Irvine, for I
hae made up my mind what I'm to do; and I'll do it;
sae it's needless for ye to pit yoursell into a bleeze;
for the surest promisers are aye the slackest payers.
It isna likely that your bad language will gar me alter
my purpose."

" If that *be* your purpose, Mr Adamson, and if you
put that purpose in execution, I wadna change conditions wi' you the day for ten thousand times a' the
gear ye are worth.   Ye're gaun to do the thing that
ye'll repent only aince—for a' the time that ye hae to
exist baith in this world and the neist, and that's a
lang lang look forrit and ayond.   Ye have assisted a
poor honest family for the purpose of taking them at
a disadvantage, and crushing them to beggars; and
when ane thinks o' that, what a heart you must hae!
Ye hae first put my poor man in prison, a place where
he little thought, and less deserved, ever to be; and
now ye are reaving his sackless family out o' their last
bit o' bread.   Look at this bit bonny innocent thing
in my arms, how it is smiling on ye!   Look at a' the
rest standing leaning against the wa's, ilka ane wi' his
een fixed on you by way o' imploring your pity!   If
ye reject thae looks, ye'll see them again in some trying moments, that will bring this ane back to your
mind; ye will see them i' your dreams; ye will see
them on your death-bed, and ye will *think* ye see

them gleaming on ye through the reek o' hell,—but it winna be them."

" Haud your tongue, woman, for ye make me feared to hear ye."

" Ay, but better be feared in time, than torfelled for ever! Better conquess your bad humour for aince, than be conquessed for it through sae mony lang ages. Ye pretend to be a religious man, Mr Adamson, and a great deal mair sae than your neighbours—do you think that religion teaches you acts o' cruelty like this? Will ye hae the face to kneel afore your Maker the night, and pray for a blessing on you and yours, and that He will forgive you your debts as you forgive your debtors? I hae nae doubt but ye will. But aih! how sic an appeal will heap the coals o' divine vengeance on your head, and tighten the belts o' burning yettlin ower your hard heart! Come forrit, bairns, and speak for yoursells, ilk ane o' ye."

" O, Maister Adamson, ye maunna turn my father and mother out o' their house and their farm; or what think ye is to come o' us?" said Thomas.

No consideration, however, was strong enough to turn Adamson from his purpose. The sale went on; and still, on the calling off of every favourite animal, Mrs Irvine renewed her anathemas.

" Gentlemen, this is the mistress's favourite cow, and gives thirteen pints of milk every day. She is valued in my roup-roll at fifteen pounds ; but we shall begin her at ten. Does any body say ten pounds for this excellent cow ? ten pounds—ten pounds ? Nobody says ten pounds ? Gentlemen, this is extraordinary ! Money is surely a scarce article here to-day. Well, then, does any gentleman say five pounds to begin this excellent cow that gives twelve pints of milk daily ? Five pounds—only five pounds !—Nobody bids five pounds ? Well, the stock must positively be sold without reserve. Ten shillings for the cow—ten shillings—ten shillings—Will nobody bid ten shillings to set the sale a-going ?"

" I'll gie five-and-twenty shillings for her," cried Adamson.

" Thank you, sir. One pound five—one pound five, and just a-going. Once—twice—*thrice*. Mr Adamson, one pound five."

Mrs Irvine came forward, drowned in tears, with the babe in her arms, and patting the cow, she said, " Ah, poor lady Bell, this is my last sight o' you, and the last time I'll clap your honest side ! And hae we really been deprived o' your support for the miserable sum o' five-and-twenty shillings ?—my curse light on the head o' him that has done it ! In the name of my destitute bairns I curse him ; and does he think that a mother's curse will sink fizzenless to the ground ? Na, na ! I see an ee that's looking down here in pity and in anger; and I see a hand that's gathering the bolts o' Heaven thegither, for some purpose that I could divine, but daurna utter. But that hand is unerring, and where it throws the bolt, there it will strike. Fareweel, poor beast! ye hae supplied us wi' mony a meal, but ye will never supply us wi' another."

This sale at Kirkheugh was on the 11th of July. On the day following, Mr Adamson went up to the folds in the hope, to shear his sheep, with no fewer than twenty-five attendants, consisting of all his own servants and cottars, and about as many neighbouring shepherds whom he had collected; it being customary for the farmers to assist one another reciprocally on these occasions. Adamson continued more than usually capricious and unreasonable all that forenoon. He was discontented with himself; and when a man is ill pleased with himself, he is seldom well pleased with others. He seemed altogether left to the influences of the Wicked One, running about in a rage, finding fault with every thing, and every person, and at times cursing bitterly, a practice to which he was not addicted; so that the sheep-shearing, that used to be a scene of hilarity among so many young and old shepherds, lads, lasses, wives, and callants, was that day turned into one of gloom and dissatisfaction.

After a number of other provoking outrages, Adamson at length, with the buisting-iron which he held in

his hand, struck a dog belonging to one of his own
shepherd boys, till the poor animal fell senseless on the
ground, and lay sprawling as in the last extremity.
This brought matters to a point which threatened nothing but anarchy and confusion ; for every shepherd's
blood boiled with indignation, and each almost wished
in his heart that the dog had been his own, that he
might have retaliated on the tyrant.   At the time the
blow was struck, the boy was tending one of the fold-
doors, and perceiving the plight of his faithful animal,
he ran to its assistance, lifted it in his arms, and holding it up to recover its breath, he wept and lamented
over it most piteously.   " My poor little Nimble !"
he cried ; " I am feared that mad body has killed ye,
and then what am I to do wanting ye ?   I wad ten
times rather he had strucken mysell !"

He had scarce said the words ere his master caught
him by the hair of the head with the one hand, and began to drag him about, while with the other he struck
him most unmercifully.   When the boy left the fold-
door, the unshorn sheep broke out, and got away to
the hill among the lambs and the clippies; and the farmer being in one of his " mad tantrums," as the servants called them, the mischance had almost put him
beside himself; and that boy, or man either, is in a
ticklish case who is in the hands of an enraged person
far above him in strength.

The sheep-shearers paused, and the girls screamed, when they saw their master lay hold of the boy. But Robert Johnston, a shepherd from an adjoining farm, flung the sheep from his knee, made the shears ring against the fold-dike, and in an instant had the farmer by both wrists, and these he held with such a grasp, that he took the power out of his arms; for Johnston was as far above the farmer in might, as the latter was above the boy.

"Mr Adamson, what are ye about?" he cried; "hae ye tint your reason a'thegither, that ye are gaun on rampauging like a madman that gate? Ye hae done the thing, sir, in your ill-timed rage, that ye ought to be ashamed of baith afore God and man."

"Are ye for fighting, Rob Johnston?" said the farmer, struggling to free himself. "Do ye want to hae a fight, lad? Because if ye do, I'll maybe gie you enough o' that."

"Na, sir, I dinna want to fight; but I winna let you fight either, unless wi' ane that's your equal; sae gie ower spraughling, and stand still till I speak to ye; for an ye winna stand to hear reason, I'll gar ye lie till ye hear it. Do ye consider what ye hae been doing even now? Do ye consider that ye hae been striking a poor orphan callant, wha has neither father nor mother to protect him, or to right his wrangs? and a' for naething, but a bit start o' natural affection? How wad ye like

sir, an ony body were to guide a bairn o' yours that
gate? and ye as little ken what they are to come to
afore their deaths, as that boy's parents did when they
were rearing and fondling ower him.   Fie for shame,
Mr Adamson! fie for shame! Ye first strak his poor
dumb brute, which was a greater sin than the tither,
for it didna ken what ye were striking it for; and then,
because the callant ran to assist the only creature he
has on the earth, and I'm feared the only true and
faithfu' friend beside, ye claught him by the hair o' the
head, and fell to the dadding him as he war your slave!
Od, sir, my blood rises at sic an act o' cruelty and injustice; and gin I thought ye worth my while, I wad
tan ye like a pellet for it."

The farmer struggled and fought so viciously, that
Johnston was obliged to throw him down twice over,
somewhat roughly, and hold him by main force.   But
on laying him down the second time, Johnston said,
" Now, sir, I just tell ye, that ye deserve to hae your
banes weel throoshen; but ye're nae match for me,
and I'll scorn to lay a tip on ye.   I'll leave ye to Him
who has declared himself the stay and shield of the
orphan; and gin some visible testimony o' his displeasure dinna come ower ye for the abusing of his ward,
I am right sair mista'en."

Adamson, finding himself fairly mastered, and that
no one seemed disposed to take his part, was obliged

to give in, and went sullenly away to tend the hirsel that stood beside the fold. In the meantime the sheep-shearing went on as before, with a little more of hilarity and glee. It is the business of the lasses to take the ewes, and carry them from the fold to the clippers; and now might be seen every young shepherd's sweetheart, or favourite, waiting beside him, helping him to clip, or holding the ewes by the hind legs to make them lie easy, a great matter for the furtherance of the operator. Others again, who thought themselves slighted, or loved a joke, would continue to act in a different manner, and plague the youths by bringing them such sheep as it was next to impossible to clip.

" Aih, Jock lad, I hae brought you a grand ane this time ! Ye will clank the shears ower her, and be the first done o' them a' !"

" My truly, Jessy, but ye hae gi'en me ane ! I declare the beast is woo to the cloots and the een holes; and afore I get the fleece broken up, the rest will be done. Ah, Jessy, Jessy ! ye're working for a mischief the day; and ye'll maybe get it."

" She's a braw sonsie sheep, Jock. I ken ye like to hae your arms weel filled. She'll amaist fill them as weel as Tibby Tod."

" There's for it now ! there's for it ! What care I for Tibby Tod, dame ? Ye are the most jealous elf, Jessy, that ever drew coat ower head. But wha was't

that sat half a night at the side of a grey stane wi' a
crazy cooper? And wha was't that gae the poor precentor the whiskings, and reduced a' his sharps to
downright flats? An ye cast up Tibby Tod ony mair
to me, I'll tell something that will gar thae wild een
reel i' your head, Mistress Jessy."

" Wow, Jock, but I'm unco wae for ye now. Poor
fellow! It's really very hard usage! If ye canna
clip the ewe, man, gie me her, and I'll tak her to anither; for I canna bide to see ye sae sair put about. I
winna bring ye anither Tibby Tod the day, take my
word on it. The neist shall be a real May Henderson
o' Firthhope-cleuch——ane, ye ken, wi' lang legs, and a
good lamb at her fit."

" Gudesake, lassie, haud your tongue, and dinna
affront baith yoursell and me. Ye are fit to gar ane's
cheek burn to the bane. I'm fairly quashed, and daurna say anither word. Let us therefore hae let-a-be for
let-a-be, which is good bairns's greement, till after the
close o' the day sky; and then I'll tell ye my mind."

" Ay, but whilk o' your minds will ye tell me,
Jock? For ye will be in five or six different anes
afore that time. Ane, to ken your mind, wad need to
be tauld it every hour o' the day, and then cast up the
account at the year's end. But how wad she settle it
then, Jock? I fancy she wad hae to multiply ilk year's

minds by dozens, and divide by four, and then we a'
ken what wad be the quotient."

" Aih wow, sirs! heard ever ony o' ye the like o'
that? For three things the sheep-fauld is disquieted,
and there are four which it cannot bear."

" And what are they, Jock?"

" A witty wench, a woughing dog, a waukit-woo'd
wedder, and a pair o' shambling shears."

After this manner did the gleesome chat go on, now
that the surly goodman had withdrawn from the scene.
But this was but one couple; every pair being engaged according to their biasses, and after their kind—
some settling the knotty points of divinity; others
telling auld-warld stories about persecutions, forays,
and fairy raids; and some whispering, in half sentences, the soft breathings of pastoral love.

But the farmer's bad humour, in the meanwhile
was only smothered, not extinguished; and, like a
flame that is kept down by an overpowering weight of
fuel, wanted but a breath to rekindle it; or like a barrel of gunpowder, that the smallest spark will set in a
blaze. That spark unfortunately fell upon it too soon.
It came in the form of an old beggar, ycleped Patie
Maxwell, a well-known, and generally a welcome
guest, over all that district. He came to the folds for
his annual present of a fleece of wool, which had never before been denied him; and the farmer being the

first person he came to, he approached him, as in respect bound, accosting him in his wonted obsequious
way.

"Weel, gudeman, how's a' wi' ye the day?"—(No
answer.)—"This will be a thrang day w'ye? How
are ye getting on wi' the clipping?"

"Nae the better o' you, or the like o' you. Gang
away back the gate ye came. What are ye coming
doiting up through amang the sheep that gate for,
putting them a' tersyversy?"

"Tut, gudeman, what does the sheep mind an auld
creeping body like me? I hae done nae ill to your
pickle sheep; and as for ganging back the road I cam,
I'll do that whan I like, and no till than."

"But I'll make you blithe to turn back, auld vaga-
bond! Do ye imagine I'm gaun to hae a' my clippers
and grippers, buisters and binders, laid half idle, gaff-
ing and giggling wi' you?"

"Why, then, speak like a reasonable man, and a
courteous Christian, as ye used to do, and I'se crack
wi' yoursell, and no gang near them."

"I'll keep my Christian cracks for others than auld
Papist dogs, I trow."

"Wha do ye ca' auld Papist dogs, Mr Adamson?
—Wha is it that ye mean to denominate by that fine-
sounding title?"

"Just you, and the like o' ye, Pate. It is weel

kenn'd that ye are as rank a Papist as ever kissed a crosier, and that ye were out in the very fore-end o' the unnatural Rebellion, in order to subvert our religion, and place a Popish tyrant on the throne. It is a shame for a Protestant parish like this to support ye, and gie you as liberal awmosses as ye were a Christian saint. For me, I can tell you, ye'll get nae mae at my hand ; nor nae rebel Papist loun amang ye."

"Dear sir, ye're surely no yoursell the day ? Ye hae kenn'd I professed the Catholic religion these thretty years—it was the faith I was brought up in, and that in which I shall dee ; and ye kenn'd a' that time that I was out in the Forty-Five wi' Prince Charles, and yet ye never made mention o' the facts, nor refused me my awmos, till the day. But as I hae been obliged t'ye, I'll haud my tongue ; only, I wad advise ye as a friend, whenever ye hae occasion to speak of ony community of brother Christians, that ye will in future hardly make use o' siccan harsh terms. Or, if ye will do't, tak care wha ye use them afore, and let it no be to the face o' an auld veteran."

"What, ye auld profane wafer-eater, and worshipper of graven images, dare ye heave your pikit kent at me ?"

"I hae heaved baith sword and spear against mony a better man ; and, in the cause o' my religion, I'll do it again."

He was proceeding, but Adamson's choler rising to an ungovernable height, he drew a race, and, running against the gaberlunzie with his whole force, made him fly heels-over-head down the hill. The old man's bonnet flew off, his meal-pocks were scattered about, and his mantle, with two or three small fleeces of wool in it, rolled down into the burn.

The servants observed what had been done, and one elderly shepherd said, " In troth, sirs, our master is no himsell the day. He maun really be looked to. It appears to me, that sin' he roupit out yon poor family yesterday, the Lord has ta'en his guiding arm frae about him. Rob Johnston, ye'll be obliged to rin to the assistance of the auld man."

" I'll trust the auld Jacobite for another shake wi' him yet," said Rob, " afore I steer my fit ; for it strikes me, if he hadna been ta'en unawares, he wad hardly hae been sae easily coupit."

The gaberlunzie was considerably astounded and stupified when he first got up his head ; but finding all his bones whole, and his old frame disencumbered of every superfluous load, he sprung to his feet, shook his grey burly locks, and cursed the aggressor in the name of the Holy Trinity, the Mother of our Lord, and all the blessed Saints above. Then approaching him with his cudgel heaved, he warned him to be on his guard, or make out of his reach, else he would

8

send him to eternity in the twinkling of an eye. The
farmer held up his staff across, to defend his head
against the descent of old Patie's piked kent, and, at
the same time, made a break in, with intent to close
with his assailant ; but, in so doing, he held down his
head for a moment, on which the gaberlunzie made a
swing to one side, and lent Adamson such a blow over
the neck, or back part of the head, that he fell violently on his face, after running two or three steps
precipitately forward. The beggar, whose eyes gleamed with wild fury, while his grey locks floated over
them like a winter cloud over two meteors of the
night, was about to follow up his blow with another
more efficient one on his prostrate foe ; but the farmer, perceiving these unequivocal symptoms of danger,
wisely judged that there was no time to lose in provi-
ding for his own safety, and, rolling himself rapidly
two or three times over, he got to his feet, and made
his escape, though not before Patie had hit him what
he called " a stiff lounder across the rumple."

The farmer fled along the brae, and the gaberlunzie
pursued, while the people at the fold were convulsed
with laughter. The scene was highly picturesque, for
the beggar could run none, and still the faster that he
essayed to run, he made the less speed. But ever and
anon he stood still, and cursed Adamson in the name
of one or other of the Saints or Apostles, brandishing

his cudgel, and stamping with his foot. The other, keeping still at a small distance, pretended to laugh at him, and at the same time uttered such bitter abuse against the Papists in general, and old Patie in particular, that, after the latter had cursed himself into a proper pitch of indignation, he always broke at him again, making vain efforts to reach him one more blow. At length, after chasing him by these starts about half a mile, the beggar returned, gathered up the scattered implements and fruits of his occupation, and came to the fold to the busy group.

Patie's general character was that of a patient, jocular, sarcastic old man, whom people liked, but dared not much to contradict; but that day his manner and mien had become so much altered, in consequence of the altercation and conflict which had just taken place, that the people were almost frightened to look at him; and as for social converse, there was none to be had with him. His countenance was grim, haughty, and had something Satanic in its lines and deep wrinkles; and ever and anon, as he stood leaning against the fold, he uttered a kind of hollow growl, with a broken interrupted sound, like a war-horse neighing in his sleep, and then muttered curses on the farmer.

The old shepherd before-mentioned, ventured, at length, to caution him against such profanity, saying, " Dear Patie, man, dinna sin away your soul, venting siccan curses as these. They will a' turn back on your ain head; for what harm can the curses of a poor sinfu' worm do to our master?"

"My curse, sir, has blasted the hopes of better men than either you or him," said the gaberlunzie, in an earthquake voice, and shivering with vehemence as he spoke. "Ye may think the like o' me can hae nae power wi' Heaven; but an I hae power wi' hell, it is sufficient to cow ony that's here. I sanna brag what effect my curse will have, but I shall say this, that either your master, or ony o' his men, had as good have auld Patie Maxwell's blessing as his curse ony time, Jacobite and Roman Catholic though he be."

It now became necessary to bring into the fold the sheep that the farmer was tending; and they were the last hirsel that was to shear that day. The farmer's face was reddened with ill-nature; but yet he now appeared to be somewhat humbled, by reflecting on the ridiculous figure he had made. Patie sat on the top of the fold-dike, and from the bold and hardy asseverations that he made, he seemed disposed to provoke a dispute with any one present who chose to take up the cudgels. While the shepherds, under fire of the gaberlunzie's bitter speeches, were sharping their shears, a thick black cloud began to rear itself over the height to the southward, the front of which seemed to be boiling—both its outsides rolling rapidly forward, and again wheeling in toward the centre. I have heard old Robin Johnston, the stout young man mentioned above, but who was a very old man when I knew him, describe the appearance of the cloud as greatly resembling a whirlpool made by the eddy of a rapid tide, or flooded river; and he declared, to his dying day, that he never saw aught in nature have a more ominous appearance. The gaberlunzie was the first to notice it, and drew the attention of the rest towards that point of the heavens by the following singular and profane remark:——" Aha, lads! see what's coming yonder. Yonder's Patie Maxwell's curse coming rowing and reeling on ye already; and what will ye say an the curse of God be coming backing it?"

" Gudesake, haud your tongue, ye profane body; ye mak me feared to hear ye," said one.——" It's a strange delusion to think that a Papish can hae ony influence wi' the Almighty, either to bring down his blessing or his curse."

" Ye speak ye ken nae what, man," answered Pate; " ye hae learned some rhames frae your poor cauld-rife Protestant Whigs about Papists, and Antichrist, and children of perdition; yet it is plain that ye haena ae spark o' the life or power o' religion in your whole frame, and dinna ken either what's truth or what's falsehood.——Ah! yonder it is coming, grim and gurly! Now

I hae called for it, and it is coming, let me see if a' the Protestants that are of ye can order it back, or pray it away again! Down on your knees, ye dogs, and set your mou's up against it, like as many spiritual cannon, and let me see if you have influence to turn aside ane o' the hailstanes that the deils are playing at chucks wi' in yon dark chamber!"

"I wadna wonder if our clipping were cuttit short," said one.

"Na, but I wadna wonder if something else were cuttit short," said Patie; "What will ye say an some o' your weazons be cuttit short? Hurraw! yonder it comes! Now, there will be sic a hurly-burly in Laverhope as never was sin' the creation o' man!"

The folds of Laverhope were situated on a gently sloping plain, in what is called "the forkings of a burn." Laver-burn runs to the eastward, and Widehope-burn runs north, meeting the other at a right angle, a little below the folds. It was around the head of this Widehope that the cloud first made its appearance, and there its vortex seemed to be impending. It descended lower and lower, with uncommon celerity, for the elements were in a turmoil. The cloud laid first hold of one height, then of another, till at length it closed over and around the pastoral group, and the dark hope had the appearance of a huge chamber hung with sackcloth. The big clear drops of rain soon began to descend, on

which the shepherds covered up the wool with blankets,
then huddled together under their plaids at the side of
the fold, to eschew the speat, which they saw was going to be a terrible one.   Patie still kept undauntedly
to the top of the dike, and Mr Adamson stood cowering at the side of it, with his plaid over his head, at a
little distance from the rest.   The hail and rain mingled, now began to descend in a way that had been seldom witnessed; but it was apparent to them all that
the tempest raged with much greater fury in Widehope-
head to the southward.—Anon a whole volume of lightning burst from the bosom of the darkness, and quivered
through the gloom, dazzling the eyes of every behold-
er;—even old Maxwell clapped both his hands on his
eyes for a space; a crash of thunder followed the flash,
that made all the mountains chatter, and shook the firmament so, that the density of the cloud was broken
up; for, on the instant that the thunder ceased, a rushing sound began in Widehope, that soon increased to a
loudness equal to the thunder itself; but it resembled
the noise made by the sea in a storm.   "Holy Virgin!"
exclaimed Patie Maxwell, "What is this? What is
this? I declare we're a' ower lang here, for the dams
of heaven are broken up;" and with that he flung himself from the dike, and fled toward the top of a rising
ground. He knew that the sound proceeded from the
descent of a tremendous water-spout; but the rest, not

conceiving what it was, remained where they were. The storm increased every minute, and in less than a quarter of an hour after the retreat of the gaberlunzie, they heard him calling out with the utmost earnestness; and when they eyed him, he was jumping like a madman on the top of the hillock, waving his bonnet, and screaming out, "Run, ye deil's buckies! Run for your bare lives!" One of the shepherds, jumping up on the dike, to see what was the matter, beheld the burn of Widehope coming down in a manner that could be compared to nothing but an ocean, whose boundaries had given way, descending into the abyss. It came with a cataract front more than twenty feet deep, as was afterwards ascertained by measurement; for it left sufficient marks to enable men to do this with precision. The shepherd called for assistance, and leaped into the fold to drive out the sheep; and just as he got the foremost of them to take the door, the flood came upon the head of the fold, on which he threw himself over the side-wall, and escaped in safety, as did all the rest of the people.

Not so Mr Adamson's ewes; the greater part of the hirsel being involved in this mighty current. The large fold nearest the burn was levelled with the earth in one second. Stones, ewes, and sheep-house, all were carried before it, and all seemed to bear the same weight. It must have been a dismal sight, to see so many fine animals tumbling and rolling in one irresistible mass. They were strong, however, and a few plunged out, and made their escape to the eastward; a greater number were carried headlong down, and thrown out on the other side of Laver-burn, upon the side of a dry hill, to which they all escaped, some of them considerably maimed; but the greatest number of all were lost, being overwhelmed among the rubbish of the fold, and entangled so among the falling dikes, and the torrent wheeling and boiling amongst them, that escape was impossible. The wool was totally swept away, and all either lost, or so much spoiled, that, when afterwards recovered, it was unsaleable.

When first the flood broke in among the sheep, and the women began to run screaming to the hills, and the despairing shepherds to fly about, unable to do any thing, Patie began a-laughing with a loud and hellish guffaw, and in that he continued to indulge till quite exhausted. " Ha, ha, ha, ha ! what think ye o' the auld beggar's curse now ? Ha, ha, ha, ha ! I think it has been backit wi' Heaven's and the deil's baith. Ha, ha, ha, ha !" And then he mimicked the thunder with the most outrageous and ludicrous jabberings, turning occasionally up to the cloud streaming with lightning and hail, and calling out,—" Louder yet, deils ! louder yet ! Kindle up your crackers, and yerk away ! Rap, rap, rap, rap—Ro-ro, ro, ro—Roo—Whush."

" I daresay that body's the vera deevil himsell in the shape o' the auld Papish beggar !" said one, not thinking that Patie could hear at such a distance.

" Na, na, lad, I'm no the deil," cried he in answer ; " but an I war, I wad let ye see a stramash ! It is a sublime thing to be a Roman Catholic amang sae mony weak apostates ; but it is a sublimer thing still to be a deil—a master-spirit in a forge like yon. Ha, ha, ha, ha ! Take care o' your heads, ye cock-chickens o' Calvin—take care o' the auld Coppersmith o' the Black Cludd !"

From the moment that the first thunder-bolt shot from the cloud, the countenance of the farmer was changed. He was manifestly alarmed in no ordinary degree ; and when the flood came rushing from the dry mountains, and took away his sheep and his folds before his eyes, he became as a dead man, making no effort to save his store, or to give directions how it might be done. He ran away in a cowering posture, as he had been standing, and took shelter in a little green hollow, out of his servants' view.

The thunder came nearer and nearer the place where the astonished hinds were, till at length they perceived the bolts of flame striking the earth around them, in every direction ; at one time tearing up its bosom, and at another splintering the rocks. Robin Johnston, in describing it, said, that " the thunnerbolts came shim-

mering out o' the cludd sae thick, that they appeared
to be linkit thegither, and fleeing in a' directions.
There war some o' them blue, some o' them red, and
some o' them like the colour o' the lowe of a candle;
some o' them diving into the earth, and some o' them
springing up out o' the earth and darting into the
heaven." I cannot vouch for the truth of this, but I am
sure my informer thought it true, or he would not have
told it; and he said farther, that when old Maxwell
saw it, he cried——" Fie, tak care, cubs o' hell! fie, tak
care! cower laigh, and sit sicker; for your auld dam is
aboon ye, and aneath ye, and a' round about ye.   O
for a good wat nurse to spean ye, like John Adamson's
lambs! Ha, ha, ha!"——The lambs, it must be observed,
had been turned out of the fold at first, and none of
them perished with their dams.

But just when the storm was at the height, and apparently passing the bounds ever witnessed in these
northern climes; when the embroiled elements were
in the state of hottest convulsion, and when our little
pastoral group were every moment expecting the next
to be their last, all at once a lovely " blue bore," frin-
ged with downy gold, opened in the cloud behind, and
in five minutes more the sun again appeared, and all
was beauty and serenity. What a contrast to the scene
so lately witnessed!

The most remarkable circumstance of the whole

was perhaps the contrast between the two burns. The burn of Laverhope never changed its colour, but continued pure, limpid, and so shallow, that a boy might have stepped over it dry-shod, all the while that the other burn was coming in upon it like an ocean broken loose, and carrying all before it. In mountainous districts, however, instances of the same kind are not infrequent in times of summer speats. Some other circumstances connected with this storm, were also described to me : The storm coming from the south, over a low-lying, wooded, and populous district, the whole of the crows inhabiting it posted away up the glen of Laverhope to avoid the fire and fury of the tempest. " There were thoosands and thoosands came up by us," said Robin, " a' laying theirsells out as they had been mad. And then, whanever the bright bolt played flash through the darkness, ilk ane o' them made a dive and a wheel to avoid the shot : For I was persuaded that they thought a' the artillery and musketry o' the haill coöntry were loosed on them, and that it was time for them to tak the gate. There were likewise several colly dogs came by us in great extremity, hinging out their tongues, and looking aye ower their shouthers, rinning straight on they kenn'dna where ; and amang other things, there was a black Highland cow came roaring up the glen, wi' her stake hanging at her neck."

When the gush of waters subsided, all the group, men and women, were soon employed in pulling out dead sheep from among rubbish of stones, banks of gravel, and pools of the burn; and many a row of carcasses was laid out, which at that season were of no use whatever, and of course utterly lost. But all the time they were so engaged, Mr Adamson came not near them; at which they wondered, and some of them remarked, that " they thought their master was fey the day, mae ways than ane."

" Ay, never mind him," said the old shepherd, " he'll come when he thinks it his ain time; he's a right sair humbled man the day, and I hope by this time he has been brought to see his errors in a right light. But the gaberlunzie is lost too. I think he be sandit in the yird, for I hae never seen him sin' the last great crash o' thunner."

" He'll be gane into the howe to wring his duds," said Robert Johnston, " or maybe to make up matters wi' your master. Gude sauf us, what a profane wretch the auld creature is ! I didna think the muckle horned deil himsell could hae set up his mou' to the heaven, and braggit and blasphemed in sic a way. He gart my heart a' grue within me, and dirle as it had been bored wi' reid-het elsins."

" Oh, what can ye expect else of a Papish ?" said the old shepherd, with a deep sigh. " They're a' deil's bairns ilk ane, and a' employed in carrying on their father's wark. It is needless to expect gude branches frae sic a stock, or gude fruit frae siccan branches."

" There's ae wee bit text that folks should never lose sight o'," said Robin, " and it's this,—' Judge not, that ye be not judged.' I think," remarked Robin, when he told the story, " I think that steekit their gabs !"

The evening at length drew on ; the women had gone away home, and the neighbouring shepherds had scattered here and there to look after their own flocks. Mr Adamson's men alone remained, lingering about the brook and the folds, waiting for their master. They had seen him go into the little green hollow, and they knew he was gone to his prayers, and were unwilling to disturb him. But they at length began to think it extraordinary that he should continue at his prayers the whole afternoon. As for the beggar, though acknowledged to be a man of strong sense and sound judgment, he had never been known to say prayers all his life, except in the way of cursing and swearing a little sometimes ; and none of them could conjecture what was become of him. Some of the rest, as it grew late, applied to the old shepherd before oft mentioned, whose name I have forgot, but he had herded with Adamson twenty years—some of the rest, I say, applied to him to go and bring their master away home, thinking that perhaps he was taken ill.

" O, I'm unco laith to disturb him," said the old
man; " he sees that the hand o' the Lord has fa'en
heavy on him the day, and he's humbling himsell afore
him in great bitterness o' spirit, I daresay. I count it
a sin to brik in on sic devotions as thae."

" Na, I carena if he should lie and pray yonder till
the morn," said a young lad, " only I wadna like to
gang hame and leave him lying on the hill, if he should
hae chanced to turn no weel. Sae, if nane o' ye will
gang and bring him, or see what ails him, I'll e'en gang
mysell;" and away he went, the rest standing still to
await the issue.

When the lad went first to the brink of the little
slack where Adamson lay, he stood a few moments, as
if gazing or listening, and then turned his back and
fled. The rest, who were standing watching his motions, wondered at this; and they said, one to another,
that their master was angry at being disturbed, and had
been threatening the lad so rudely, that it had caused
him to take to his heels. But what they thought most
strange was, that the lad did not fly towards them, but
straight to the hill; nor did he ever so much as cast
his eyes in their direction; so deeply did he seem to
be impressed with what had passed between him
and his master. Indeed, it rather appeared that he
did not know what he was doing; for, after running a
space with great violence, he stood and looked back,

and then broke to the hill again—always looking first
over the one shoulder, and then over the other. Then
he stopped a second time, and returned cautiously towards the spot where his master reclined ; and all the
while he never so much as once turned his eyes in the
direction of his neighbours, or seemed to remember
that they were there. His motions were strikingly er-
ratic ; for all the way, as he returned to the spot where
his master was, he continued to advance by a zigzag
course, like a vessel beating up by short tacks ; and several times he stood still, as on the very point of retreating. At length he vanished from their sight in the
little hollow.

It was not long till the lad again made his appearance, shouting and waving his cap for them to come
likewise ; on which they all went away to him as fast
as they could, in great amazement what could be the
matter. When they came to the green hollow, a shocking spectacle presented itself : There lay the body of
their master, who had been struck dead by the lightning ; and, his right side having been torn open, his
bowels had gushed out, and were lying beside the body. The earth was rutted and ploughed close to his
side, and at his feet there was a hole scooped out, a
full yard in depth, and very much resembling a grave.
He had been cut off in the act of prayer, and the body
was still lying in the position of a man praying in the

field. He had been on his knees, with his elbows leaning on the brae, and his brow laid on his folded hands ;
his plaid was drawn over his head, and his hat below
his arm ; and this affecting circumstance proved a
great source of comfort to his widow afterwards, when
the extremity of her suffering had somewhat abated.

No such awful visitation of Providence had ever
been witnessed, or handed down to our hinds on the
ample records of tradition, and the impression which
it made, and the interest it excited, were also without
a parallel.   Thousands visited the spot, to view the
devastations made by the flood, and the furrows formed by the electrical matter ; and the smallest circumstances were inquired into with the most minute curiosity :   above all, the still and drowsy embers of su-
perstition were rekindled by it into a flame, than
which none had ever burnt brighter, not even in the
darkest days of ignorance ; and by the help of it a
theory was made out and believed, that for horror is
absolutely unequalled.   But as it was credited in its
fullest latitude by my informant, and always added by
him at the conclusion of the tale, I am bound to mention the circumstances, though far from vouching them
to be authentic.

It was asserted, and pretended to have been proved,
that old Peter Maxwell *was not in the glen of Laverhope that day,* but at a great distance in a different

county, and that it was the devil who attended the folds in his likeness. It was farther believed by all the people at the folds, that it was the last explosion of the whole that had slain Mr Adamson; for they had at that time observed the side of the brae, where the little green slack was situated, covered with a sheet of flame for a moment. And it so happened, that thereafter the profane gaberlunzie had been no more seen; and therefore they said—and here was the most horrible part of the story—there was no doubt of his being the devil, waiting for his prey, and that he fled away in that sheet of flame, carrying the soul of John Adamson along with him.

I never saw old Pate Maxwell,—for I believe he died before I was born; but Robin Johnston said, that to his dying day, he denied having been within forty miles of the folds of Laverhope on the day of the thunder-storm, and was exceedingly angry when any one pretended to doubt the assertion. It was likewise reported, that at six o'clock afternoon a stranger had called on Mrs Irvine, and told her, that John Adamson, and a great part of his stock, had been destroyed by the lightning and the hail. Mrs Irvine's house was five miles distant from the folds; and more than that, the farmer's death was not so much as known of by mortal man until two hours after Mrs Irvine received this information. The storm exceeded any thing remembered, either for its violence or consequences, and these mysterious circumstances having been bruited abroad, gave it a hold on the minds of the populace, never to be erased but by the erasure of existence.   It fell out on the 12th of July, 1753.

The death of Mr Copland of Minnigapp, in Annandale, forms another era of the same sort.   It happened, if I mistake not, on the 18th of July, 1804.   It was one of those days by which all succeeding thunder-storms have been estimated, and from which they are dated, both as having taken place so many years before, and so long after.

Adam Copland, Esquire, of Minnigapp, was a gentleman esteemed by all who knew him.   Handsome in his person, and elegant in his manners, he was the ornament of rural society, and the delight of his family and friends ; and his loss was felt as no common misfortune.   As he occupied a pastoral farm of considerable extent, his own property, he chanced likewise to be out at his folds on the day above-mentioned, with his own servants, and some neighbours, weaning a part of his lambs, and shearing a few sheep. About mid-day the thunder, lightning, and hail, came on, and deranged their operations entirely ; and, among other things, a part of the lambs broke away from the folds, and being in great fright, they continued to run on.   Mr Copland and a shepherd of his, named Thomas

Scott, pursued them, and, at the distance of about half a mile from the folds, they turned them, mastered them, after some running, and were bringing them back to the fold, when the dreadful catastrophe happened. Thomas Scott was the only person present, of course ; and though he was within a few steps of his master at the time, he could give no account of any thing. I am well acquainted with Scott, and have questioned him about the particulars fifty times ; but he could not so much as tell me how he got back to the fold ; whether he brought the lambs with him or not ; how long the storm continued ; nor, indeed, any thing after the time that his master and he turned the lambs. That circumstance he remembered perfectly, but thenceforward his mind seemed to have become a blank. I should likewise have mentioned, as an instance of the same kind of deprivation of consciousness, that when the young lad who went first to the body of Adamson was questioned why he fled from the body at first, he denied that ever he fled ; he was not conscious of having fled a foot, and never would have believed it, if he had not been seen by four eye-witnesses. The only things of which Thomas Scott had any impressions were these : that, when the lightning struck his master, he sprung a great height into the air, much higher, he thought, than it was possible for any man to leap by his own exertion. He also thinks,

that the place where he fell dead was at a considerable
distance from that on which he was struck and leaped
from the ground; but when I inquired if he judged
that it would be twenty yards or ten yards, he could
give no answer—he could not tell. He only had an
impression that he saw his master spring into the air,
all on fire; and, on running up to him, he found him
quite dead. If Scott was correct in this, (and he being a man of plain good sense, truth, and integrity,
there can scarce be a reason for doubting him,) the
circumstance would argue that the electric matter by
which Mr Copland was killed issued out of the earth.
He was speaking to Scott with his very last breath;
but all that the survivor could do, he could never remember what he was saying. Some melted drops of
silver were standing on the case of his watch, as well
as on some of the buttons of his coat, and the body
never stiffened like other corpses, but remained as
supple as if every bone had been softened to jelly.
He was a married man, scarcely at the prime of life,
and left a young widow and only son to lament his
loss. On the spot where he fell there is now an obelisk
erected to his memory, with a warning text on it, relating to the shortness and uncertainty of human life.

CHAPTER III.

THE PRODIGAL SON.

" BRING me my pike-staff, daughter Matilda,—the one with the head turned round like crummy's horn; I find it easiest for my hand. And do you hear, Matty?—Stop, I say; you are always in such a hurry. —Bring me likewise my best cloak,—not the tartan one, but the grey marled one, lined with green flannel. I go over to Shepherd Gawin's to-day, to see that poor young man who is said to be dying."

" I would not go, father, were I you. He is a great reprobate, and will laugh at every good precept; and, more than that, you will heat yourself with the walk, get cold, and be confined again with your old complaint." -

" What was it you said, daughter Matilda? Ah, you said that which was very wrong. God only knows who are reprobates, and who are not. We can judge from nought but external evidence, which is a false ground to build calculations upon; but He knows the heart, with all our motives of action, and judges very differently from us. You said very wrong, daughter. But women will always be speaking unadvisedly. Always rash! always rash!——Bring me my cloak, daughter, for as to my being injured by my walk, I am going on my Master's business; my life and health are in his hands, and let him do with me as seemeth good in his sight; I will devote all to his service the little while I have to sojourn here."

" But this young man, father, is not only wicked himself, but he delights in the wickedness of others: He has ruined all his associates, and often not without toiling for it with earnest application. Never did your own heart yearn more over the gaining of an immortal soul to God and goodness, than this same young profligate's bosom has yearned over the destruction of one."

" Ah! it is a dismal picture, indeed! but not, perhaps, so bad as you say. Women are always disposed to exaggerate, and often let their tongues outrun their judgments. Bring me my cloak and my staff, daughter Mat. Though God withdraw his protecting arm from a fellow-creature for a time, are we to give all up for lost? Do you not know that his grace aboundeth to the chief of sinners?"

" I know more of this youth than you do, my dear father; would to Heaven I knew less! and I advise you to stay at home, and leave him to the mercy of that God whom he has offended. Old age and decrepitude are his derision, and he will mock at and laugh you to scorn, and add still more pangs to the hearts of his disconsolate parents. It was he, who, after much travail, overturned the principles of your beloved grandson, which has cost us all so much grief, and so many tears."

" That is indeed a bitter consideration; nevertheless it shall be got over. I will not say, The Lord reward him according to his works, although the words almost brooded on my tongue; but I will say, in the sincerity of a Christian disposition, May the Lord of mercy forgive him, and open his eyes to his undone state before it be too late, and the doors of forgiveness be eternally shut! Thanks to my Maker, I now feel as I ought! Go bring me my cloak, daughter Matilda; not that tartan one, with the gaudy spangles, but my comfortable grey marled one, with the green flannel lining."

" Stay till I tell you one thing more, father."

" Well, what is it? Say on, daughter, I'll hear you. Surely you are not desirous that this young man's soul should perish? Women's prejudices are always too strong, either one way or another. But I will hear you, daughter—I will hear you. What is it?"

" You knew formerly somewhat of the evil this profligate youth did to your grandson, but you do not

know that he has most basely betrayed his sister, your
darling Euphemia."

Old Isaac's head sunk down, while some tears involuntarily dropped on his knee; and to conceal his
emotion, he remained silent, save that he uttered a few
stifled groans. Natural affection and duty were at
strife within him, and for a time neither of them would
yield. His daughter perceived the struggle, and contented herself with watching its effects.

"Where is my cloak, daughter Matilda?" said he,
at length, without raising his head.

"It is hanging on one of the wooden knags in the
garret, sir," said she.

"Ay. Then you may let it hang on the knag where
it is all day. It is a weary world this! and we are
all guilty creatures! I fear I cannot converse and pray
with the ruthless seducer of both my children."

"Your resolution is prudent, sir. All efforts to re-
gain such a one are vain. He is not only a reprobate,
and an outcast from his Maker, but a determined and
avowed enemy to his laws and government."

"You do not know what you say, daughter," said
old Isaac, starting to his feet, and looking her sternly
in the face. "If I again hear you presume to prejudge
any accountable and immortal being in such a manner, I shall be more afraid of your own state than of
his. While life remains, we are in a land where re-

5

pentance is to be had and hoped for, and I will not hear the mercy of God arraigned. Bring me my cloak and my staff instantly, without another word. When I think of the country beyond the grave, and of the eternal fate that awaits this hapless prodigal, all my injuries vanish, and my trust in the Lord is strengthened anew. I shall at least pray with him, and for him; if he will not hear me, my Father who is in heaven may hear me, and haply He will open the victim's eyes to the hope that is set before him; for the hearts of all the children of men are in his hands, and as the rivers of water He turneth them whithersoever He pleaseth."

So old Isaac got his staff in his hand that had the head turned round like the horn of a cow, and also his cloak round his shoulders, not the tartan one with its gaudy spangles, but the grey marled one lined with green flannel. Well might old Isaac be partial to that cloak, for it was made for him by a beloved daughter who had been removed from him and from her family at the age of twenty-three. She was the mother of his two darlings, Isaac and Euphemia, mentioned before; and the feelings with which he put on the mantle that day can only be conceived by those who have learned to count all things but loss save Jesus Christ, and him crucified; and how few are the number who attain this sublime and sacred height!

"The blessing of him that is ready to perish shall

light on the head of my father," said Matilda, as she followed with her eye the bent figure of the old man hasting with tottering steps over the moor, on the road that led to Shepherd Gawin's ; and when he vanished from her view on the height, she wiped her eyes, drew the window screen, and applied herself to her work.

Isaac lost sight of his own home, and came in view of Shepherd Gawin's at the same instant ; but he only gave a slight glance back to his own, for the concern that lay before him dwelt on his heart. It was a concern of life and death, not only of a temporal, but of a spiritual and eternal nature ; and where the mortal concerns are centred, on that place, or towards that place, will the natural eye be turned. Isaac looked only at the dwelling before him : All wore a solemn stillness about the place that had so often resounded with rustic mirth ; the cock crowed not at the door as was his wont, nor strutted on the top of his old dung-hill, that had been accumulating there for ages, and had the appearance of a small green mountain ; but he sat on the kailyard dike, at the head of his mates, with his feathers ruffled, and every now and then his one eye turned up to the sky, as if watching some appearance there of which he stood in dread. The blithesome collies came not down the green to bark and frolic half in kindness and half in jealousy ; they lay coiled up on the shelf of the hay-stack, and as the stranger approached, lifted up their heads and viewed him with a sullen and sleepy eye, then, uttering a low and stifled growl, muffled their heads again between their hind feet, and shrouded their social natures in the very depth of sullenness.

"This is either the abode of death, or deep mourning, or perhaps both," said old Isaac to himself, as he approached the house; "and all the domestic animals are affected by it, and join in the general dismay. If this young man has departed with the eyes of his understanding blinded, I have not been in the way of my duty. It is a hard case that a blemished lamb should be cast out of the flock, and no endeavour made by the shepherd to heal or recall it; that the poor stray thing should be left to perish, and lost to its Master's fold. It behoveth not a faithful shepherd to suffer this; and yet—Isaac, thou art the man! May the Lord pardon his servant in this thing!"

The scene continued precisely the same until Isaac reached the solitary dwelling. There was no one passing in or out by the door, nor any human creature to be seen stirring, save a little girl, one of the family, who had been away meeting the carrier to procure some medicines, and who approached the house by a different path. Isaac was first at the door, and on reaching it he heard a confused noise within, like the sounds of weeping and praying commingled. Unwill-

ing to break in upon them, ignorant as he was how
matters stood with the family, he paused, and then with
a soft step retreated to meet the little girl that approached, and make some inquiries of her. She tried
to elude him by running past him at a little distance,
but he asked her to stop and tell him how all was
within. She did not hear what he said, but guessing
the purport of his inquiry, answered, " He's nae better,
sir."—" Ah me ! still in the same state of suffering ?"
—" Aih no,—no ae grain,—I tell ye he's nae better
ava." And with that she stepped into the house, Isaac
following close behind her, so that he entered without
being either seen or announced. The first sounds that
he could distinguish were the words of the dying youth;
they had a hoarse whistling sound, but they were the
words of wrath and indignation. As he crossed the
hallan he perceived the sick man's brother, the next to
him in age, sitting at the window with his elbow leaning on the table, and his head on his closed fist, while
the tints of sorrow and anger seemed mingled on his
blunt countenance. Farther on stood his mother and
elder sister leaning on each other, and their eyes shaded
with their hands, and close by the sick youth's bedside ; beyond these kneeled old Gawin the shepherd,
his fond and too indulgent father. He held the shrivelled hand of his son in his, and with the other that
of a damsel who stood by his side : And Isaac heard

him conjuring his son in the name of the God of heaven. Here old Isaac's voice interrupted the affecting scene. " Peace be to this house,—may the peace of the Almighty be within its walls," said he, with an audible voice. The two women uttered a stifled shriek, and the dying man a " Poh! poh!" of abhorrence. Old Gawin, though he did not rise from his knees, gazed round with amazement in his face ; and looking first at his dying son, and then at old Isaac, he drew a full breath, and said, with a quivering voice, " Surely the hand of the Almighty is in this !"

There was still another object in the apartment well worthy of the attention of him who entered—it was the damsel who stood at the bedside ; but then she stood with her back to Isaac, so that he could not see her face, and at the sound of his voice, she drew her cloak over her head, and retired behind the bed, sobbing so, that her bosom seemed like to rend. The cloak was similar to the one worn that day by old Isaac, for, be it remembered, he had not the gaudy tartan one about him, but the russet grey plaid made to him by his beloved daughter. Isaac saw the young woman retiring behind the bed, and heard her weeping ; but a stroke like that of electricity seemed to have affected the nerves of all the rest of the family on the entrance of the good old man, so that his attention was attracted by those immediately under his eye. The mother and

daughter whispered to each other in great perplexity.
Old Gawin rose from his knees ; and not knowing well
what to say or do, he diligently wiped the dust from
the knee-caps of his corduroy breeches, even descending to the minutiæ of scraping away some specks more
adhesive than the rest, with the nail of his mid finger.
No one welcomed the old man, and the dying youth
in the bed grumbled these bitter words, " I see now
on what errand Ellen was sent ! Confound your officiousness !"

" No, Graham, you are mistaken.   The child was
at T——r to meet the carrier for your drogs," said old
Gawin.

" Poh ! poh ! all of a piece with the rest of the
stuff you have told me.   Come hither, Ellen, and let
me see what the doctor has sent."——The girl came near,
and gave some vials with a sealed direction.

" So you got these at T——r, did you ?"

" Yes, I got them from Jessy Clapperton ; the carrier was away."

" Lying imp ! who told you to say that ? Answer
me !"——The child was mute and looked frightened.——
" Oh ! I see how it is ! You have done very well, my
dear, very cleverly, you give very fair promise.   Get
me some clothes, pray——I will try if I can leave this
house."

" Alas, my good friends, what is this ?" said Isaac ;

" the young man's reason, I fear, is wavering. Good Gawin, why do you not give me your hand ? I am extremely sorry for your son's great bodily sufferings, and for what you and your family must suffer mentally on his account. How are you?"

" Right weel, sir—as weel as may be expected," said Gawin, taking old Isaac's hand, but not once lifting his eyes from the ground to look the good man in the face.

" And how are you, good dame?" continued Isaac, shaking hands with the old woman.

" Right weel, thanks t'ye, sir. It is a cauld day this. Ye'll be cauld?"

" Oh no, I rather feel warm."

" Ay, ye have a comfortable plaid for a day like this ; a good plaid it is."

" I like to hear you say so, Agnes, for that plaid was a Christmas present to me, from one who has now been several years in the cold grave. It was made to me by my kind and beloved daughter Euphy. But enough of this—I see you have some mantles in the house of the very same kind."

" No; not the same. We have none of the same here."

" Well, the same or nearly so,—it is all one. My sight often deceives me now."—The family all looked at one another.—" But enough of this," continued old

Isaac, " I came not thus far to discuss such matters.
The sick young man, from what I heard, I fear, is incapable of spiritual conversation ?"

" Yes, I am," said he, from the bed, with a squeak-
ing voice; " and I would this moment that I were
dead !   Why don't you give me my clothes ?   Sure
never was a poor unfortunate being tormented as I
am ! Won't you have pity on me, and let me have a
little peace for a short time ?   It is not long I will
trouble you.   Is it not mean and dastardly in you all
to combine against an object that cannot defend himself ?"

" Alack, alack !" said old Isaac, " the calmness of
reason is departed for the present.   I came to converse
a little with him on that which concerns his peace
here, and his happiness hereafter : to hold the mirror
up to his conscience, and point out an object to him,
of which, if he take not hold, all his hope is a wreck."

" I knew it ! I knew it !" vociferated the sick man.
" A strong and great combination : but I'll defeat it,—
ha, ha, ha ! I tell you, Father Confessor, I have no
right or part in the object you talk of.   I will have no
farther concern with her.   She shall have no more of
me than you shall have.   If the devil should have all,
that is absolute——Will that suffice ?"

" Alas ! he is not himself," said old Isaac, " and
has nearly been guilty of blasphemy.   We must not

irritate him farther. All that we can do is to join in prayer that the Lord will lay no more upon him than he is able to bear, that he will heal his wounded spirit, and restore him to the use of reason ; and that, in the midst of his wanderings, should he blaspheme, the sin may not be laid to his charge."

Gawin was about to speak, and explain something that apparently affected him ; the dying youth had likewise raised himself on his elbow, and, with an angry countenance, was going to reply ; but when the old man took off his broad-brimmed hat, and discovered the wrinkled forehead and the thin snowy hair waving around it, the sight was so impressive that silence was imposed on every tongue. He sung two stanzas of a psalm, read a chapter of the New Testament, and then kneeling by the bedside, prayed for about half an hour, with such fervency of devotion, that all the family were deeply affected. It was no common-place prayer, nor one so general that it suited any case of distress ; every sentence of it spoke home to the heart, and alluded particularly to the very state of him for whom the petitions were addressed to heaven. Old Gawin gave two or three short sighs, which his wife hearing, she wiped her eyes with her apron. Their fair daughter made the same sort of noise that one does who takes snuff, and the innocent youth, their second son, who leaned forward on the table instead of kneeling, let two tears fall on the board, which he formed with his forefinger into the initials of his name ; the little girl looked from one to another, and wondered what ailed them all, then casting down her eyes, she tried to look devout, but they would not be restrained.   The dying youth, who at the beginning testified the utmost impatience, by degrees became the most affected of all. His features first grew composed, then rueful, and finally he turned himself on his face in humble prostration.   Isaac pleaded fervently with the Almighty that the sufferer's days might be lengthened, and that he might not be cut off in the bloom of youth, and exuberance of levity—at that season when man is more apt to speak than calculate, and to act than consider, even though speech should be crime, and action irretrievable ruin.   " Spare and recover him, O merciful Father, yet for a little while," said he, " that he may have his eyes opened to see his ruined state both by nature and by wicked works ; for who among us liveth and sinneth not, and what changes may be made in his dispositions in a few years or a few months by thy forbearance ?   Thou takest no pleasure in the death of sinners, but rather that all should repent, and turn unto thee, and live ; therefore, for his immortal soul's sake, and for the sake of what thy Son hath suffered for ruined man, spare him till he have time and space to repent.   Should his youthful mind have been tainted

with the prevailing vice of infidelity, so that he hath
been tempted to lift up his voice against the most sacred truths ; and should he, like all the profane, have
been following his inclinations rather than his judgment, how is he now prepared to abide the final result ?
or to be ushered into the very midst of those glorious
realities which he hath hitherto treated as a fiction ?
And how shall he stand before thee, when he discovers,
too late, that there is indeed a God, whose being and
attributes he hath doubted, a Saviour whom he hath
despised, a heaven into which he cannot enter, and a
hell which he can never escape ? Perhaps he hath been
instrumental in unhinging the principles of others, and
of misleading some unwary being from the paths of
truth and holiness ; and in the flush of reckless depravity, may even have deprived some innocent, loving,
and trusting being of virtue, and left her a prey to
sorrow and despair ; and with these and more grievous
crimes on his head,—all unrepented and unatoned,—
how shall he appear before thee ?"

At this part of the prayer, the sobs behind the bed
became so audible, that it made the old man pause
in the midst of his fervent supplications ; and the dying youth was heard to weep in suppressed breathings.
Isaac went on, and prayed still for the sufferer as one
insensible to all that passed ; but he prayed so earnestly for his forgiveness, for the restoration of his right

reason, and for health and space for repentance and amendment, that the sincerity of his heart was apparent in every word and every tone.

When he rose from his knees there was a deep silence ; no one knew what to say, or to whom to address himself ; for the impression made on all their minds was peculiarly strong. The only motion made for a good while was by the soft young man at the table, who put on his bonnet as he was wont to do after prayers ; but remembering that the Minister was present, he slipped it off again by the ear, as if he had been stealing it from his own head. At that instant the dying youth stretched out his hand. Isaac saw it, and looking to his mother, said he wanted something. " It is yours—your hand that I want," said the youth, in a kind and expressive tone. Isaac started, he had judged him to be in a state of delirium, and his surprise may be conceived when he heard him speak with calmness and composure. He gave him his hand, but from what he had heard fall from his lips before, knew not how to address him. " You *are* a good man," said the youth, " God in heaven reward you !"

" What is this I hear ?" cried Isaac, breathless with astonishment. " Have the disordered senses been rallied in one moment ? Have our unworthy prayers indeed been heard at the throne of Omnipotence, and answered so suddenly ? Let us bow ourselves with gratitude and adoration. And for thee, my dear young friend, be of good cheer; for there are better things intended towards thee. Thou shalt yet live to repent of thy sins, and to become a chosen vessel of mercy in the house of him that saved thee."

"If I am spared in life for a little while," said the youth, "I shall make atonement for some of my transgressions, for the enormity of which I am smitten to the heart."

"Trust to no atonement you can make of yourself," cried Isaac fervently. "It is a bruised reed, to which, if you lean, it will go into your hand and pierce it; a shelter that will not break the blast. You must trust to a higher atonement, else your repentance shall be as stubble, or as chaff that the wind carrieth away."

"So disinterested!" exclaimed the youth. "Is it my wellbeing alone over which your soul yearns? This is more than I expected to meet with in humanity! Good father, I am unable to speak more to you to-day, but give me your hand, and promise to come back to see me on Friday. If I am spared in life, you shall find me all that you wish, and shall never more have to charge me with ingratitude."

In the zeal of his devotion, Isaac had quite forgot all personal injuries; he did not even remember that there were such beings as his grandchildren in existence at that time; but when the young man said, that " he should find him all that he wished, and that he would no more be ungrateful," the sobs and weeping behind the bed grew so audible, that all farther exchange of sentiments was interrupted. The youth grasped old Isaac's hand, and motioned for him to go away; and he was about to comply, out of respect for the feelings of the sufferer, but before he could withdraw his hand from the bed, or rise from the seat on which he had just sat down, the weeping fair one burst from behind the bed; and falling on his knees with her face, she seized his hand with both hers, kissed it an hundred times, and bathed it all over with her tears. Isaac's heart was at all times soft, and at that particular time he was in a mood to be melted quite; he tried to soothe the damsel, though he himself was as much affected as she was—but as her mantle was still over her head, how could he know her? His old dim eyes were, moreover, so much suffused with tears, that he did not perceive that mantle to be the very same with his own, and that one hand must have been the maker of both. " Be comforted," said old Isaac; " he will mend—He will mend, and be yet a stay to you and to them all—be of good comfort, dear love."

When he had said this, he wiped his eyes hastily and impatiently with the lap of his plaid, seized his old pike-staff; and as he tottered across the floor, drawing up his plaid around his waist, its purple rus-

tic colours caught his eye, dim as it was ; and he perceived that it was not his tartan one with the gaudy
spangles, but the grey marled one that was made to
him by his beloved daughter. Who can trace the links
of association in the human mind ? The chain is more
angled, more oblique, than the course marked out by
the bolt of heaven—as momentarily formed, and as
quickly lost. In all cases, they are indefinable, but on
the mind of old age, they glance like dreams and visions of something that have been, and are for ever
gone. The instant that Isaac's eye fell on his mantle,
he looked hastily and involuntarily around him, first
on the one side and then on the other, his visage ma-
nifesting trepidation and uncertainty. "Pray what
have you lost, sir ?" said the kind and officious dame.
"I cannot tell what it was that I missed," said old
Isaac, "but methought I felt as if I had left something
behind me that was mine." Isaac went away, but left
not a dry eye in the dwelling which he quitted.

On leaving the cottage he was accompanied part of
the way by Gawin, in whose manner there still remained an unaccountable degree of embarrassment.
His conversation laboured under a certain restraint, in-
somuch that Isaac, who was an observer of human nature, could not help taking notice of it ; but those who
have never witnessed, in the same predicament, a home-
bred, honest countryman, accustomed to speak his

thoughts freely at all times, can form no conception of
the appearance that Gawin made. From the time that
the worthy old man first entered his cot, till the time
they parted again on the height, Gawin's lips were curled, the one up, and the other down, leaving an inordi-
nate extent of teeth and gums displayed between them ;
whenever his eyes met those of his companion, they
were that instant withdrawn, and, with an involuntary
motion, fixed on the summit of some of the adjacent
hills ; and when they stopped to converse, Gawin was
always laying on the ground with his staff, or beating
some unfortunate thistle all to pieces. The one family
had suffered an injury from the other, of a nature so
flagrant in Gawin's eyes, that his honest heart could not
brook it ; and yet so delicate was the subject, that
when he essayed to mention it, his tongue refused the
office. " There has a sair misfortune happened," said
he once, " that ye aiblins dinna ken o'.——But it's nae
matter ava !" And with that he fell on and beat a
thistle, or some other opposing shrub, most unmercifully.

There was, however, one subject on which he spoke
with energy, and that was the only one in which old
Isaac was for the time interested. It was his son's religious state of mind. He told Isaac, that he had formed a correct opinion of the youth, and that he was indeed a scoffer at religion, because it had become fa-

shionable in certain college classes, where religion was
never mentioned but with ridicule ; but that his infidelity sprung from a perverse and tainted inclination,
in opposition to his better judgment, and that if he
could have been brought at all to think or reason on
the subject, he would have thought and reasoned
aright ; this, however, he had avoided by every means,
seeming horrified at the very mention of the subject,
and glad to escape from the tormenting ideas that it
brought in its train.——" Even the sight of your face to-
day," continued Gawin, " drove him into a fit of temporary derangement. But from the unwonted docili-
ty he afterwards manifested, I have high hopes that
this visit of yours will be accompanied by the blessing
of Heaven. He has been a dear lad to me ; for the
sake of getting him forret in his lair, I hae pinched
baith mysell and a' my family, and sitten down wi'
them to mony a poor and scrimpit meal. But I never
grudged that, only I hae whiles been grieved that the
rest o' my family hae gotten sae little justice in their
schooling. And yet, puir things, there has never ane
o' them grieved my heart,—which he has done aftener
than I like to speak o'. It has pleased Heaven to pu-
nish me for my partiality to him ; but I hae naething
for it but submission.——Ha ! do ye ken, sir, that that
day I first saw him mount a poopit, and heard him begin a discourse to a croudit congregation, I thought a'

my pains and a' my pinching poverty overpaid. For the
first quarter of an hour I was sae upliftit, that I hardly
kenn'd whether I was sitting, standing, or flying in the
air, or whether the kirk was standing still, or rinning
round about. But, alake! afore the end o' his twa dis-
courses, my heart turned as cauld as lead, and it has
never again hett in my breast sinsyne. They were twa
o' thae cauldrife moral harangues, that tend to uplift
poor wrecked, degenerate human nature, and rin down
divine grace. There was nae dependence to be heard
tell o' there, beyond the weak arm o' sinfu' flesh; and
oh, I thought to mysell, that will afford sma' comfort,
my man, to either you or me, at our dying day!"

Here the old shepherd became so much overpower-
ed, that he could not proceed, and old Isaac took up
the discourse, and administered comfort to the sorrow-
ing father: then shaking him kindly by the hand, he
proceeded on his way, while Gawin returned slowly
homeward, still waging war with every intrusive and
superfluous shrub in his path. He was dissatisfied
with himself because he had not spoken his mind to a
person who so well deserved his confidence, on a subject that most of all preyed on his heart.

Matilda, who sat watching the path by which her
father was to return home, beheld him as soon as he
came in view, and continued to watch him all the way
with that tender solicitude which is only prompted by

the most sincere and disinterested love.——" With what agility he walks!" exclaimed she to herself; " bless me, sirs, he is running! He is coming pacing down yon green sward as if he were not out of his teens yet. I hope he has been successful in his mission, and prevailed with that abandoned profligate to make some amends to my hapless niece."

How different are the views of different persons! and how various the objects of their pursuit! Isaac thought of no such thing. He rejoiced only in the goodness and mercy of his Maker, and had high hopes that he would make him (unworthy as he was) instrumental in gaining over an immortal soul to Heaven and happiness. He sung praises to Heaven in his heart, and the words of gratitude and thankfulness hung upon his tongue. His daughter never took her eye from him, in his approach to his little mansion. Her whole dependence was on her father——her whole affection was centred in him: she had been taught from her infancy to regard him as the first and best of men; and though she had now lived with him forty years, he had never in one instance done an action to lessen that esteem, or deface that pure image of uprightness and sincerity, which her affectionate heart had framed. When he came in, her watchful kindness assailed him in a multitude of ways——every thing was wrong; she would have it that his feet were damp, although he assured her of the contrary—his right-hand sleeve was wringing wet ; and there was even a dampness between his shoulders, which was exceedingly dangerous, as it was so nearly opposite the heart. In short, old Isaac's whole apparel had to be shifted piecemeal, though not without some strong remonstrances on his part, and the good-natured quotation, several times repeated, from the old song :

> " Nought's to be won at woman's hand,
>   Unless ye gie her a' the plea."

When she had got him all made comfortable to her mind, and his feet placed in slippers well-toasted before the fire, she then began her inquiries. " How did you find all at Gawin's to-day, now when I have gotten time to speir ?"

" Why, daughter Matty, poorly enough, very poorly. But, thanks be to God, I think I left them somewhat better than I found them."

" I am so glad to hear that ! I hope you have taken Graham over the coals about Phemy ?"

" Eh ! about Phemy ?"

" You know what I told you before you went away ? You were not so unnatural as to forget your own flesh and blood, in communing with the man who has wronged her ?"

" I did not think more of the matter ; and if I had, there would have been no propriety in mentioning it, as none of the family spoke of it to me. And how was I assured that there was no mis-statement? Women are always so rash-spoken, and so fond of exaggeration, that I am afraid to trust them at the first word; and besides, my dear Matty, you know they are apt to see things double sometimes."

" Well, my dear father, I must say that your wit, or raillery, is very ill timed, considering whom it relates to. Your grand-daughter has been most basely deceived, under a pretence of marriage; and yet you will break your jokes on the subject!"

" You know, Matty, I never broke a joke on such a subject in my life. It was you whom I was joking; for your news cannot always be depended on. If I were to take up every amour in the parish, upon the faith of your first hints, and to take the delinquents over the coals, as you recommend, I should often commit myself sadly."

Matilda was silenced. She asked for no instances, in order to deny the insinuation; but she murmured some broken sentences, like one who has been fairly beat in an argument, but is loath to yield. It was rather a hard subject for the good lady; for ever since she had bidden adieu to her thirtieth year, she had become exceedingly jealous of the conduct of the younger portion of her sex. But Isaac was too kind-hearted to exult in a severe joke; he instantly added, as a palli-

ative, " But I should hold my tongue. You have
many means of hearing, and coming to the truth of
such matters, that I have not."

" I wish this were false, however," said Matilda,
turning away her face from the fire, lest the flame
should scorch her cheek ; " but I shall say no more
about it, and neither, I suppose, will you, till it be out
of time. Perhaps it may not be true, for I heard,
since you went away, that she was to be there to-day,
by appointment of his parents, to learn his final determination, which may be as much without foundation
as the other part of the story. If she had been there,
you must have seen her, you know."

" Eh ?" said Isaac, after biting his lip, and making a
long pause ; " What did you say, daughter Matty ?
Did you say my Phemy was to have been there to-
day ?"

" I heard such a report, which must have been un-
true, because, had she been there, you would have met
with her."

" There was a lass yonder," said Isaac. " How
many daughters has Gawin ?"

" Only one who is come the length of woman, and
whom you see in the kirk every day capering with her
bobbs of crimson ribbons, and looking at Will Fergu-
son."

" It is a pity women are always so censorious," said

Isaac—" always construing small matters the wrong way. It is to be hoped these little constitutional failings will not be laid to their charge.—So Gawin has but one daughter ?"

" I said, one that is a grown-up woman. He has, besides, little Ellen ; a pert idle creature, who has an eye in her head that will tell tales some day."

" Then there was indeed another damsel," said old Isaac, " whom I did not know, but took her for one of the family. Alake, and wo is me ! Could I think it was my own dear child hanging over the couch of a dying man ! The girl that I saw was in tears, and deeply affected. She even seized my hand, and bathed it with tears. What could she think of me, who neither named nor kissed her, but that I had cast her off and renounced her ? But no, no, I can never do that ; I will forgive her as heartily as I would beg for her forgiveness at the throne of mercy. We are all fallible and offending creatures ; and a young maid, that grows up as a willow by the water-courses, and who is in the flush of youth and beauty, ere ever she has had a moment's time for serious reflection, or one trial of worldly experience—that such a one should fall a victim to practised guilt, is a consequence so natural, that, however deeply to be regretted, it is not matter of astonishment. Poor misguided Phemy ! Did you indeed kneel at my knee, and bathe my hand with your affec-

tionate tears, without my once deigning to acknowledge
you?   And yet how powerful are the workings of
nature!   They are indeed the workings of the Deity
himself: for when I arose, all unconscious of the presence of my child, and left her weeping, I felt as if I
had left a part of my body and blood behind me."

" So she was indeed there, whining and whimpering
over her honourable lover ?" said Matilda.   " I wish
I had been there, to have told her a piece of my mind !
The silly, inconsiderate being, to allow herself to be
deprived of fair fame and character by such a worthless profligate, bringing disgrace on all connected with
her !   And then to go whimpering over his sick-bed !
—O dear love, you must marry me, or I am undone !
I have *loved* you with all my heart, you know, and you
must make me your wife.   I am content to beg my
bread with you, now that I have *loved* you so dearly !
only you must marry me.   Oh dear ! Oh dear ! what
shall become of me else !"

" Dear daughter Matilda, where is the presumptuous
being of the fallen race of Adam who can say, Here
will I stand in my own strength ? What will the best
of us do, if left to ourselves, better than the erring, in-
experienced being, whose turning aside you so bitterly
censure ?   It is better that we lament the sins and
failings of our relatives, my dear Matty, than rail

against them, putting ourselves into sinful passion, and thereby adding one iniquity to another."

The argument was kept up all that evening, and all next day, with the same effect; and if either of the disputants had been asked what it was about, neither could have told very precisely: the one attached a blame, which the other did not deny; only there were different ways of speaking about it. On the third day, which was Friday, old Isaac appeared at breakfast in his Sunday clothes, giving thus an intimation of a second intended visit to the house of Gawin the shepherd. The first cup of tea was scarcely poured out, till the old subject was renewed, and the debate seasoned with a little more salt than was customary between the two amiable disputants. Matilda disapproved of the visit, and tried, by all the eloquence she was mistress of, to make it appear indecorous. Isaac defended it on the score of disinterestedness and purity of intention; but finding himself hard pressed, he brought forward his promise, and the impropriety of breaking it. Matty would not give up her point; she persisted in it, till she spoiled her father's breakfast, made his hand shake so, that he could scarcely put the cup to his head, and, after all, staggered his resolution so much, that at last he sat in silence, and Matty got all to say herself. She now accounted the conquest certain, and valuing herself on the influence she possessed, she began to overburden her old father with all manner of kindness and teasing officiousness. Would he not take this, and refrain from that, and wear one part of dress in preference to another that he had on? There was no end of controversy with Isaac, however kind might be the intent. All that he said at that time was, " Let me alone, dear Matty; let me have some peace. Women are always overwise—always contrary."

When matters were at this pass, the maid-servant came into the room, and announced that a little girl of shepherd Gawin's wanted to speak with the Minister. " Alas, I fear the young man will be at his rest!" said Isaac. Matilda grew pale, and looked exceedingly alarmed, and only said, " she hoped not." Isaac inquired of the maid, but she said the girl refused to tell her any thing, and said she had orders not to tell a word of aught that had happened about the house.

" Then something *has* happened," said Isaac. " It must be as I feared! Send the little girl ben."

Ellen came into the parlour with a beck as quick and as low as that made by the water ouzel, when standing on a stone in the middle of the water; and, without waiting for any inquiries, began her speech on the instant, with, " Sir—hem—heh—my father sent me, sir —hem—to tell ye that ye warna to forget your promise to come ower the day, for that there's muckle need for yer helping hand yonder—sir; that's a', sir."

" You may tell your father," said Isaac, " that I will come as soon as I am able. I will be there by twelve o'clock, God willing."

" Are you wise enough, my dear father, to send such a message ?" remonstrated Matilda. " You are not able to go a journey to-day. I thought I had said enough about that before.——You may tell your father," continued she, turning to Ellen, " that my father cannot come the length of his house to-day."

" I'll tell my father what the Minister bade me,' replied the girl. " I'll say, sir, that ye'll be there by twall o'clock ;——will I, sir ?"

" Yes, by twelve o'clock," said Isaac.

Ellen had no sooner made her abrupt curtsey, and left the room, than Matilda, with the desperation of a general who sees himself on the point of being driven from a position which it had cost him much exertion to gain, again opened the fire of her eloquence upon her father. " Were I you," said she, " I would scorn to enter their door, after the manner in which the profligate villain has behaved: first, to make an acquaintance with your grandson at the College——pervert all his ideas of rectitude and truth——then go home with him to his father's house, during the vacation, and there live at heck and manger, no lady being in the house save your simple and unsuspecting Phemy, who now is reduced to the necessity of going to a shepherd's cottage, and begging to be admitted to the alliance of a family, the best of whom is far beneath her, to say nothing of the unhappy individual in question. Wo is me, that I have seen the day !"

" If the picture be correctly drawn, it is indeed very bad ; but I hope the recent sufferings of the young man will have the effect of restoring him to the principles in which he was bred, and to a better sense of his heinous offences.   I must go and see how the family fares, as in duty and promise bound.   Content yourself, dear daughter.   It may be that the unfortunate youth has already appeared at that bar from which there is no appeal."

This consideration, as it again astounded, so it put to silence the offended dame, who suffered her father to depart on his mission of humanity without farther opposition ; and old Isaac again set out, meditating as he went, and often conversing with himself, on the sinfulness of man, and the great goodness of God.   So deeply was he wrapt in contemplation, that he scarcely cast an eye over the wild mountain scenery by which he was surrounded, but plodded on his way, with eyes fixed on the ground, till he approached the cottage.   He was there aroused from his reverie, by the bustle that appeared about the door.   The scene was changed indeed from that to which he introduced himself two days before.   The collies came yelping and wagging their tails to meet him, while the inmates of the dwelling were peeping out at the door, and as quickly vanishing again into the interior. There were also a pair or two of neighbouring shepherds sauntering about the side of the kail-yard dike, all dressed in their Sunday apparel, and every thing bespeaking some " occasion," as any uncommon occurrence is generally denominated.

" What can it be that is astir here to-day?" said Isaac to himself.——" Am I brought here to a funeral or corpse-chesting, without being apprised of the event? It must be so. What else can cause such a bustle about a house where trouble has so long prevailed? Ah! there is also old Robinson, my session-clerk and precentor. He is the true emblem of mortality: then it is indeed all over with the poor young man!"

Now Robinson had been at so many funerals all over the country, and was so punctual in his attendance on all within his reach, that to see him pass, with his staff, and black coat without the collar, was the very same thing as if a coffin had gone by. A burial was always a good excuse for giving the boys the play, for a refreshing walk into the country, and was, besides, a fit opportunity for moral contemplation, not to say any thing of hearing the country news. But there was also another motive, which some thought was the most powerful inducement of any with the old Dominie. It arose from that longing desire after preeminence which reigns in every human breast, and which no man fails to improve, however small the circle may be in which it can be manifested. At every funeral, in the absence of the Minister, Robinson was called on to say grace; and when they were both present, whenever the Parson took up his station in one apartment, the Dominie took up his in another, and thus had an equal chance, for the time, with his superior. It was always shrewdly suspected, that the Clerk tried to outdo the Minister on such occasions, and certainly made up in length what he wanted in energy. The general remarks on this important point amounted to this, " that the Dominie was langer than the Minister, and though he was hardly just sae conceese, yet he meant as weel;" and that, " for the maist part, he was *stronger on the grave.*" Suffice it, that the appearance of old Robinson, in the present case, confirmed Isaac in the belief of the solemnity of the scene awaiting him; and as his mind was humbled to acquiesce in the Divine will, his mild and reverend features were correspondent therewith. He thought of the disappointment and sufferings of the family, and had already begun in his heart to intercede for them at the throne of Mercy.

When he came near to the house, out came old Gawin himself. He had likewise his black coat on, and his Sunday bonnet, and a hand in each coat-pocket; but for all his misfortune and heavy trials, he strode to the end of the house with a firm and undismayed step.——Ay, he is quite right, thought Isaac to himself; that man has his trust where it should be, fixed on the Rock of Ages; and he has this assurance, that the Power on whom he trusts can do nothing wrong. Such a man can look death in the face, undismayed, in all his steps and inroads.

Gawin spoke to some of his homely guests, then turned round, and came to meet Isaac, whom he saluted, by taking off his bonnet, and shaking him heartily by the hand.——The bond of restraint had now been removed from Gawin's lips, and his eye met the Minister's with the same frankness it was wont. The face of affairs was changed since they had last parted.

" How's a' w'ye the day, sir?——How's a' w'ye?—— I'm unco blythe to see ye," said Gawin.

" Oh, quite well, think you. How are you yourself? And how are all within?"

" As weel as can be expectit, sir—as weel as can be expectit."

" I am at a little loss, Gawin——Has any change taken place in family circumstances since I was here?"

" Oh, yes; there has indeed, sir; a material change —I hope for the better."

Gawin now led the way, without further words, into the house, desiring the Minister to follow him, and

" tak' care o' his head and the bauks, and no fa' ower the bit stirk, for it was sure to be lying i' the dark."

When Isaac went in, there was no one there but the goodwife, neatly dressed in her black stuff gown, and check apron, with a close 'kerchief on her head, well crimped in the border, and tied round the crown and below the chin with a broad black ribbon. She also saluted the Minister with uncommon frankness— " Come away, sir, come away. Dear, dear, how are ye the day ? It's but a slaitery kind o' day this, as I was saying to my man, there ; Dear, dear, Gawin, says I, I wish the Minister may be nae the waur o' coming ower the muir the day. That was joost what I said. And dear, dear, sir, how's Miss Matty, sir ? Oh, it is lang sin' I hae seen her. I like aye to see Miss Matty, ye ken, to get a rattle frae her about the folk, ye ken, and a' our neighbours, that fa' into sinfu' gates ; for there's muckle sin gangs on i' the parish. Ah, ay ! I wat weel that's very true, Miss Matty, says I. But what can folk help it ? ye ken, folk are no a' made o' the same metal, as the airn tangs,—like you——"

—" Bless me with patience !" said Isaac in his heart ; " this poor woman's misfortunes have crazed her ! What a salutation for the house of mourning !" Isaac looked to the bed, at the side of which he had so lately kneeled in devotion, and he looked with a reverent dread, but the corpse was not there ! It was neatly spread with a clean coverlid.——It is best to conceal the pale and ghostly features of mortality from the gazer's eye, thought Isaac. It is wisely done, for there is nothing to be seen in them but what is fitted for corruption.

" Gawin, can nae ye tak' the Minister ben the house, or the rest o' the clanjamphery come in ?" said the talkative dame.——" Hout, ay, sir, step your ways ben the house. We hae a ben end and a but end the day, as weel as the best o' them. And ye're ane o' our ain folk, ye ken. Ah, ay ! I wat weel that's very true ! As I said to my man, Gawin, quo' I, whenever I see our Minister's face, I think I see the face of a friend."

" Gudewife, I hae but just ae word to say, by way o' remark," said Gawin ; " folk wha count afore the change-keeper, hae often to count twice, and sae has the herd, wha counts his hogs afore Beltan.——Come this way, sir ; follow me, and tak' care o' your head and the bauks."

Isaac followed into the rustic parlour, where he was introduced to one he little expected to see sitting there. This was no other than the shepherd's son, who had so long been attended on as a dying person, and with whom Isaac had so lately prayed, in the most fervent devotion, as with one of whose life little hope was entertained. There he sat, with legs like two poles, hands like the hands of a skeleton ; yet his emaciated

E 2

features were lighted up with a smile of serenity and joy. Isaac was petrified. He stood still on the spot, even though the young man rose up to receive him. He deemed he had come there to see his lifeless form laid in the coffin, and to speak words of comfort to the survivors. He was taken by surprise, and his heart thrilled with unexpected joy.

"My dear young friend, do I indeed see you thus?" he said, taking him kindly and gently by the hand. "God has been merciful to you, above others of your race. I hope, in the mercy that has saved you from the gates of death, that you feel grateful for your deliverance; for, trust me, it behoves you to do so, in no ordinary degree."

"I shall never be able to feel as I ought, either to my deliverer or to yourself," said he. "Till once I heard the words of truth and seriousness from your mouth, I have not dared, for these many years, to think my own thoughts, speak my own words, or perform the actions to which my soul inclined. I have been a truant from the school of truth; but have now returned, with all humility, to my Master, for I feel that I have been like a wayward boy, groping in the dark, to find my way, though a path splendidly lighted up lay open for me. But of these things I long exceedingly to converse with you, at full length and full leisure. In the meantime, let me introduce you to other friends who are longing for some little notice. This is my sister, sir ; and——shake hands with the Minister, Jane——And do you know this young lady, sir, with the mantle about her, who seems to expect a word from you, acknowledging old acquaintance ?"

" My eyes are grown so dim now," said old Isaac, " that it is with difficulty I can distinguish young people from one another, unless they speak to me. But she will not look up. Is this my dear young friend, Miss Mary Sibbet ?"

" Nay, sir, it is not she. But I think, as you two approach one another, your plaids appear very nearly the same."

" Phemy ! My own child Phemy ! Is it yourself ? Why did you not speak ?——But you have been an alien of late, and a stranger to me. Ah, Phemy ! Phemy ! I have been hearing bad news of you. But I did not believe them——no, I *would not* believe them."

Euphemia for a while uttered not a word, but keeping fast hold of her grandfather's hand, she drew it under her mantle, and crept imperceptibly a degree nearer to his breast. The old man waited for some reply, standing as in the act of listening ; till at length, in a trembling whisper, scarcely audible, she repeated these sacred words——" Father, forgive me, for I knew not what I did !" The expression had the effect desired on Isaac's mind. It brought to his remembrance that gracious petition, the most fully fraught with mercy and forgiveness that ever was uttered on earth, and bowed his whole soul at once to follow the pattern of his great Master. His eye beamed with exultation in his Redeemer's goodness, and he answered, " Yes, my child, yes. He whose words you have unworthily taken, will not refuse the petition of any of his repentant children, however great their enormities may have been ; and why should such a creature as I am presume to pretend indignation and offence, at aught further than his high example warrants ? May the Almighty forgive you as I do !"

" May Heaven bless and reward you !" said the young man. " But she is blameless—blameless as the babe on the knee. I alone am the guilty person, who infringed the rights of hospitality, and had nearly broken the bonds of confidence and love. But I am here today to make, or offer at least, what amends is in my power—to offer her my hand in wedlock ; that whether I live or die, she may live without dishonour. But, reverend sir, all depends on your fiat. Without your approbation she will consent to nothing ; saying, that she had offended deeply by taking her own will once, but nought should ever induce her to take it unadvisedly again. It was for this purpose that we sent for you so expressly to-day, namely, that I might entreat your consent to our union. I could not be removed from

home, so that we could not all meet, to know one another's mind, in any other place. We therefore await
your approbation with earnest anxiety, as that on which
our future happiness depends."

After some mild and impressive reprehensions, Isaac's
consent was given in the most unqualified manner, and
the names were given in to the old Dominie's hand,
with proper vouchers, for the publication of the bans.
The whole party dined together at old Gawin's. I was
there among the rest, and thought to enjoy the party exceedingly ; but the party was too formal, and too much
on the reserve before the Minister. I noted down, when
I went home, all the conversation, as far as I could
remember it, but it is not worth copying. I see that
Gawin's remarks are all measured and pompous, and,
moreover, delivered in a sort of bastard English, a language which I detest. He considered himself as now
to be nearly connected with the *Manse Family*, and
looking forward to an eldership in the church, deemed
it incumbent on him to talk in a most sage and instruc-
tive manner. The young shepherd, and an associate
of his, talked of dogs, Cheviot tups, and some remarkably bonny lasses that sat in the west gallery of the
church. John Grierson of the Hope recited what they
called " lang skelps o' metre," a sort of homely rhymes,
that some of them pronounced to be " far ayont Burns's
fit." And the goodwife ran bustling about ; but when-

ever she could get a little leisure, she gave her tongue
free vent, without regard either to Minister or Dominie.   She was too well trained in the old homely
Scotch, to attempt any of the flights, which to Gawin,
who was more sparing in his speech, were more easy
to be accomplished. "Dear, dear, sirs, can nae ye eat
away ?   Ye hae nae the stamacks o' as mony cats.
Dear, dear, I'm sure an the flesh be nae good, it sude
be good, for it never saw either braxy or breakwind,
bleer-ee nor Beltan pock, but was the cantiest crock o'
the Kaim-law.   Dear, dear, Johnie Grierson, tak' another rive o't, and set a good example ; as I said to my
man there, Gawin, says I, it's weel kenn'd ye're nae
flae-bitten about the gab ; and I said very true too."

Many such rants did she indulge in, always reminding
her guests that " it was a names-gieing-in, whilk was,
o' a' ither things, the ane neist to a wedding," and often hinting at their new and honourable alliance, scarcely even able to keep down the way in which it was
brought about ; for she once went so far as to say,
" As I said to my gudeman, Gawin, says I, for a' the
fy-gae-to ye hae made, it's weel kenn'd faint heart never wan fair lady. Ay, weel I wat, that's very true, says
I ; a bird in the hand is worth twa on the bush.——Won
a' to and fill yoursells, sirs ; there's routh o' mair where
that came frae.   It's no aye the fattest foddering that
mak's the fu'est aumry—and that's nae lee."

Miss Matilda, the Minister's maiden daughter, was in towering indignation about the marriage, and the connexion with a shepherd's family; and it was rumoured over all the parish that she would never countenance her niece any more. How matters went at first it is perhaps as well for Miss Matilda's reputation, in point of good-nature, that I am not able to say; but the last time I was at the Manse, the once profligate and freethinking student had become Helper to old Isaac, and was beloved and revered by all the parish, for the warmth of his devotion, and soundness of his principles. His amiable wife Euphemia had two sons, and their aunt Matty was nursing them with a fondness and love beyond that which she bore to life itself.

In conclusion, I have only further to remark, that I have always considered the prayers of that good old man as having been peculiarly instrumental in saving a wretched victim, not only from immediate death, but from despair of endless duration.

CHAPTER IV.

THE SCHOOL OF MISFORTUNE.

THE various ways in which misfortunes affect different minds, are often so opposite, that in contemplating them, we may well be led to suppose the human soul animated and directed in some persons by corporeal functions, formed after a different manner from those of others——persons of the same family frequently differing most widely in this respect.

It will appear, on a philosophic scrutiny of human feelings, that the extremes of laughing and crying are more nearly allied than is sometimes believed. With children, the one frequently dwindles, or breaks out into the other. I once happened to sit beside a negro, in the pit of the Edinburgh theatre, while the tragedy of Douglas was performing. As the dialogue between Old Norval and Lady Randolph proceeded, he grew more and more attentive; his eyes grew very large, and seemed set immovably in one direction; the tears started from them; his features went gradually awry; his under-lip curled and turned to one side; and just when I expected that he was going to cry outright, he burst into the most violent fit of laughter.

I have a female friend, on whom unfortunate accidents have the singular effect of causing violent laughter, which, with her, is much better proportioned to the calamity, than crying is with many others of the sex. I have seen the losing of a rubber at whist, when there was every probability that her party would gain it, cause her to laugh till her eyes streamed with tears. The breaking of a tureen, or set of valuable china, would quite convulse her. Danger always makes her sing, and misfortunes laugh. If we hear her in any apartment of the farm-house, or the offices, singing very loud, and very quick, we are sure something is on the point of going wrong with her; but if we hear her burst out a-laughing, we know that it is past redemption. Her memory is extremely defective; indeed she scarcely seems to retain any perfect recollection of past events; but her manners are gentle, easy, and engaging; her temper good, and her humour inexhaustible; and, with all her singularities, she certainly enjoys a greater share of happiness than her chequered fortune could possibly have bestowed on a mind differently constituted.

I have another near relation, who, besides being possessed of an extensive knowledge in literature, and a

refined taste, is endowed with every qualification requisite to constitute the valuable friend, the tender parent, and the indulgent husband ; yet his feelings, and
his powers of conception, are so constructed, as to ren-
der him a constant prey to corroding care.   No man
can remain many days in his company without saying,
in his heart, " that man was made to be unhappy."
What others view as slight misfortunes, affect him
deeply ; and in the event of any such happening to
himself, or those that are dear to him, he will groan
from his inmost soul, perhaps for a whole evening after
it first comes to his knowledge, and occasionally, for
many days afterwards, as the idea recurs to him.   Indeed, he never wants something to make him miserable ; for, on being made acquainted with any favour-
able turn of fortune, the only mark of joy that it pro-
duces is an involuntary motion of the one hand to
scratch the other elbow ; and his fancy almost instan-
taneously presents to him such a number of difficulties,
dangers, and bad consequences attending it, that though
I have often hoped to awake him to joy by my tidings,
I always left him more miserable than I found him.

I have another acquaintance whom we denominate " the Knight," who falls upon a method totally different to overcome misfortunes.   In the event of any
cross accident, or vexatious circumstance, happening to
him, he makes straight towards his easy chair—sits

calmly down upon it—clenches his right hand, with the
exception of his fore-finger, which is suffered to continue straight—strikes his fist violently against his left
shoulder—keeps it in that position, with his eyes fixed
on one particular point, till he has cursed the event and
all connected with it most heartily,—then, with a countenance of perfect good-humour, he indulges in a pleasant laugh, and if it is possible to draw a comical or ridiculous inference from the whole, or any part of the
affair, he is sure to do it, that the laugh may be kept
up.   If he fails in effecting this, he again resumes his
former posture, and consigns all connected with the
vexatious circumstance to the devil ; then takes another
good hearty laugh ; and in a few minutes the affair is no
more heard or thought of.

   John Leggat is a lad about fifteen, a character of
great singularity, whom nature seems to have formed
in one of her whims. He is not an entire idiot, for he
can perform many offices about his master's house—
herd the cows, and run errands too, provided there be
no dead horses on the road, nor any thing extremely
ugly ; for, if there be, the time of his return is very uncertain.   Among other anomalies in his character, the
way that misfortunes affect him is not the least striking.
He once became warmly attached to a young hound,
which was likewise very fond of him, paying him all
the grateful respect so often exhibited by that faithful

animal. John loved him above all earthly things—
some even thought that he loved him better than his
own flesh and blood. The hound one day came to an
untimely end. John never got such sport in his life ;
he was convulsed with laughter when he contemplated
the features of his dead friend. When about his ordinary business, he was extremely melancholy ; but whenever he came and looked at the carcass, he was transported with delight, and expressed it by the most extravagant raptures. He next attached himself to a tur-
key-cock, which he trained to come at his call, and pursue and attack such people as he pointed out for that
purpose. John was very fond of this amusement ; but
it proved fatal to his favourite—an irritated passenger
knocked it dead at a stroke. This proved another
source of unbounded merriment to John ; the stiff half-
spread wing, the one leg stretched forward, and the
other back, were infinitely amusing ; but the abrupt
crook in his neck—his turned-up eye and open bill
were quite irresistible—John laughed at them till he
was quite exhausted. Few ever loved their friends
better than John did while they were alive ; no man
was ever so much delighted with them after they were
dead.

The most judicious way of encountering misfortunes
of every kind, is to take up a firm resolution never to
shrink from them when they cannot be avoided, nor

yet be tamely overcome by them, or add to our anguish by useless repining, but, by a steady and cheerful perseverance, endeavour to make the best of whatever untoward event occurs. To do so, still remains in our power; and it is a grievous loss indeed, with regard to fortune or favour, that perseverance will not, sooner or later, overcome. I do not recommend a stupid insensible apathy with regard to the affairs of life, nor yet that listless inactive resignation which persuades a man to put his hands in his bosom, and saying, It is the will of Heaven, sink under embarrassments without a struggle. The contempt which is his due will infallibly overtake such a man, and poverty and wretchedness will press hard upon his declining years.

I had an old and valued friend in the country, who, on any cross accident happening that vexed his associates, made always the following observations: " There are just two kinds of misfortunes, gentlemen, at which it is folly either to be grieved or angry; and these are, things that can be remedied, and things that cannot be remedied." He then proved, by plain demonstration, that the case under consideration belonged to one or other of these classes, and showed how vain and unprofitable it was to be grieved or angry at it. This maxim of my friend's may be rather too comprehensive; but it is nevertheless a good one; for a resolution to that effect cannot fail of leading a man to the proper mode of action. It indeed comprehends all things whatsoever, and is as much as to say, that a man should never suffer himself to grow angry at all; and, upon the whole, I think, if the matter be candidly weighed, it will appear, that the man who suffers himself to be transported with anger, or teased by regret, is commonly, if not always, the principal sufferer by it, either immediately, or in future. Rage is unlicensed, and runs without a curb. It lessens a man's respectability among his contemporaries; grieves and hurts the feelings of those connected with him; harrows his own soul; and transforms a rational and accountable creature into the image of a fiend.

Impatience under misfortunes is certainly one of the failings of our nature, which contributes more than any other to imbitter the cup of life, and has been the immediate cause of more acts of desperate depravity than any passion of the human soul. The loss of fortune or favour is particularly apt to give birth to this tormenting sensation; for, as neither the one nor the other occurs frequently without some imprudence or neglect of our own having been the primary cause, so the reflection on that always furnishes the gloomy retrospect with its principal sting.

So much is this the case that I hold it to be a position almost incontrovertible, that out of every twenty worldly misfortunes, nineteen occur in consequence of our own imprudence. Many will tell you, it was owing to such and such a friend's imprudence that they sustained all their losses. No such thing. Whose imprudence or want of foresight was it that trusted such a friend, and put it in his power to ruin them, and reduce the families that depended on them for support, from a state of affluence to one of penury and bitter regret? If the above position is admitted, then there is, as I have already remarked, but one right and proper way in which misfortunes ought to affect us; namely, by stirring us up to greater circumspection and perseverance. Perseverance is a noble and inestimable virtue! There is scarcely any difficulty or danger that it will not surmount. Whoever observes a man bearing up under worldly misfortunes, with undaunted resolution, will rarely fail to see that man ultimately successful. And it may be depended on, that circumspection in business is a quality so absolutely necessary, that without it the success of any one will only be temporary.

The present Laird of J——s——y, better known by the appellation of Old Sandy Singlebeard, was once a common hired shepherd, but he became master of the virtues above recommended, for he had picked them up in the severe school of misfortune. I have heard him relate the circumstances myself, oftener than once. "My father had bought me a stock of sheep,"

said he, " and fitted me out as a shepherd ; and from
the profits of these, I had plenty of money to spend,
and lay out on good clothes ; so that I was accounted
a thriving lad, and rather a dashing blade among the
lasses.   Chancing to change my master at a term, I
sold my sheep to the man who came in my place, and
bought those of the shepherd that went from the flock
to which I was engaged.   But when the day of payment came, the man who bought my sheep could not
pay them, and without that money, I had not where-
with to pay mine own.   He put me off from week to
week, until the matter grew quite distressing ; for, as
the price of shepherds' stock goes straight onward
from one hand to another, probably twenty, or perhaps
forty people, were all kept out of their right by this
backwardness of my debtor.   I craved him for the
money every two or three days, grumbled, and threatened a prosecution, till at last my own stock was
poinded.   Thinking I should be disgraced beyond recovery, I exerted what little credit I had, and borrow-
ed as much as relieved my stock ; and then, being a
good deal exasperated, resorted immediately to legal
measures, as they are called, in order to recover the
debt due to me, the non-payment of which had alone
occasioned my own difficulties.   Notwithstanding every exertion, however, I could never draw a farthing
from my debtor, and only got deeper and deeper into

8

expenses to no purpose. Many a day it kept me bare and busy before I could clear my feet, and make myself as free and independent as I was before. This was the beginning of my misfortunes, but it was but the beginning; year after year I lost and lost, until my little all was as good as three times sold off at the ground; and at last I was so reduced, that I could not say the clothes I wore were my own.

" This will never do, thought I; they shall crack well that persuade me to sell at random again.——Accordingly, I thenceforth took good care of all my sales that came to any amount. My rule was, to sell my little things, such as wool, lambs, and fat sheep, worth the money; and not to part with them till I got the price in my hand. This plan I never rued; and people finding how the case stood, I had always plenty of merchants; so that I would recommend it to every man who depends for procuring the means of living on business such as mine. What does it signify to sell your stock at a great price, merely for a boast, if you never get the money for it? It will be long ere that make any one rich or independent! This did all very well, but still I found, on looking over my accounts at the end of the year, that there were a great many items in which I was regularly taken in. My shoemaker charged me half-a-crown more for every pair of shoes than I could have bought them for in a market for ready money; the smith, threepence more for shoeing them. My haberdasher's and tailor's accounts were scandalous. In shirts, stockings, knives, razors, and even in shirt-neck buttons, I found myself taken in to a certain amount. But I was never so astonished, as to find out, by the plain rules of addition and subtraction, assisted now and then by the best of all practical rules—(I mean the one that says, ' if such a thing will bring such a thing, what will such and such a number bring ?')—to find, I say, that the losses and profits in small things actually come to more at the long-run, than any casual great slump loss, or profit, that usually chances to a man in the course of business. Wo to the man who is not aware of this ! He is labouring for that which will not profit him. By a course of strict economy, I at length not only succeeded in clearing off the debt I had incurred, but saved as much money as stocked the farm of Windlestrae-knowe. That proved a fair bargain; so, when the lease was out, I took Doddysdamms in with it; and now I am, as you see me, the Laird of J—s—y, and farmer of both these besides. My success has been wholly owing to this :—misfortune made me cautious—caution taught me a lesson which is not obvious to every one, namely *the mighty importance of the two right-hand columns in addition.* The two left-hand ones, those of pounds and shillings, every one knows the value of. With a man of any common abilities, those will take care of themselves ; but he that neglects the pence and farthings is a goose !"——

Any one who reads this will set down old Single-beard as a miser ; but I scarcely know a man less deserving the character. If one is present to hear him settling an account with another, he cannot help thinking him niggardly, owing to his extraordinary avidity in small matters ; but there is no man whom customers like better to deal with, owing to his high honour and punctuality. He will not pocket a farthing that is the right of any man living, and he is always on the watch lest some designing fellow overreach him in these minute particulars. For all this, he has assisted many of his poor relations with money and credit, when he thought them deserving it, or judged that it could be of any benefit to them ; but always with the strictest injunctions of secrecy, and an assurance, that, if ever they hinted the transaction to any one, they forfeited all chance of farther assistance from him. The consequence of this has always been, that while he was doing a great deal of good to others by his credit, he was railing against the system of giving credit all the while ; so that those who knew him not, took him for a selfish, contracted, churlish old rascal.

He was once applied to in behalf of a nephew, who had some fair prospects of setting up in business. He thought the stake too high, and declined it ; for it was a rule with him, never to credit any one so far as to put it in his power to distress him, or drive him into any embarrassment.   A few months afterwards, he consented to become bound for one half of the sum required, and the other half was made up by some less wealthy relations in conjunction.   The bonds at last became due, and I chanced to be present on a visit to my old friend Singlebeard, when the young man came to request his uncle's quota of the money required.   I knew nothing of the matter, but I could not help noticing the change in old Sandy's look, the moment that his nephew made his appearance.   I suppose he thought him too foppish to be entirely dependent on the credit of others, and perhaps judged his success in business, on that account, rather doubtful.   At all events, the old Laird had a certain quizzical, dissatisfied look, that I never observed before ; and all his remarks were in conformity with it.   In addressing the young man, too, he used a degree of familiarity which might be warranted by his seniority and relationship, and the circumstances in which his nephew stood to him as an obliged party ; but it was intended to be as provoking as possible, and obviously did not fail to excite a good deal of uneasy feeling.

" That's surely a very fine horse of yours, Jock ?" said the Laird.——" Hech, man, but he is a sleek ane !

How much corn does he eat in a year, this hunter of yours, Jock?"

"Not much, sir, not much. He is a very fine horse that, uncle. Look at his shoulder; and see what limbs he has; and what a pastern!—How much do you suppose such a horse would be worth, now, uncle?"

"Why, Jock, I cannot help thinking he is something like Geordy Dean's daughter-in-law,—nought but a spindle-shankit devil! I would not wonder if he had cost you eighteen pounds, that greyhound of a creature?"

"What a prime judge you are! Why, uncle, that horse cost eighty-five guineas last autumn. He is a real blood horse that; and has won a great deal of valuable plate."

"Oh! that, indeed, alters the case! And have you got all that valuable plate?"

"Nay, nay; it was before he came to my hand."

"That was rather a pity now, Jock—I cannot help thinking that was a great pity; because if you had got the plate, you would have had something you could have called your own.—So, you don't know how much corn that fellow eats in a year?"

"Indeed I do not; he never gets above three feeds in a day, unless when he is on a journey, and then he takes five or six."

" Then take an average of four: four feeds are worth two shillings at least, as corn is selling.   There is fourteen shillings a-week: fourteen times fifty-two —why, Jock, there is L.36, 8s. for horse's corn; and there will be about half as much, or more, for hay, besides: on the whole, I find he will cost you about L.50 a-year at livery.——I suppose there is an absolute necessity that a manufacturer should keep such a horse ?"

" O ! God bless you, sir, to be sure.   We must gather in money and orders, you know.   And then, consider the ease and convenience of travelling on such a creature as that, compared with one of your vile low-bred hacks; one goes through the country as he were flying, on that animal."

Old Sandy paddled away from the stable, towards the house, chuckling and laughing to himself; but again turned round, before he got half-way.——" Right, Jock ! quite right.   Nothing like gathering in plenty of money and orders.   But, Jock, hark ye——I do not think there is any necessity for *flying* when one is on such a commission.   You should go leisurely and slowly through the towns and villages, keeping all your eyes about you, and using every honest art to obtain good customers.   How can you do this, Jock, if you go as you were flying through the country ? People, instead of giving you a good order, will come to their shop-door, and say——There goes the Flying Manufacturer !——Jock, they say a rolling stone never gathers any moss. How do you think a flying one should gather it ?"

The dialogue went on in the same half-humorous, half-jeering tone all the forenoon, as well as during dinner, while a great number of queries still continued to be put to the young man ; as——How much his lodgings cost him a-year ? The answer to this astounded old Sandy. His comprehension could hardly take it in ; he opened his eyes wide, and held up his hands, exclaiming, with a great burst of breath, " What enormous profits there must be in your business !" and then the Laird proceeded with his provoking interrogatories——How much did his nephew's fine boots and spurs cost ? what was his tailor's bill yearly ? and every thing in the same manner ; as if the young gentleman had come from a foreign country, of which Sandy Singlebeard wished to note down every particular. The nephew was a little in the fidgets, but knowing the ground on which he stood, he answered all his uncle's queries but too truly, impressing on his frugal mind a far greater idea of his own expenditure than was necessary, and which my old friend could not help viewing as utterly extravagant.

Immediately on the removal of the cloth, the young gentleman withdrew into another room, and sending

for his uncle to speak with him, he there explained
the nature of his errand, and how absolutely necessary
it was for him to have the money, for the relief of his
bond. Old Sandy was off in a twinkling. He had no
money for him—not one copper!—not the value of a
hair of his thin grey beard should he have from him!
He had other uses for his money, and had won it too
hardly to give it to any one to throw away for him on
grand rooms and carpets, upon flying horses, and four-
guinea boots!

They returned to the parlour, and we drank some
whisky toddy together.   There was no more gibing
and snappishness.   The old man was civil and attentive, but the face of the young one exhibited marks of
anger and despair. He took his leave, and went away
abruptly enough; and I began to break some jests on
the Flying Manufacturer, in order to try the humour
of my entertainer.   I soon found it out; old Singlebeard's shaft was shot, and he now let me know he
had a different opinion of his nephew from what had
been intimated by the whole course of his conversation with the young man himself.   He said he was a
good lad; an ingenious and honest one; that he scarcely knew a better of his years; but he wanted to curb
a little that *upsetting spirit* in him, to which every
young man new to business was too much addicted.

The young gentleman went to his other friends in

a sad pickle, and represented himself to them as ruined beyond all redress ; reprobating all the while the inconsistency of his uncle, and his unaccountable and ill-timed penury.

The most part of the young gentleman's relations were in deep dismay, in consequence of the Laird's refusal to perform his engagement. But one of them, after listening seriously to the narration, instead of being vexed, only laughed immoderately at the whole affair, and said he had never heard any thing so comic and truly ludicrous. " Go your ways home, and mind your business," said he ; " you do not know any thing of old uncle Sandy : leave the whole matter to me, and I shall answer for his share of the concern."

" You will be answerable at your own cost, then," said the nephew. " If the money is not paid till he advance it, the sum will never be paid on this side of time. —You may as well try to extract it from the rock on the side of the mountain."

" Go your ways," said the other. " It is evident that you can do nothing in the business ; but were the sum three times the amount of what it is, I shall be answerable for it."

It turned out precisely as this gentleman predicted ; but no man will conceive old Sandy's motive for refusing that which he was in fact bound to perform : He could not bear to have it known that he had done so

liberal and generous an action, and wished to manage
matters so, that his nephew might believe the money
to have been raised in some other way attended with
the utmost difficulty.   He could not put his nephew to
the same school in which he himself had been taught,
namely, the School of Actual Adversity ; but he wanted to give him a touch of Ideal Misfortune ; that he
might learn the value of independence.

CHAPTER V.

GEORGE DOBSON'S EXPEDITION TO HELL.

THERE is no phenomenon in nature less understood, and about which greater nonsense is written, than dreaming. It is a strange thing. For my part, I do not understand it, nor have I any desire to do so ; and I firmly believe that no philosopher that ever wrote knows a particle more about it than I do, however elaborate and subtle the theories he may advance concerning it. He knows not even what sleep is, nor can he define its nature, so as to enable any common mind to comprehend him ; and how, then, can he define that ethereal part of it, wherein the soul holds intercourse with the external world ?——how, in that state of abstraction, some ideas force themselves upon us, in spite of all our efforts to get rid of them ; while others, which we have resolved to bear about with us by night as well as by day, refuse us their fellowship, even at periods when we most require their aid ?

No, no ; the philosopher knows nothing about either ;

and if he says he does, I entreat you not to believe
him. He does not know what mind is ; even his own
mind, to which one would think he has the most direct
access : far less can he estimate the operations and
powers of that of any other intelligent being. He
does not even know, with all his subtlety, whether it
be a power distinct from his body, or essentially the
same, and only incidentally and temporarily endowed
with different qualities. He sets himself to discover
at what period of his existence the union was established. He is baffled; for Consciousness refuses the intelligence, declaring, that she cannot carry him far
enough back to ascertain it. He tries to discover the
precise moment when it is dissolved, but on this Consciousness is altogether silent ; and all is darkness and
mystery ; for the origin, the manner of continuance,
and the time and mode of breaking up of the union between soul and body, are in reality undiscoverable by
our natural faculties—are not patent, beyond the pos-
sibility of mistake : but whosoever can read his Bible,
and solve a dream, can do either, without being sub-
jected to any material error.

It is on this ground that I like to contemplate, not
the theory of dreams, but the dreams themselves ; because they prove to the unlettered man, in a very for-
cible manner, a distinct existence of the soul, and its
lively and rapid intelligence with external nature, as

well as with a world of spirits with which it has no
acquaintance, when the body is lying dormant, and
the same to the soul as if sleeping in death.

I account nothing of any dream that relates to the
actions of the day; the person is not sound asleep who
dreams about these things; there is no division between matter and mind, but they are mingled together
in a sort of chaos—what a farmer would call compost
—fermenting and disturbing one another. I find that
in all dreams of that kind, men of every profession
have dreams peculiar to their own occupations; and,
in the country, at least, their import is generally understood. Every man's body is a barometer. A thing
made up of the elements must be affected by their
various changes and convulsions; and so the body assuredly is. When I was a shepherd, and all the com-
forts of my life depended so much on good or bad
weather, the first thing I did every morning was strictly to overhaul the dreams of the night; and I found
that I could calculate better from them than from the
appearance and changes of the sky. I know a keen
sportsman, who pretends that his dreams never deceive
him. If he dream of angling, or pursuing salmon in
deep waters, he is sure of rain; but if fishing on dry
ground, or in waters so low that the fish cannot get
from him, it forebodes drought; hunting or shooting
hares, is snow, and moorfowl, wind, &c. But the most

extraordinary professional dream on record is, without
all doubt, that well-known one of George Dobson,
coach-driver in Edinburgh, which I shall here relate ;
for though it did not happen in the shepherd's cot, it
has often been recited there.

· George was part proprietor and driver of a hackney-
coach in Edinburgh, when such vehicles were scarce ;
and one day a gentleman, whom he knew, came to
him and said :—" George, you must drive me and my
son here out to ———," a certain place that he named,
somewhere in the vicinity of Edinburgh.

" Sir," said George, " I never heard tell of such a
place, and I cannot drive you to it unless you give me
very particular directions."

" It is false," returned the gentleman ; " there is no
man in Scotland who knows the road to that place better than you do.   You have never driven on any other
road all your life ; and I insist on your taking us."

" Very well, sir," said George, " I'll drive you to
hell, if you have a mind ; only you are to direct me on
the road."

" Mount and drive on, then," said the other ; " and
no fear of the road."

George did so, and never in his life did he see his
horses go at such a noble rate ; they snorted, they
pranced, and they flew on ; and as the whole road appeared to lie down-hill, he deemed that he should soon

come to his journey's end.   Still he drove on at the same rate, far, far down-hill,——and so fine an open road he never travelled,——till by degrees it grew so dark that he could not see to drive any farther.   He called to the gentleman, inquiring what he should do ; who answered, that this was the place they were bound to, so he might draw up, dismiss them, and return.   He did so, alighted from the dickie, wondered at his foaming horses, and forthwith opened the coach-door, held the rim of his hat with the one hand, and with the other demanded his fare.

" You have driven us in fine style, George," said the elder gentleman, " and deserve to be remembered ; but it is needless for us to settle just now, as you must meet us here again to-morrow precisely at twelve o'clock."

" Very well, sir," said George ; " there is likewise an old account, you know, and some toll-money ;" which indeed there was.

" It shall be all settled to-morrow, George, and moreover, I fear there will be some toll-money to-day."

" I perceived no tolls to-day, your honour," said George.

" But I perceived one, and not very far back neither, which I suspect you will have difficulty in repassing without a regular ticket.   What a pity I have no change on me !"

" I never saw it otherwise with your honour," said George, jocularly; " what a pity it is you should always suffer yourself to run short of change!"

" I will give you that which is as good, George," said the gentleman; and he gave him a ticket written with red ink, which the honest coachman could not read. He, however, put it into his sleeve, and inquired of his employer where that same toll was which he had not observed, and how it was that they did not ask toll from him as he came through? The gentleman replied, by informing George that there was no road out of that domain, and that whoever entered it must either remain in it, or return by the same path; so they never asked any toll till the person's return, when they were at times highly capricious; but that the ticket he had given him would answer his turn. And he then asked George if he did not perceive a gate, with a number of men in black standing about it.

" Oho! Is yon the spot?" says George; " then, I assure your honour, yon is no toll-gate, but a private entrance into a great man's mansion; for do not I know two or three of the persons yonder to be gentlemen of the law, whom I have driven often and often? and as good fellows they are, too, as any I know—men who never let themselves run short of change! Good day.——Twelve o'clock to-morrow?"

" Yes, twelve o'clock noon, precisely;" and with

that, George's employer vanished in the gloom, and left him to wind his way out of that dreary labyrinth the best way he could.   He found it no easy matter, for his lamps were not lighted, and he could not see an ell before him—he could not even perceive his horses' ears; and what was worse, there was a rushing sound, like that of a town on fire, all around him, that stunned his senses, so that he could not tell whether his horses were moving or standing still.   George was in the greatest distress imaginable, and was glad when he perceived the gate before him, with his two identical friends, men of the law, still standing.   George drove boldly up, accosted them by their names, and asked what they were doing there; they made him no answer, but pointed to the gate and the keeper. George was terrified to look at this latter personage, who now came up and seized his horses by the reins, refusing to let him pass.   In order to introduce himself, in some degree, to this austere toll-man, George asked him, in a jocular manner, how he came to employ his two eminent friends as assistant gate-keepers?·

"Because they are among the last comers," replied the ruffian, churlishly.   "You will be an assistant here, to-morrow."

"The devil I will, sir?"

"Yes, the devil you will, sir."

"I'll be d——d if I do then—that I will."

" Yes, you'll be d——d if you do——that you will."

" Let my horses go in the meantime, then, sir, that I may proceed on my journey."

" Nay."

" Nay?——Dare you say nay to me, sir ? My name is George Dobson, of the Pleasance, Edinburgh, coach-driver, and coach-proprietor too; and no man shall say *nay* to me, as long as I can pay my way.   I have his Majesty's license, and I'll go and come as I choose—— and that I will.   Let go my horses there, and tell me what is your demand."

" Well, then, I'll let your horses go," said the keep-er; " but I'll keep yourself for a pledge."   And with that he let go the horses, and seized honest George by the throat, who struggled in vain to disengage himself, and swore, and threatened, according to his own con-fession, most bloodily.   His horses flew off like the wind, so swift, that the coach seemed flying in the air, and scarcely bounding on the earth once in a quarter of a mile.   George was in furious wrath, for he saw that his grand coach and harness would all be broken to pieces, and his gallant pair of horses maimed or de-stroyed; and how was his family's bread now to be won !——He struggled, threatened, and prayed in vain; ——the intolerable toll-man was deaf to all remon-strances.   He once more appealed to his two genteel acquaintances of the law, reminding them how he had of late driven them to Roslin on a Sunday, along with two ladies, who, he supposed, were their sisters, from their familiarity, when not another coachman in town would engage with them. But the gentlemen, very ungenerously, only shook their heads, and pointed to the gate. George's circumstances now became desperate, and again he asked the hideous toll-man what right he had to detain him, and what were his charges.

" What right have I to detain you, sir, say you? Who are you that make such a demand here? Do you know where you are, sir?"

" No, faith, I do not," returned George ; " I wish I did. But I *shall* know, and make you repent your insolence too. My name, I told you, is George Dobson, licensed coach-hirer in Pleasance, Edinburgh ; and to get full redress of you for this unlawful interruption, I only desire to know where I am."

" Then, sir, if it can give you so much satisfaction to know where you are," said the keeper, with a malicious grin, " you *shall* know, and you may take instruments by the hands of your two friends there, instituting a legal prosecution. Your redress, you may be assured, will be most ample, when I inform you that you are in HELL ! and out at this gate you pass no more."

This was rather a damper to George, and he began to perceive that nothing would be gained in such a place by the strong hand, so he addressed the inexorable toll-

man, whom he now dreaded more than ever, in the following terms : " But I must go home at all events, you
know, sir, to unyoke my two horses, and put them up,
and to inform Chirsty Halliday, my wife, of my engagement.   And, bless me ! I never recollected till this
moment, that I am engaged to be back here to-morrow
at twelve o'clock, and see, here is a free ticket for my
passage this way."

The keeper took the ticket with one hand, but still
held George with the other. " Oho ! were you in with
our honourable friend, Mr R—— of L——y ?" said he.
" He has been on our books for a long while ;—however, this will do, only you must put your name to it
likewise ; and the engagement is this—You, by this in-
strument, engage your soul, that you will return here
by to-morrow at noon."

" Catch me there, billy !" says George.   " I'll engage no such thing, depend on it ;—that I will not."

" Then remain where you are," said the keeper,
" for there is no other alternative.   We like best for
people to come here in their own way,—in the way of
their business ;" and with that he flung George backward, heels-over-head down hill, and closed the gate.

George, finding all remonstrance vain, and being desirous once more to see the open day, and breathe the
fresh air, and likewise to see Chirsty Halliday, his wife,
and set his house and stable in some order, came up

again, and in utter desperation, signed the bond, and was suffered to depart. He then bounded away on the track of his horses, with more than ordinary swiftness, in hopes to overtake them; and always now and then uttered a loud Wo! in hopes they might hear and obey, though he could not come in sight of them. But George's grief was but beginning; for at a well-known and dangerous spot, where there was a tan-yard on the one hand, and a quarry on the other, he came to his gallant steeds overturned, the coach smashed to pieces, Dawtie with two of her legs broken, and Duncan dead. This was more than the worthy coachman could bear, and many degrees worse than being in hell. There, his pride and manly spirit bore him up against the worst of treatment; but here, his heart entirely failed him, and he laid himself down, with his face on his two hands, and wept bitterly, bewailing, in the most deplorable terms, his two gallant horses, Dawtie and Duncan.

While lying in this inconsolable state, some one took hold of his shoulder, and shook it; and a well-known voice said to him, "Geordie! what is the matter wi' ye, Geordie?" George was provoked beyond measure at the insolence of the question, for he knew the voice to be that of Chirsty Halliday, his wife. "I think you needna ask that, seeing what you see," said George. "O, my poor Dawtie, where are a' your jink-ings and prancings now, your moopings and your win-

cings? I'll ne'er be a proud man again—bereaved o'
my bonny pair!"

"Get up, George; get up, and bestir yourself," said
Chirsty Halliday, his wife. "You are wanted directly, to bring in the Lord President to the Parliament
House. It is a great storm, and he must be there by
nine o'clock.—Get up—rouse yourself, and make ready
—his servant is waiting for you."

"Woman, you are demented!" cried George.
"How can I go and bring in the Lord President, when
my coach is broken in pieces, my poor Dawtie lying
with twa of her legs broken, and Duncan dead? And,
moreover, I have a previous engagement, for I am
obliged to be in hell before twelve o'clock."

Chirsty Halliday now laughed outright, and continued long in a fit of laughter; but George never
moved his head from the pillow, but lay and groaned,—
for, in fact, he was all this while lying snug in his bed;
while the tempest without was roaring with great violence, and which circumstance may perhaps account
for the rushing and deafening sound which astounded
him so much in hell. But so deeply was he impressed with the idea of the reality of his dream, that he
would do nothing but lie and moan, persisting and believing in the truth of all he had seen. His wife now
went and informed her neighbours of her husband's
plight, and of his singular engagement with Mr R——

of L——y at twelve o'clock. She persuaded one friend to harness the horses, and go for the Lord President; but all the rest laughed immoderately at poor coachy's predicament.   It was, however, no laughing to him; he never raised his head, and his wife becoming at last uneasy about the frenzied state of his mind, made him repeat every circumstance of his adventure to her, (for he would never believe or admit that it was a dream,) which he did in the terms above narrated; and she perceived, or dreaded, that he was becoming somewhat feverish.   She went out, and told Dr Wood of her husband's malady, and of his solemn engagement to be in hell at twelve o'clock.

" He maunna keep it, dearie. He maunna keep that engagement at no rate," said Dr Wood.   " Set back the clock an hour or twa, to drive him past the time, and I'll ca' in the course of my rounds.   Are ye sure he hasna been drinking hard ?"——She assured him he had not.——" Weel, weel, ye maun tell him that he maunna keep that engagement at no rate.   Set back the clock, and I'll come and see him.   It is a frenzy that maunna be trifled with.   Ye maunna laugh at it, dearie,——maunna laugh at it.   Maybe a nervish fever, wha kens."

The Doctor and Chirsty left the house together, and as their road lay the same way for a space, she fell a-telling him of the two young lawyers whom

George saw standing at the gate of hell, and whom the porter had described as two of the last comers. When the Doctor heard this, he stayed his hurried, stooping pace in one moment, turned full round on the woman, and fixing his eyes on her, that gleamed with a deep, unstable lustre, he said, " What's that ye were saying, dearie ? What's that ye were saying ? Repeat it again to me, every word." She did so. On which the Doctor held up his hands, as if palsied with astonishment, and uttered some fervent ejaculations. " I'll go with you straight," said he, " before I visit another patient. This is wonderfu' ! it is terrible ! The young gentlemen are both at rest—both lying corpses at this time ! Fine young men—I attended them both—died of the same exterminating disease—Oh, this is wonderful ; this is wonderful !"

The Doctor kept Chirsty half running all the way down the High Street and St Mary's Wynd, at such a pace did he walk, never lifting his eyes from the pavement, but always exclaiming now and then, " It is wonderfu' ! most wonderfu' !" At length, prompted by woman's natural curiosity, Chirsty inquired at the Doctor if he knew any thing of their friend Mr R——of L——y. But he shook his head, and replied, " Na, na, dearie,—ken naething about him. He and his son are baith in London,—ken naething about him ; but the tither is awfu'—it is perfectly awfu' !"

5

When Dr Wood reached his patient, he found him very low, but only a little feverish; so he made all haste to wash his head with vinegar and cold water, and then he covered the crown with a treacle plaster, and made the same application to the soles of his feet, awaiting the issue.   George revived a little, when the Doctor tried to cheer him up by joking him about his dream; but on mention of that he groaned, and shook his head.   "So you are convinced, dearie, that it is nae dream?" said the Doctor.

"Dear sir, how could it be a dream?" said the patient.   "I was there in person, with Mr R—— and his son; and see, here are the marks of the porter's fingers on my throat."——Dr Wood looked, and distinctly saw two or three red spots on one side of his throat, which confounded him not a little.——"I assure you, sir," continued George, "it was no dream, which I know to my sad experience.   I have lost my coach and horses, —and what more have I?—signed the bond with my own hand, and in person entered into the most solemn and terrible engagement."

"But ye're no to keep it, I tell ye," said Dr Wood; "ye're no to keep it at no rate.   It is a sin to enter into a compact wi' the deil, but it is a far greater ane to keep it.   Sae let Mr R—— and his son bide where they are yonder, for ye sanna stir a foot to bring them out the day."

" Oh, oh, Doctor !" groaned the poor fellow, " this is not a thing to be made a jest o'! I feel that it is an engagement that I cannot break.   Go I must, and that very shortly.   Yes, yes, go I must, and go I will, although I should borrow David Barclay's pair."   With that he turned his face towards the wall, groaned deeply, and fell into a lethargy, while Dr Wood caused them to let him alone, thinking if he would sleep out the appointed time, which was at hand, he would be safe ; but all the time he kept feeling his pulse, and by degrees showed symptoms of uneasiness.   His wife ran for a clergyman of famed abilities, to pray and converse with her husband, in hopes by that means to bring him to his senses ; but after his arrival, George never spoke more, save calling to his horses, as if encouraging them to run with great speed ; and thus in imagination driving at full career to keep his appointment, he went off in a paroxysm, after a terrible struggle, precisely within a few minutes of twelve o'clock.

A circumstance not known at the time of George's death made this singular professional dream the more remarkable and unique in all its parts.   It was a terrible storm on the night of the dream, as has been already mentioned, and during the time of the hurricane, London smack went down off Wearmouth about three in the morning.   Among the sufferers were the Hon. Mr R—— of L——y, and his son!   George could not know aught of this at break of day, for it was not known in Scotland till the day of his interment; and as little knew he of the deaths of the two young lawyers, who both died of the small-pox the evening before.

CHAPTER VI.

THE SOUTERS OF SELKIRK.

I HAVE heard an amusing story of a young man
whose name happened to be the same as that of the
hero of the preceding chapter—George Dobson.   He
was a shoemaker, a very honest man, who lived at the
foot of an old street, called the Back Row, in the town
of Selkirk.   He was upwards of thirty, unmarried, had
an industrious old stepmother, who kept house for
him, and of course George was what is called " a bein
bachelor," or " a chap that was gayan weel to leeve."
He was a cheerful happy fellow, and quite sober, except when on the town-council, when he sometimes
took a glass with the magistrates of his native old bo-
rough, of whose loyalty, valour, and antiquity, there
was no man more proud.

Well, one day, as George was sitting in his *shop*, as
he called it, (though no man now-a-days would call
that a shop in which there was nothing to sell,) sewing
away at boots and shoes for his customers, whom he

could not half hold in whole leather, so great was the demand over all the country for George Dobson's boots and shoes—he was sitting, I say, plying away, and singing with great glee,—

> " Up wi' the Souters o' Selkirk,
>   And down wi' the Earl o' Hume,
> And up wi' a' the brave billies
>   That sew the single-soled shoon !
> And up wi' the yellow, the yellow ;
>   The yellow and green hae doon weel ;
> Then up wi' the lads of the Forest,
> -   But down wi' the Merse to the deil !"

The last words were hardly out of George's mouth, when he heard a great noise enter the Back Row, and among the voices one making loud proclamation, as follows :—

> " Ho yes !—Ho yes !
> Souters ane, Souters a',
> Souters o' the Back Raw,
> There's a gentleman a-coming
> Wha will ca' ye *Souters* a'."

" I wish he durst," said George. " That will be the Earl o' Hume wha's coming. He has had us at ill-will for several generations. Bring my aik staff into the shop, callant, and set it down beside me here— and ye may bring ane to yoursell too.—I say, callant, stop. Bring my grandfather's auld sword wi' ye. I wad like to see the Earl o' Hume, or ony o' his cronies, come and cast up our honest calling and occupation till us !"

George laid his oak staff on the cutting-board before him, and leaned the old two-edged sword against the wall, at his right hand.   The noise of the proclamation went out at the head of the Back Row, and died in the distance ; and then George began again, and sung the Souters of Selkirk with more obstreperous glee than ever.——The last words were not out of his mouth, when a grand gentleman stepped into the shop, clothed in light armour, with a sword by his side and pistols in his breast.   He had a livery-man behind him, and both the master and man were all shining in gold.——This is the Earl o' Hume in good earnest, thought George to himself ; but, nevertheless, he shall not danton me.

" Good morrow to you, Souter Dobson," said the gentleman.   " What song is that you were singing ?"

George would have resented the first address with a vengeance, but the latter question took him off it unawares, and he only answered, " It is a very good sang, sir, and ane of the auldest——What objections have you to it ?"

" Nay, but what is it about ?" returned the stranger ; " I want to hear what you say it is about."

" I'll sing you it over again, sir," said George, " and then you may judge for yoursell.   Our sangs up here-awa dinna speak in riddles and parables ; they're gayan downright ;" and with that George gave it him over again full birr, keeping at the same time a sharp look-out on all his guest's movements; for he had no doubt now that it was to come to an engagement between them, but he was determined not to yield an inch, for the honour of old Selkirk.

When the song was done, however, the gentleman commended it, saying, it was a spirited old thing, and, without doubt, related to some of the early Border feuds. "But how think you the Earl of Hume would like to hear this?" added he. George, who had no doubt all this while that the Earl of Hume was speaking to him, said good-naturedly, "We dinna care muckle, sir, whether the Earl o' Hume take the sang ill or weel. I'se warrant he has heard it mony a time ere now, and, if he were here, he wad hear it every day when the school looses, and Wattie Henderson wad gie him it every night."

"Well, well, Souter Dobson, that is neither here nor there. That is not what I called about. Let us to business. You must make me a pair of boots in your very best style," said the gentleman, standing up, and stretching forth his leg to be measured.

"I'll make you no boots, sir," said George, nettled at being again called Souter. "I have as many regular customers to supply as hold me busy from one year's end to the other. I cannot make your boots—you may get them made where you please."

"You *shall* make them, Mr Dobson," said the stranger;

" I am determined to try a pair of boots of your making, cost what they will. Make your own price, but let
me have the boots by all means ; and, moreover, I want
them before to-morrow morning."

This was so conciliatory and so friendly of the Earl,
that George, being a good-natured fellow, made no
farther objection, but took his measure, and promised
to have them ready.   " I will pay them now," said the
gentleman, taking out a purse of gold ; but George refused to accept of the price till the boots were produced.   " Nay, but I will pay them now," said the
gentleman ; " for, in the first place, it will ensure me of
the boots, and, in the next place, I may probably leave
town to-night, and make my servant wait for them.
What is the cost ?"

" If they are to be as good as I can make them, sir,
they will be twelve shillings."

" Twelve shillings, Mr Dobson ! I paid thirty-six for
these I wear in London, and I expect yours will be a
great deal better.   Here are two guineas, and be sure
to make them good."

"I cannot, for my life, make them worth the half of
that money," said George.   " We have no materials
in Selkirk that will amount to one-third of it in value."
However, the gentleman flung down the gold, and went
away, singing the Souters of Selkirk.

" He is a most noble fellow that Earl of Hume,"

said George to his apprentice. " I thought he and I should have had a battle, but we have parted on the best possible terms."

" I wonder how you could bide to be *Souter'd* yon gate !" said the boy.

George scratched his head with the awl, bit his lip, and looked at his grandfather's sword. He had a great desire to follow the insolent gentleman ; for he found that he had inadvertently suffered a great insult without resenting it.

After George had shaped the boots with the utmost care, and of the best and finest Kendal leather, he went up the Back Row to seek assistance, so that he might have them ready at the stated time ; but never a stitch of assistance could George obtain, for the gentleman had trysted a pair of boots in every shop in the Row, paid for them all, and called every one of the shoe-makers Souter twice over.

Never was there such a day in the Back Row of Selkirk ! What could it mean ? Had the gentleman a whole regiment coming up, all of the same size, and the same measure of leg ? Or was he not rather an army agent, come to take specimens of the best workmen in the country ? This last being the prevailing belief, every Selkirk Souter threw off his coat, and fell a-slashing and cutting of Kendal leather ; and such a

G 2

forenoon of cutting, and sewing, and puffing, and roset-
ing, never was in Selkirk since the battle of Flodden-
field.

George's shop was the nethermost of the street, so
that the stranger guests came all to him first ; so, scarcely had he taken a hurried dinner, and begun to sew
again, and, of course, to sing, when in came a fat gentleman, exceedingly well mounted with sword and pistols ; he had fair curled hair, red cheeks that hung over
his stock, and a liveryman behind him. " Merry be
your heart, Mr Dobson ! but what a plague of a song
is that you are singing ?" said he. George looked very
suspicious-like at him, and thought to himself, Now I
could bet any man two gold guineas that this is the
Duke of Northumberland, another enemy to our town ;
but I'll not be cowed by him neither, only I could have
wished I had been singing another song when his Grace
came into the shop.——These were the thoughts that ran
through George's mind in a moment, and at length he
made answer——" We reckon it a good sang, my lord,
and ane o' the auldest."

" Would it suit your convenience to sing that last
verse over again ?" said the fat gentleman ; and at the
same time he laid hold of his gold-handled pistols.

" O certainly, sir," said George ; " but at the same
time I must take a lesson in manners from my supe-
riors ;" and with that he seized his grandfather's cut-

and-thrust sword, and cocking that up by his ear, he sang out with fearless glee—

> " The English are dolts, to a man, a man—
> Fat puddings to fry in a pan, a pan—
>   Their Percys and Howards
>   We reckon but cowards—
> But turn the Blue Bonnets wha can, wha can !"

George now set his joints in such a manner, that the moment the Duke of Northumberland presented his pistol, he might be ready to cleave him, or cut off his right hand, with his grandfather's cut-and-thrust sword; but the fat gentleman durst not venture the issue—he took his hand from his pistol, and laughed till his big sides shook. "You are a great original, Dobson," said he; "but you are nevertheless a brave fellow—a noble fellow—a Souter among a thousand, and I am glad I have met with you in this mood too. Well, then, let us proceed to business. You must make me a pair of boots in your very best style, George, and that without any loss of time."

"O Lord, sir, I would do that with the greatest pleasure, but it is a thing entirely out of my power," said George, with a serious face.

"Pooh, pooh ! I know the whole story," said the fat gentleman. "You are all hoaxed and made fools of this morning; but the thing concerns me very much, and I'll give you five guineas, Mr Dobson, if you will

make me a pair of good boots before to-morrow at this
time."

"I wad do it cheerfully for the fifth part o' the price,
my lord," said George; "but it is needless to speak
about that, it being out o' my power.   But what way
are we hoaxed? I dinna account ony man made a fool
of wha has the cash in his pocket as weel as the goods
in his hand.".

"You are all made fools of together, and I am the
most made a fool of, of any," said the fat gentleman.
"I betted a hundred guineas with a young Scottish
nobleman last night, that he durst not go up the Back
Row of Selkirk, calling all the way,

> ' Souters ane, Souters a',
> Souters o' the Back Raw ;'

and yet, to my astonishment, you have let him do so,
and insult you all with impunity; and he has won."

"Confound the rascal!" exclaimed George.   "If
we had but taken him up!   But we took him for our
friend, come to warn us, and lay all in wait for the audacious fellow who was to come up behind."

"And a good amends you took of him when he
came!" said the fat gentleman.   "Well, after I had
taken the above bet, up speaks another of our company,
and he says—' Why make such account of a few poor
cobblers, or Souters, or how do you call them?   I'll
bet a hundred guineas, that I'll go up the Back Row

after that gentleman has set them all agog, and I'll call every one of them *Souter* twice to his face.' I took the bet in a moment : ' You dare not, for your blood, sir,' says I. ' You do not know the spirit and bravery of the men of Selkirk. They will knock you down at once, if not tear you to pieces.' But I trusted too much to your spirit, and have lost my two hundred guineas, it would appear. Tell me, in truth, Mr Dobson, did you suffer him to call you *Souter* twice to your face without resenting it ?"

George bit his lip, scratched his head with the awl, and gave the lingles such a yerk, that he made them both crack in two. " D——n it ! we're a' affrontit thegither !" said he, in a half whisper, while the apprentice-boy was like to burst with laughter at his master's mortification.

" Well, I have lost my money," continued the gentleman ; " but I assure you, George, the gentleman wants no boots. He has accomplished his purpose, and has the money in his pocket ; but as it will avail me, I may not say how much, I entreat that you will make me a pair. Here is the money,——here are five guineas, which I leave in pledge ; only let me have the boots. Or suppose you make these a little wider, and transfer them to me ; that is very excellent leather, and will do exceedingly well ; I think I never saw better ;" and he stood leaning over George, handling the leather.   " Now, do you consent to let me have them ?"

" I can never do that, my lord," says George, " having the other gentleman's money in my pocket.   If you should offer me ten guineas, it would be the same thing."

" Very well, I will find those who will," said he, and off he went, singing,

> " Turn the Blue Bonnets wha can, wha can."

" This is the queerest day about Selkirk that I ever saw," said George ; " but really this Duke of Northumberland, to be the old hereditary enemy of our town, is a real fine, frank fellow."

" Ay, but he *Souter'd* ye, too," said the boy.

" It's a lee, ye little blackguard."

" I heard him ca' you a Souter amang a thousand, master ; and that taunt will be heard tell o' yet."

" I fancy, callant, we maun let that flee stick to the wa'," said George ; and sewed away, and sewed away, and got the boots finished next day at twelve o'clock. Now, thought he to himself, I have thirty shillings by this bargain, and so I'll treat our magistrates to a hearty glass this afternoon ; I hae muckle need o' a slockening, and the Selkirk bailies never fail a friend.— George put his hand into his pocket to clink his two gold guineas; but never a guinea was in George's pocket,

nor plack either! His countenance changed, and fell
so much, that the apprentice noticed it, and suspected
the cause; but George would confess nothing, though,
in his own mind, he strongly suspected the Duke of
Northumberland of the theft, *alias*, the fat gentleman
with the fair curled hair, and the red cheeks hanging
over his stock.

George went away up among his brethren of the
awl in the Back Row, and called on them every one;
but he soon perceived, from their blank looks, and their
disinclination to drink that night, that they were all in
the same predicament with himself. The fat gentleman
with the curled hair had visited every one of them, and
got measure for a pair of ten-guinea boots, but had not
paid any of them; and, somehow or other, every man
had lost the price of the boots which he had received in
the morning. Whom to blame for this, nobody knew;
for the whole day over, and a good part of the night,
from the time the proclamation was made, the Back
Row of Selkirk was like a cried fair; all the idle people
in the town and the country about were there, wonder-
ing after the man who had raised such a demand for
boots. After all, the Souters of Selkirk were left neither richer nor poorer than they were at the beginning,
but every one of them had been four times called a *Souter* to his face,—a title of great obloquy in that town,
although the one of all others that the townsmen ought

to be proud of. And it is curious that they are proud
of it when used collectively ; but apply it to any of
them as a term of reproach, and you had better call him
the worst name under heaven.

This was the truth of the story ; and the feat was
performed by the late Duke of Queensberry, when Earl
of March, and two English noblemen then on a tour
through this country. Every one of them gained his
bet, through the simplicity of the honest Souters ; but
certainly the last had a difficult part to play, having
staked two hundred guineas that he would take all the
money from the Souters that they had received from
the gentleman in the morning, and call every one of
them *Souter* to his face. He got the price entire from
every one, save Thomas Inglis, who had drunk the
half of his before he got to him ; but this being proved,
the English gentleman won.

George Dobson took the thing most amiss. He
had been the first taken in all along, and he thought a
good deal about it. He was, moreover, a very honest
man, and in order to make up the boots to the full
value of the money he had received, he had shod them
with silver, which took two Spanish dollars, and he had
likewise put four silver tassels to the tops, so that they
were splendid boots, and likely to remain on his hand.
In short, though he did not care about the loss, he
took the hoax very sore to heart.

Shortly after this, he was sitting in his shop, work-ing away, and not singing a word, when in comes a fat gentleman, with fair curled hair, and red cheeks, but they were *not* hanging over his cravat ; and he says, " Good morning, Dobson. You are very quiet and contemplative this morning."

" Ay, sir ; folk canna be aye alike merry."

" Have you any stomach for taking measure of a pair of boots this morning ?"

" Nah ! I'll take measure o' nae mae boots to stran-gers ; I'll stick by my auld customers."——He is very like my late customer, thought George, but his tongue is not the same. If I thought it were he, I would nick him !

" I have heard the story of the boots, George," said the visitor, " and never heard a better one. I have laughed very heartily at it ; and I called principally to inform you, that if you will call at Widow Wilson's, in Hawick, you will get the price of your boots."

" Thank you, sir," said George ; and the gentle-man went away ; Dobson being now persuaded he was *not* the Duke of Northumberland, though astonishing-ly like him. George had not sewed a single yerking, ere the gentleman came again into the shop, and said, " You had better measure me for these boots, Dobson. I intend to be your customer in future."

" Thank you, sir, but I would rather not, just now."

"Very well; call then at Widow Wilson's, in Hawick, and you shall get *double* payment for the boots you have made."——George thanked him again, and away he went; but in a very short space he entered the shop again, and again requested George to measure him for a pair of boots. George became suspicious of the gentleman, and rather uneasy, as he continued to haunt him like a ghost; and so, merely to be quit of him, he took the measure of his leg and foot. "It is very near the measure of these fine silver-mounted ones, sir," said George; "you had better just take them."

"Well, so be it," said the stranger. "Call at Widow Wilson's, in Hawick, and you shall have *triple* payment for your boots. Good day."

"O, this gentleman is undoubtedly wrong in his mind," said George to himself. "This beats all the customers I ever met with! Ha——ha——ha! Come to Widow Wilson's, and you shall have payment for your boots,——double payment for your boots,——*triple* payment for your boots! Oh! the man's as mad as a March hare! He——he——he——he!"

"Hilloa, George," cried a voice close at his ear, "what's the matter wi' ye? Are ye gane daft? Are ye no gaun to rise to your wark the day?"

"Aich! Gudeness guide us, mother, am I no up yet?" cried George, springing out of his bed; for he had been all the while in a sound sleep, and dreaming.

"What gart ye let me lie sae lang? I thought I had been i' the shop!"

—"Shop!" exclaimed she; "I daresay, then, you thought you had found a fiddle in't. What were ye guffawing and laughing at?"

"O! I was laughing at a fat man, and the payment of a pair o' boots at Widow Wilson's, in Hawick."

"Widow Wilson's, i' Hawick!" exclaimed his mother, holding up both her hands; "Gude forgie me for a great leear, if I hae dreamed about ony body else, frae the tae end o' the night to the tither!"

"Houts, mother, haud your tongue; it is needless to heed your dreams, for ye never gie ower dreaming about somebody."

"And what for no, lad? Hasna an auld body as good a right to dream as a young ane? Mrs Wilson's a throughgaun quean, and clears mair than a hunder a-year by the Tannage. I'se warrant there sall something follow thir dreams; I get the maist o' my dreams redd."

George was greatly tickled with his dream about the fat gentleman and the boots, and so well convinced was he that there was some sort of meaning in it, that he resolved to go to Hawick the next market day, and call on Mrs Wilson, and settle with her; although it was a week or two before his usual term of payment, he

thought the money would scarcely come wrong. So
that day he plied and wrought as usual; but instead of
his favourite ditties relating to the Forest, he chanted,
the whole day over, one as old as any of them; but I
am sorry I recollect only the chorus and a few odd
stanzas of it.

ROUND ABOUT HAWICK.

We'll round about Hawick, Hawick,
  Round about Hawick thegither;
We'll round about Hawick, Hawick,
  And in by the bride's gudemither.
    Sing, Round about Hawick, &c.

And as we gang by we will rap,
  And drink to the luck o' the bigging;
For the bride has her tap in her lap,
  And the bridegroom his tail in his rigging.
    Sing, Round about Hawick, &c.

There's been little luck i' the deed;
  We're a' in the dumps thegither;
Let's gie the bridegroom a sheep's head,
  But gie the bride brose and butter.
    Sing, Round about Hawick, &c.

Then a' the gudewives i' the land
  Came flocking in droves thegither,
A' bringing their bountith in hand,
  To please the young bride's gudemither.
    Sing, Round about Hawick, &c.

The black gudewife o' the Braes
  Gae baby-clouts no worth a button;

But the auld gudewife o' Penchrice
  Cam in wi' a shouder o' mutton.
    Sing, Round about Hawick, &c.

Wee Jean o' the Coate gae a pun',
  A penny, a plack, and a boddle;
But the wife at the head o' the town
  Gae nought but a lang pin-todle.*
    Sing, Round about Hawick, &c.

The mistress o' Bortugh cam ben,
  Aye blinking sae couthy and canny;
But some said she had in her han'
  A kipple o' bottles o' branny.
    Sing, Round about Hawick, &c.

And some brought dumples o' woo,
  And some brought flitches o' bacon,
And kebbucks and cruppocks enow;
  But Jenny Muirhead brought a capon.
    Sing, Round about Hawick, &c.

Then up cam the wife o' the Mill,
  Wi' the cog, and the meal, and the water;
For she likit the joke sae weel
  To gie the bride brose and butter.
    Sing, Round about Hawick, &c.

And first she pat in a bit bread,
  And then she pat in a bit butter,
And then she pat in a sheep's head,
  Horns and a' thegither!
    Sing, Round about Hawick, Hawick,
      Round about Hawick thegither;
    Round about Hawick, Hawick,
      Round about Hawick for ever

---

* A pin-cushion.

On the Thursday following, George, instead of going to *the shop*, dressed himself in his best Sunday clothes, and, with rather a curious face, went ben to his stepmother, and inquired " what feck o' siller she had about her ?"

" Siller ! Gudeness forgie you, Geordie, for an evendown waster and a profligate ! What are ye gaun to do wi' siller the day ?"

" I have something ado ower at Hawick, and I was thinking it wad be as weel to pay her account when I was there."

" Oho, lad ! are ye there wi' your dreams and your visions o' the night, Geordie ? Ye're aye keen o' sangs, man ; I can pit a vera gude ane i' your head. There's an unco gude auld thing they ca', Wap at the widow, my laddie.   D'ye ken it, Geordie ?   Siller ! quo he ! Hae ye ony feck o' siller, mother ! Whew ! I hae as muckle as will pay the widow's account sax times ower ! Ye may tell her that frae me.   Siller ! lack-a-day !——But, Geordie, my man——Auld wives' dreams are no to be regardit, ye ken.   Eh ?"

After putting half a dozen pairs of trysted shoes, and the identical silver-mounted boots, into the cadger's creels——then the only regular carriers——off set George Dobson to Hawick market, a distance of nearly eleven new-fashioned miles, but then accounted only eight and three quarters ; and after parading the Sandbed, Slitterick Bridge, and the Tower Knowe, for the space of an hour, and shaking hands with some four or five acquaintances, he ventured east-the-gate to pay Mrs Wilson her account. He was kindly welcomed, as every good and regular customer was, by Mrs Wilson. They settled amicably, and in the course of business George ventured several sly, jocular hints, to see how they would be taken, vexed that his grand and singular dream should go for nothing. No, nothing would pass there but sterling cent per cent. The lady was deaf and blind to every effort of gallantry, valuing her own abilities too highly ever to set a man a second time at the head of her flourishing business. Nevertheless, she could not be blind to George's qualifications—he knew that was impossible,—for in the first place he was a goodly person, with handsome limbs and broad square shoulders; of a very dark complexion, true, but with fine, shrewd, manly features; was a burgess and councillor of the town of Selkirk, and as independent in circumstances as she was.

Very well; Mrs Wilson knew all this—valued George Dobson accordingly, and would not have denied him any of those good points more than Gideon Scott would to a favourite Cheviot tup, in any society whatever; but she had such a sharp, cold, business manner, that George could discover no symptoms where the price of the boots was to come from. In

8

order to conciliate matters as far as convenient, if not
even to stretch a point, he gave her a farther order,
larger than the one just settled ; but all that he elicited was thanks for his custom, and one very small glass
of brandy ; so he drank her health, and a good husband to her. Mrs Wilson only courtseyed, and thanked
him coldly, and away George set west-the-street, with
a quick and stately step, saying to himself that the expedition of the silver-mounted boots was all up.

As he was posting up the street, an acquaintance of
his, a flesher, likewise of the name of Wilson, eyed
him, and called him aside. " Hey, George, come this
way a bit. How are ye ? How d'ye do, sir ? What
news about Selkirk ? Grand demand for boots there
just now, I hear—eh ? Needing any thing in my way
the day ?—Nae beef like that about your town. Come
away in, and taste the gudewife's bottle. I want to
hae a crack wi' ye, and get measure of a pair o' boots.
The grandest story yon, sir, I ever heard—eh ?—Needing a leg o' beef ?—Better ? Never mind, come away
in."

George was following Mr Wilson into the house,
having as yet scarcely got a word said,—and he liked
the man exceedingly,—when one pulled his coat, and a
pretty servant girl smirked in his face and said, " Maister Dabsen, thou maun cum awa yest-the-gate and

speak till Mistress Wulsin; there's sumtheyng forgot
atween ye. Thou maun cum directly."

" Haste ye, gae away, rin!" says Wilson, pushing
him out at the door, " that's a better bait than a poor
flesher's dram. There's some comings and gangings
yonder. A bien birth and a thrifty dame. Grip to,
grip to, lad! I'se take her at a hunder pund the quarter. Let us see you as ye come back again."

George went back, and there was Mrs Wilson standing in the door to receive him.

" I quite forgot, Mr Dobson—I beg pardon. But
I hope, as usual, you will take a family-dinner with me
to-day?"

" Indeed, Mrs Wilson, I was just thinking to mysell that you were fey, and that we two would never
bargain again, for I never paid you an account before
that I did not get the offer of my dinner."

" A very stupid neglect! But, indeed, I have so
many things to mind, and so hard set with the world,
Mr Dobson; you cannot conceive, when there's only a
woman at the head of affairs——"

" Ay, but sic a woman," said George, and shook his
head.

" Well, well, come at two. I dine early. No cere_
mony, you know. Just a homely dinner, and no drinking." So saying, she turned and sailed into the house
very gracefully; and then turning aside, she looked out

at the window after him, apostrophizing him thus—
" Ay, ye may strut away west-the-street, as if I were
looking after you.   Shame fa' the souter-like face o'
ye ; I wish you had been fifty miles off the day !   If
it hadna been fear for affronting a good steady customer,
you shoudna hae been here.   For there's my brother
coming to dinner, and maybe some o' his cronies ; and
he'll be sae ta'en wi' this merry souter chield, that I ken
weel they'll drink mair than twice the profits o' this bit
order.   My brother maun hae a' his ain will too !
Folk maun aye bow to the bush they get bield frae,
else I should take a staup out o' their punch cogs the
night."

George attended at ten minutes past two, to be as
fashionable as the risk of losing his kale would permit
—gave a sharp wooer-like rap at the door, and was
shown by the dimpling Border maid into *The* ROOM,
—which, in those days, meant the only sitting apartment of a house.   Mrs Wilson being absent to super-
intend the preparations for dinner, and no one to introduce the parties to each other, think of George's utter
amazement, when he saw the identical fat gentleman,
who came to him thrice in his dream, and ordered him
to come to Widow Wilson's and get payment of his
boots !   He was the very gentleman in every respect,
every inch of him, and George could have known him
among a thousand.   It was not the Duke of Northum-

berland, but he that was so very like him, with fair curled hair, and red cheeks, which did not hang over his cravat. George felt as if he had been dropped into another state of existence, and hardly knew what to think or say. He had at first very nigh run up and taken the gentleman's hand, and addressed him as an old acquaintance, but luckily he recollected the equivocal circumstances in which they met, which was not actually in *the shop*, but in George's little bed-closet in the night, or early in the morning.

In short, the two sat awkward enough, till, at last, Mrs Wilson entered, in most brilliant attire, and really a handsome fine woman ; and with her a country lady, with something in her face extremely engaging. Mrs Wilson immediately introduced the parties to each other thus :—" Brother, this is Mr Dobson, boot and shoemaker in Selkirk ;—as honest a young man, and as good a payer, as I know.—Mr Dobson, this is Mr Turnbull, my brother, the best friend I ever had ; and this is his daughter Margaret."

The parties were acquainted in one minute, for Mr Turnbull was a frank kind-hearted gentleman ; ay, they were more than acquainted, for the very second or third look that George got of Margaret Turnbull, he loved her. And during the whole afternoon, every word that she spoke, every smile that she smiled, and every happy look that she turned on another, added to his flame; so that long ere the sun leaned his elbow on Skelfhill Pen, he was deeper in love than, perhaps, any other souter in this world ever was. It is needless to describe Miss Turnbull; she was just what a woman should be, and not exceeding twenty-five years of age. What a mense she would be to the town of Selkirk, and to a boot and shoemaker's parlour, as well as to the top of the councillors' seat every Sunday!

When the dinner was over, the brandy bottle went round, accompanied with the wee wee glass, in shape of the burr of a Scots Thistle. When it came to Mr Turnbull, he held it up between him and the light,— " Keatie, whaten a niff-naff of a glass is this? let us see a feasible ane."

" If it be over little, you can fill it the oftener, brother. I think a big dram is so vulgar!"

" That's no the thing, Keatie. The truth is, that ye're a perfect she Nabal, and ilka thing that takes the value of a plack out o' your pocket, is vulgar, or improper, or something that way. But I'll tell you, Keatie, my woman, what you shall do: Set down a black bottle on this hand o' me, and twa clear anes on this, and the cheeny bowl atween them, and I'll let you see what I'll do. I ken o' nane within the ports o' Hawick can afford a bowl better than you. Nane o' your half bottles and quarter bottles at a time; now Keatie, ye ken, ye hae a confoundit trick o' that; but

I hae some hopes that I'll learn ye good manners by and by."

"Dear brother, I'm sure you are not going to drink your bottles here? Think what the town would say, if I were to keep cabals o' drinkers in my sober house."

"Do as I bid you now, Keatie, and lippen the rest to me.—Ah, she is a niggard, Mr Dobson, and has muckle need of a little schooling to open her heart."

The materials were produced, and Mr Turnbull, as had been predicted, did not spare them. Other two Wilsons joined them immediately after dinner, the one a shoemaker, and the other our friend the flesher, and a merrier afternoon has seldom been in Hawick. Mr Turnbull was perfectly delighted with George;—he made him sing "The Souters o' Selkirk," "Turn the Blue Bonnets," and all his best things; but when he came to "Round about Hawick," he made him sing it six times over, and was never weary of laughing at it, and identifying the characters with those then living. Then the story of the boots was an inexhaustible joke, and the likeness between Mr Turnbull and the Duke of Northumberland an acceptable item. At length Mr Turnbull got so elevated, that he said, "Ay, man! and they are shod wi' silver, and silver tassels round the top? I wad gie a bottle o' wine for a sight o' them."

"It shall cost you nae mair," said George, and in three minutes he set them on the table. Mr Turnbull

tried them on, and walked through and through the
room with them, singing—

> " With silver he was shod before—
> With burning gold behind."

They fitted exactly ; and before sitting down, he offered
George the original price, and got them.

It became late rather too soon for our group, but the
young lady grew impatient to get home, and Mr Turnbull was obliged to prepare for going ; nothing, however, would please him, save that George should go
with him all night ; and George being, long before this
time, over head and ears in love, accepted of the invi-
tation, and the loan of the flesher's bay mare, and went
with them.   Miss Margaret had soon, by some kind of
natural inspiration, discovered our jovial Souter's partiality for her ; and in order to open the way for a ban-
ter, (the best mode of beginning a courtship,) she fell on
and rallied him most severely about the boots and the
Soutering, and particularly about letting himself be
robbed of the two guineas.   This gave George an opportunity of retaliating so happily, that he wondered
at himself, for he acknowledged that he said things that
he never believed he could have had the face to say to
a lady before.

The year after that, the two were married in the
house of Mrs Wilson, and Mr Turnbull paid down a
hundred pounds to George on the day he brought her

from that house a bride. Now, thought George to himself, I have been twice most liberally paid for my boots in that house. My wife, perhaps, will stand for the third payment, which I hope will be the best of all ; but I still think there is to be another one beside.——He was not wrong, for after the death of his worthy father-in-law, he found himself entitled to the third of his whole effects ; the transfer of which, nine years after his marriage, was made over to him in the house of his friend, Mrs Wilson.

CHAPTER VII.

THE LAIRD OF CASSWAY.

THERE is an old story which I have often heard related, about a great Laird of Cassway, in an outer corner of Dumfries-shire, of the name of Beattie, and his two sons. The incidents of the story are of a very extraordinary nature. This Beattie had occasion to be almost constantly in England, because, as my informant said, he took a great hand in government affairs, from which I conclude that the tradition had its rise about the time of the Civil Wars ; for about the close of that time, the Scotts took the advantage of the times to put the Beatties down, who, for some previous ages, had maintained the superiority of that district.

Be that as it may, the Laird of Cassway's second son, Francis, fell desperately in love with a remarkably beautiful girl, the eldest daughter of Henry Scott of Drumfielding, a gentleman, but still only a retainer, and far beneath Beattie of Cassway, both in point of wealth and influence. Francis was a scholar newly returned from the University—was tall, handsome, of a pale complexion, and gentlemanly appearance, while Thomas, the eldest son, was fair, ruddy, and stout-made, a perfect picture of health and good-humour,— a sportsman, a warrior, and a jovial blade ; one who would not suffer a fox to get rest in the whole moor district. He rode the best horse, kept the best hounds, played the best fiddle, danced the best country bumpkin, and took the stoutest draught of mountain dew, of any man between Erick Brae and Teviot Stone, and was altogether that sort of a young man, that whenever he cast his eyes on a pretty girl, either at chapel or weapon-shaw, she would hide her face, and giggle as if tickled by some unseen hand.

Now, though Thomas, or the Young Laird, as he was called, had only spoke once to Ellen Scott in his life, at which time he chucked her below the chin, and bid the devil take him if ever he saw as bonny a face in his whole born days ; yet, for all that, Ellen loved him. It could not be said that she was *in love* with him, for a maiden's heart must be won before it is given absolutely away ; but hers gave him the preference to any other young man. She loved to see him, to hear of him, and to laugh at him ; and it was even observed by the domestics, that Tam Beattie o' the Cassway's name came oftener into her conversation than there was any good reason for.

Such was the state of affairs when Francis came home, and fell desperately in love with Ellen Scott; and his father being in England, and he under no restraint, he went frequently to visit her. She received him with a kindness and affability that pleased him to the heart; but he little wist that this was only a spontaneous and natural glow of kindness towards him because of his connexions, and rather because he was the Young Laird of Cassway's only brother, than the poor but accomplished Francis Beattie, the scholar from Oxford.

He was, however, so much delighted with her, that he asked her father's permission to pay his addresses to her. Her father, who was a prudent and sensible man, answered him in this wise—" That nothing would give him greater delight than to see his beloved Ellen joined with so accomplished and amiable a young gentleman in the bonds of holy wedlock, provided his father's assent was previously obtained. But as he himself was subordinate to another house, not on the best terms with the house of Cassway, he would not take it on him to sanction any such connexion without the Old Laird's full consent. That, moreover, as he, Francis Beattie, was just setting out in life, as a lawyer, there was but too much reason to doubt that a matri-

monial connexion with Ellen at that time would be
highly imprudent; therefore it was not to be thought
further of till the Old Laird was consulted. In the
meantime, he should always be welcome to his house,
and to his daughter's company, as he had the same dependence on his honour and integrity, as if he had been
a son of his own."

The young man thanked him affectionately, and
could not help acquiescing in the truth of his remarks,
promised not to mention matrimony farther, till he had
consulted his father, and added—" But indeed you
must excuse me, if I avail myself of your permission
to visit here often, as I am sensible that it will be impossible for me to live for any space of time out of my
dear Ellen's sight." He was again assured of welcome,
and the two parted mutually pleased.

Henry Scott of Drumfielding was a widower, with
six daughters, over whom presided Mrs Jane Jerdan,
their maternal aunt, an old maid, with fashions and
ideas even more antiquated than herself. No sooner
had the young wooer taken his leave, than she bounced
into the room, the only sitting apartment in the house,
and said, in a loud important whisper, " What's that
young swankey of a lawyer wanting, that he's aye
hankering sae muckle about our town? I'll tell you
what, brother Harry, it strikes me that he wants to
make a wheelwright o' your daughter Nell. Now, gin

he axes your consent to ony siccan thing, dinna ye
grant it. That's a'. Take an auld fool's advice gin ye
wad prosper. Folk are a' wise ahint the hand, and sae
will ye be."

· " Dear, Mrs Jane, what objections can you have to
Mr Francis Beattie, the most accomplished young gentleman of the whole country ?"

" 'Complished gentleman ! 'Complished kirn-milk !
I'll tell you what, brother Harry,——afore I were a land-
less lady, I wad rather be a tailor's layboard. What
has he to maintain a lady spouse with ? The wind o'
his lungs, forsooth !——thinks to sell that for goud in
goupings. Hech me ! Crazy wad they be wha wad
buy it ; and they wha trust to crazy people for their
living will live but crazily. Take an auld fool's advice gin ye wad prosper, else ye'll be wise ahint the
hand. Have nae mair to do with him——Nell's bread
for his betters ; tell him that, Or, by my certy, gin I
meet wi' him face to face, *I'll* tell him."

" It would be unfriendly in me to keep aught a secret from you, sister, considering the interest you have
taken in my family. I *have* given him my consent to
visit my daughter, but at the same time have restrict-
ed him from mentioning matrimony until he have consulted his father."

" And what is the visiting to gang for, then ? Away
wi' him ! Our Nell's food for his betters. What wad

you think an she could get the Young Laird, his brother, wi' a blink o' her ee ?"

" Never speak to me of that, Mrs Jane. I wad rather see the poorest of his shepherd lads coming to court my child than see him ;" and with these words Henry left the room.

Mrs Jane stood long, making faces, shaking her apron with both hands, nodding her head, and sometimes giving a stamp with her foot. " I have set my face against that connexion," said she ; " our Nell's no made for a lady to a London lawyer. It wad set her rather better to be Lady of Cassway. The Young Laird, for me ! I'll hae the branks of love thrown over the heads o' the twasome, tie the tangs thegither, and then let them gallop like twa kippled grews. My brother Harry's a simple man ; he disna ken the credit that he has by his daughters—thanks to some other body than him ! Niece Nell has a shape, an ee, and a lady-manner that wad kilhab the best lord o' the kingdom, were he to come under their influence and my manoovres. She's a Jerdan a' through ; and that I'll let them ken ! Folk are a' wise ahint the hand ; credit only comes by catch and keep. Goodnight to a' younger brothers, puffings o' love vows, and sabs o' wind ! Gie me the good green hills, the gruff wedders, and bob-tail'd yowes ; and let the Law and the Gospel-men sell the wind o' their lungs as dear as they can."

In a few days, Henry of Drumfielding was called
out to attend his Chief on some expedition; on which
Mrs Jane, not caring to trust her message to any other
person, went over to Cassway, and invited the Young
Laird to Drumfielding to see her niece, quite convinced that her charms and endowments would at once
enslave the elder brother as they had done the younger.
Tam Beattie was delighted at finding such a good back
friend as Mrs Jane, for he had not failed to observe,
for a twelvemonth back, that Ellen Scott was very
pretty, and, either through chance or design, he asked
Mrs Jane if the young lady was privy to this invita-
tion.

" *She* privy to it !" exclaimed Mrs Jane, shaking
her apron. " Ha, weel I wat, no ! She wad soon hae
flown in my face wi' her gibery and her jaukery, had
I tauld her my errand; but the gowk kens what the
tittling wants, although it is not aye crying, *Give, give,*
like the horse loch-leech."

" Does the horse-leech really cry that, Mrs Jane ?
I should think, from a view of its mouth, that it could
scarcely cry any thing," said Tom.

" Are ye sic a reprobate as to deny the words o' the
Scripture, sir ? Hech, wae's me ! what some folk hae
to answer for ! We're a' wise ahint the hand. But
hark ye,—come ye ower in time, else I am feared she
may be settled for ever out o' your reach. Now, I

canna bide to think on that, for I have always thought you twa made for ane anither. Let me take a look o' you frae tap to tae—O yes—made for ane anither. Come ower in time, before billy Harry come hame again; and let your visit be in timeous hours, else I'll gie you the back of the door to keep.—Wild reprobate!" she exclaimed to herself, on taking her leave; "to deny that the horse loch-leech can speak! Ha—he—The Young Laird is the man for me!"

Thomas Beattie was true to his appointment, as may be supposed, and Mrs Jane having her niece dressed in style, he was perfectly charmed with her; and really it cannot be denied that Ellen was as much delighted with him. She was young, gay, and frolicsome, and Ellen never spent a more joyous and happy afternoon, or knew before what it was to be in a presence that delighted her so much. While they sat conversing, and apparently better satisfied with the company of each other than was likely to be regarded with indifference by any other individual aspiring to the favour of the young lady, the door was opened, and there entered no other than Francis Beattie! When Ellen saw her devoted lover appear thus suddenly, she blushed deeply, and her glee was damped in a moment. She looked rather like a condemned criminal, or at least a guilty creature, than what she really was,—a being over whose mind the cloud of guilt had never cast its shadow.

Francis loved her above all things on earth or in heaven, and the moment he saw her so much abashed at being surprised in the company of his brother, his spirit was moved to jealousy—to maddening and uncontrolable jealousy. His ears rang, his hair stood on end, and the contour of his face became like a bent bow. He walked up to his brother with his hand on his hilt, and, in a state of excitement which rendered his words inarticulate, addressed him thus, while his teeth ground together like a horse-rattle :

" Pray, sir, may I ask you of your intentions, and of what you are seeking here ?"

" I know not, Frank, what right you have to ask any such questions ; but you will allow that I have a right to ask at you what *you* are seeking here at present, seeing you come so very inopportunely ?"

" Sir," said Francis, whose passion could stay no farther parley, " dare you put it to the issue of the sword this moment ?"

" Come now, dear Francis, do not act the fool and the madman both at a time. Rather than bring such a dispute to the issue of the sword between two brothers who never had a quarrel in their lives, I propose that we bring it to a much more temperate and decisive issue here where we stand, by giving the maiden her choice. Stand you there at that corner of the room, I at this, and Ellen Scott in the middle ; let us both ask her, and to whomsoever she comes, the prize be his. Why should we try to decide, by the loss of one of our lives, what we cannot decide, and what may be decided in a friendly and rational way in one mi‑ nute ?"

" It is easy for you, sir, to talk temperately and with indifference of such a trial, but not so with me. This young lady is dear to my heart."

" Well, but so is she to mine. Let us, therefore, appeal to the lady at once, whose claim is the best ; and as your pretensions are the highest, do you ask her first."

" My dearest Ellen," said Francis, humbly and af‑ fectionately, " you know that my whole soul is devo‑ ted to your love, and that I aspire to it only in the most honourable way ; put an end to this dispute there‑ fore by honouring me with the preference which the unequivocal offer of my hand merits."

Ellen stood dumb and motionless, looking steadfast‑ ly down at the hem of her green jerkin, which she was nibbling with both her hands. She dared not lift an eye to either of the brothers, though apparently con‑ scious that she ought to have recognised the claims of Francis.

" Ellen, I need not tell you that I love you," said

Thomas, in a light and careless manner, as if certain that his appeal would be successful; " nor need I attempt to tell how dearly and how long I will love you, for in faith I cannot. Will you make the discovery for yourself by deciding in my favour ?"

Ellen looked up. There was a smile on her lovely face; an arch, mischievous, and happy smile, but it turned not on Thomas. Her face turned to the contrary side, but yet the beam of that smile fell not on Francis, who stood in a state of as terrible suspense between hope and fear, as a Roman Catholic sinner at the gate of heaven, who has implored of St Peter to open the gate, and awaits a final answer. The die of his fate was soon cast, for Ellen, looking one way, yet moving another, straightway threw herself into Thomas Beattie's arms, exclaiming, " Ah, Tom! I fear I am doing that which I shall rue, but I must trust to your generosity; for, bad as you are, I like you the best!"

Thomas took her in his arms, and kissed her; but before he could say a word in return, the despair and rage of his brother, breaking forth over every barrier of reason, interrupted him. " This is the trick of a coward, to screen himself from the chastisement he deserves. But you escape me not thus! Follow me if you dare!" And as he said this, Francis rushed from the house, shaking his naked sword at his brother.

Ellen trembled with agitation at the young man's

rage ; and while Thomas still continued to assure her
of his unalterable affection, Mrs Jane Jerdan entered,
plucking her apron so as to make it twang like a bow-
string.

" What's a' this, Squire Tummas ?   Are we to be
babbled out o' house and hadding by this rapturous*
young lawyer o' yours ?   By the souls o' the Jerdans,
I'll kick up sic a stoure about his lugs as shall blind the
juridical een o' him !   It's queer that men should study
the law only to learn to break it.   Sure am I, nae gentleman, that hasna been bred a lawyer, wad come into
a neighbour's house bullyragging that gate wi' sword
in hand, malice prepense in his eye, and venom on his
tongue.   Just as a lassie hadna her ain freedom o'
choice, because a fool has been pleased to ask her ?
Hand the grip you hae, Niece Nell ; ye hae made a
wise choice for aince.   Tam's the man for my money !
Folk are a' wise ahint the hand, but real wisdom lies
in taking time by the forelock.   But, Squire Tam, the
thing that I want to ken is this—Are you going to put
up wi' a' that bullying and threatening, or do ye
propose to chastise the fool according to his folly ?"

" In truth, Mrs Jane, I am very sorry for my brother's behaviour, and could not with honour yield any
more than I did to pacify him.   But he must be hum-

* Rapturous, i. e. outrageous.

bled. It will not do to suffer him to carry matters with so high a hand."

" Now, wad ye be but advised and leave him to me, I would play him sic a plisky as he shouldna forget till his dying day. By the souls o' the Jerdans, I would! Now promise to me that ye winna fight him."

" O promise, promise!" cried Ellen vehemently, " for the sake of heaven's love, promise my aunt that."

Thomas smiled and shook his head, as much as if he had said, " You do not know what you are asking." Mrs Jane went on.

" Do it then—do it with a vengeance, and remember this, that wherever ye set the place o' combat, be it in hill or dale, deep linn or moss hagg, I shall have a thirdsman there to encourage you on. I shall give you a meeting you little wot of."

Thomas Beattie took all this for words of course, as Mrs Jane was well known for a raving, ranting old maid, whose vehemence few regarded, though a great many respected her for the care she had taken of her sister's family, and a greater number still regarded her with terror, as a being possessed of superhuman powers ; so after many expressions of the fondest love for Ellen, he took his leave, his mind being made up how it behoved him to deal with his brother.

I forgot to mention before, that old Beattie lived at Nether Cassway with his family ; and his eldest son

Thomas at Over Cassway, having, on his father's entering into a second marriage, been put in possession of that castle, and these lands. Francis, of course, lived in his father's house when in Scotland ; and it was thus that his brother knew nothing of his frequent visits to Ellen Scott.

That night, as soon as Thomas went home, he dispatched a note to his brother to the following purport : That he was sorry for the rudeness and unreasonableness of his behaviour. But if, on coming to himself, he was willing to make an apology before his mistress, then he (Thomas) would gladly extend to him the right hand of love and brotherhood ; but if he refused this, he would please to meet him on the Crook of Glen-dearg next morning by the sun-rising. Francis returned for answer that he would meet him at the time and place appointed. There was then no farther door of reconciliation left open, but Thomas still had hopes of managing him even on the combat field.

Francis slept little that night, being wholly set on revenge for the loss of his beloved mistress ; and a little after day-break he arose, and putting himself in light armour, proceeded to the place of rendezvous. He had farther to go than his elder brother, and on coming in sight of the Crook of Glen-dearg, he perceived the latter there before him. He was wrapt in his cavalier's cloak, and walking up and down the Crook with impassioned strides, on which Francis soliloquized as follows, as he hasted on :—" Ah ha! so Tom is here before me!   This is what I did not expect, for I did not think the flagitious dog had so much spirit or courage in him as to meet me.   I am glad he has! for how I long to chastise him, and draw some of the pampered blood from that vain and insolent heart, which has bereaved me of all I held dear on earth!"

In this way did he cherish his wrath till close at his brother's side, and then, addressing him in the same insolent terms, he desired him to cease his cowardly cogitations and draw.   His opponent instantly wheeled about, threw off his horseman's cloak, and presented his sword ; and behold the young man's father stood before him, armed and ready for action!   The sword fell from Francis's hand, and he stood appalled as if he had been a statue, unable either to utter a word or move a muscle.

" Take up thy sword, caitiff, and let it work thy ruthless work of vengeance here. Is it not better that thou shouldst pierce this old heart, worn out with care and sorrow, and chilled by the ingratitude of my race, than that of thy gallant and generous brother, the representative of our house, and the Chief of our name ? Take up thy sword, I say, and if I do not chastise thee as thou deservest, may Heaven reft the sword of justice from the hand of the avenger !"

" The God of Heaven forbid that I should ever lift my sword against my honoured father !" said Francis.

" Thou darest not, thou traitor and coward !" returned the father.——" I throw back the disgraceful terms in thy teeth which thou used'st to thy brother. Thou camest here boiling with rancour, to shed his blood ; and when I appear in person for him, thou darest not accept the challenge."

" You never did me wrong, my dear father ; but my brother has wronged me in the tenderest part."

" Thy brother never wronged thee intentionally, thou deceitful and sanguinary fratricide. It was thou alone who forced this quarrel upon him ; and I have great reason to suspect thee of a design to cut him off, that the inheritance and the maid might both be thine own. But here I swear by the arm that made me, and the Redeemer that saved me, if thou wilt not go straight and kneel to thy brother for forgiveness, confessing thy injurious treatment, and swearing submission to thy natural Chief, I will banish thee from my house and presence for ever, and load thee with a parent's curse, which shall never be removed from thy soul till thou art crushed to the lowest hell."

The young scholar, being utterly astounded at his father's words, and at the awful and stern manner in which he addressed him, whom he had never before reprimanded, was wholly overcome. He kneeled to his parent, and implored his forgiveness, promising, with tears, to fulfil every injunction which it would please him to enjoin ; and on this understanding, the two parted on amicable and gracious terms.

Francis went straight to the tower of Over Cassway, and inquired for his brother, resolved to fulfil his father's stern injunctions to the very letter. He was informed his brother was in his chamber in bed, and indisposed. He asked the porter farther, if he had not been forth that day, and was answered, that he had gone forth early in the morning in armour, but had quickly returned, apparently in great agitation, and betaken himself to his bed. Francis then requested to be taken to his brother, to which the servant instantly assented, and led him up to the chamber, never suspecting that there could be any animosity between the two only brothers ; but on John Burgess opening the door, and announcing the Tutor, Thomas, being in a nervous state, was a little alarmed. " Remain in the room there, Burgess," said he.—" What, brother Frank, are you seeking here at this hour, armed capapee? I hope you are not come to assassinate me in my bed ?"

" God forbid, brother," said the other ; " here John, take my sword down with you, I want some private conversation with Thomas." John did so, and the following conversation ensued ; for as soon as the door closed, Francis dropt on his knees, and said, " O,

8

my dear brother, I have erred grievously, and am come
to confess my crime, and implore your pardon."

"We have both erred, Francis, in suffering any
earthly concern to incite us against each other's lives.
We have both erred, but you have my forgiveness
cheerfully ; here is my hand on it, and grant me thine
in return. Oh, Francis, I have got an admonition this
morning, that never will be erased from my memory,
and which has caused me to see my life in a new light.
What or whom think you I met an hour ago on my
way to the Crook of Glen-dearg to encounter you?"

"Our father, perhaps."

"You have seen him, then ?"

"Indeed I have, and he has given me such a repri-
mand for severity, as son never before received from
a parent."

"Brother Frank, I must tell you, and when I do,
you will not believe me——It *was not* our father whom
we both saw this morning."

"It was no other whom I saw. What do you
mean ? Do you suppose that I do not know my own
father ?"

"I tell you it was not, and could not be. I had an
express from him yesterday. He is two hundred miles
from this, and cannot be in Scotland sooner than three
weeks hence."

194   THE SHEPHERD'S CALENDAR.

" You astonish me, Thomas. This is beyond human comprehension !"

" It is true—that I avouch, and the certainty of it has sickened me at heart. You must be aware that he came not home last night, and that his horse and retinue have not arrived."

" He was not at home, it is true, nor have his horse and retinue arrived in Scotland. Still there is no denying that our father is here, and that it was he who spoke to and admonished me."

" I tell you it is impossible. A spirit hath spoke to us in our father's likeness, for he is not, and cannot be, in Scotland at this time. My faculties are altogether confounded by the event, not being able to calculate on the qualities or condition of our monitor. An evil spirit it certainly could not be, for all its admonitions pointed to good. I sorely dread, Francis, that our father is no more—that there has been another engagement, that he has lost his life, and that his soul has been lingering around his family before taking its final leave of this sphere. I believe that our father is dead ; and for my part I am so sick at heart, that my nerves are all unstrung. Pray, do you take horse and post off for Salop, from whence his commission to me yesterday was dated, and see what hath happened to our revered father."

" I cannot, for my life, give credit to this, brother,

or that it was any other being but my father himself who rebuked me. Pray allow me to tarry another day at least, before I set out. Perhaps our father may appear in the neighbourhood, and may be concealing himself for some secret purpose.—Did you tell him of our quarrel ?"

" No. He never asked me concerning it, but charged me sharply with my intent on the first word, and adjured me, by my regard for his blessing, and my hope in heaven, to desist from my purpose."

" Then he knew it all intuitively ; for when I first went in view of the spot appointed for our meeting, I perceived him walking sharply to and fro, wrapped in his military cloak. He never so much as deigned to look at me, till I came close to his side, and thinking it was yourself, I fell to upbraiding him, and desired him to draw. He then threw off his cloak, drew his sword, and, telling me he came in your place, dared me to the encounter. But he knew all the grounds of our quarrel minutely, and laid the blame on me. I own I am a little puzzled to reconcile circumstances, but am convinced my father is near at hand. I heard his words, and saw his eyes flashing anger and indignation. Unfortunately I did not touch him, which would have put an end to all doubts ; for he did not present the hand of reconciliation to me, as I expected he would have done, on my yielding implicitly to all his injunctions."

The two brothers then parted, with protestations of mutual forbearance in all time coming, and with an understanding, as that was the morning of Saturday, that if their father, or some word of him, did not reach home before the next evening, the Tutor of Cassway was to take horse for the county of Salop, early on Monday morning.

Thomas, being thus once more left to himself, could do nothing but toss and tumble in his bed, and reflect on the extraordinary occurrence of that morning ; and, after many troubled cogitations, it at length occurred to his recollection what Mrs Jane Jerdan had said to him :—" Do it then.   Do it with a vengeance !—But remember this, that wherever ye set the place of combat, be it in hill or dale, deep linn, or moss hagg, I shall have a thirdsman there to encourage you on.   I shall give you a meeting you little wot of."

If he was confounded before, he was ten times more so at the remembrance of these words, of most ominous import.

At the time he totally disregarded them, taking them for mere rodomontade ; but now the idea was to him terrible, that his father's spirit, like the prophet's of old, should have been conjured up by witchcraft : and then again he bethought himself that no witch

would have employed her power to prevent evil. In
the end, he knew not what to think, and so, taking the
hammer from its rest, he gave three raps on the pipe
drum, for there were no bells in the towers of those
days, and up came old John Burgess, Thomas Beattie's henchman, huntsman, and groom of the chambers,
one who had been attached to the family for fifty
years, and he says, in his slow West-Border tongue,
" How's tou now, callan' ?—Is tou ony betterlins ?
There has been tway stags seen in the Bloodhope-Linns
tis mworning already."

" Ay, and there has been something else seen, John,
that lies nearer to my heart, to-day." John looked at
his master with an inquisitive eye and quivering lip,
but said nothing. The latter went on, " I am very
unwell to-day, John, and cannot tell what is the matter with me. I think I am bewitched."

" It's very like tou is, callan. I pits nae doubt on't
at a'."

" Is there any body in this moor district who.n you
ever heard blamed for the horrible crime of witchcraft ?"

" Ay, that there is ; mair than ane or tway. There's
our neighbour, Lucky Jerdan, for instance, and her
niece Nell,—the warst o' the pair, I doubt." John said
this with a sly stupid leer, for he had admitted the old
lady to an audience with his master the day before, and

had eyed him afterwards bending his course towards Drumfielding.

" John, I am not disposed to jest at this time ; for I am disturbed in mind, and very ill. Tell me, in reality, did you ever hear Mrs Jane Jerdan accused of being a witch ?"

" Why, look thee, master, I dares nae say she's a wotch ; for Lucky has mony good points in her character. But it's weel kenned she has mair power nor her ain, for she can stwop a' the plews in Eskdale wi' a wave o' her hand, and can raise the dead out o' their graves, just as a matter o' cwoorse."

" That, John, is an extraordinary power indeed. But did you never hear of her sending any living men to their graves ? For as that is rather the danger that hangs over me, I wish you would take a ride over and desire Mrs Jane to come and see me. Tell her I am ill, and request of her to come and see me."

" I shall do that, callan'. But are tou sure it is the auld wotch I'm to bring ? For it strikes me the young ane maybe has done the deed ; and if sae, she is the fittest to effect the cure. But I sall bring the auld ane— Dinna flee intil a rage, for I sall bring the auld ane ; though, gude forgie me, it is unco like bringing the houdy."

Away went John Burgess to Drumfielding ; but Mrs Jane would not move for all his entreaties. She sent

back word to his master, to "rise out o' his bed, for
he wad be waur if ony thing ailed him; and if he had
aught to say to auld Jane Jerdan, she would be ready
to hear it at hame, though he behoved to remember
that it wasna ilka subject under the sun that she could
thole to be questioned anent."

With this answer John was forced to return, and
there being no accounts of old Beattie having been seen
in Scotland, the young men remained all the Sabbath-
day in the utmost consternation at the apparition of
their father they had seen, and the appalling rebuke they
had received from it. The most incredulous mind could
scarce doubt that they had had communion with a supernatural being; and not being able to draw any other
conclusion themselves, they became persuaded that their
father was dead; and accordingly, both prepared for
setting out early on Monday morning towards the county of Salop, from whence they had last heard of him.

But just as they were ready to set out, when their
spurs were buckled on and their horses bridled, Andrew
Johnston, their father's confidential servant, arrived
from the place to which they were bound. He had
rode night and day, never once stinting the light gallop, as he said, and had changed his horse seven times.
He appeared as if his ideas were in a state of derangement and confusion; and when he saw his young masters standing together, and ready-mounted for a jour-

ney, he stared at them as if he scarcely believed his
own senses.   They of course asked immediately about
the cause of his express; but his answers were equivocal, and he appeared not to be able to assign any motive.   They asked him concerning their father, and if
any thing extraordinary had happened to him.   He
would not say either that there had, or that there had
not; but inquired, in his turn, if nothing extraordinary
had happened with them at home.   They looked to one
another, and returned him no answer; but at length
the youngest said, "Why, Andrew, you profess to have
ridden express for the distance of two hundred miles;
now, you surely must have some guess for what purpose you have done this?   Say, then, at once, what
your message is: Is our father alive?"

"Ye—es; I think he is."

"You *think* he is?   Are you uncertain, then?"

"I am certain he is not *dead*,—at least was not when
I left him.   But—hum—certainly there has a change
taken place.   Hark ye, masters—can a man be said to
be in life when he is out of himself?"

"Why, man, keep us not in this thrilling suspense.
—Is our father well?"

"No—not *quite* well.   I am sorry to say, honest
gentleman, that he is not.   But the truth is, my masters, now that I see you well and hearty, and about to
take a journey in company, I begin to suspect that I

have been posted all this way on a fool's errand; and not another syllable will I speak on the subject, till I have had some refreshment, and if you still insist on hearing a ridiculous story, you shall hear it then."

When the matter of the refreshment had been got over to Andrew's full satisfaction, he began as follows:

" Why, faith, you see, my masters, it is not easy to say my errand to you, for in fact I have none. Therefore, all that I can do is to tell you a story,—a most ridiculous one it is, as ever sent a poor fellow out on the gallop for the matter of two hundred miles or so. On the morning before last, right early, little Isaac, the page, comes to me, and he says,—' Johnston, thou must go and visit measter. He's bad.'

" ' Bad!' says I. ' Whaten way is he bad?'

" ' Why,' says he, ' he's so far ill as he's not well, and desires to see you without one moment's delay. He's in fine taking, and that you'll find; but whatfor do I stand here? Lword, I never got such a fright. Why, Johnston, does thou know that measter hath lwost himself?'

" ' How lost himself? rabbit,' says I, ' speak plain out, else I'll have thee lug-hauled, thou dwarf!' for my blood rose at the imp, for fooling at any mishap of my master's. But my choler only made him worse, for there is not a greater deil's-buckie in all the Five Dales.

" 'Why, man, it is true that I said,' quoth he, laughing; 'the old gurly squoir hath lwost himself; and it
will be grand sport to see thee going calling him at all
the steane-crosses in the kingdom, in this here way—
Ho yes! and a two times ho yes! and a *three* times
ho yes! Did any body no see the better half of my
measter, Laird of the twa Cassways, Bloodhope, and
Pantland, which was amissing overnight, and is supposed to have gone a-wool-gathering? If any body hath
seen that better part of my measter, whilk contains as
mooch wit as a man could drive on a hurlbarrow, let
them restore it to me, Andrew Johnston, piper, trum-
peter, whacker, and wheedler, to the same great and
noble squoir; and high shall be his reward——Ho yes!'

" 'The devil restore thee to thy right mind!' said I,
knocking him down, and leaving him sprawling in the
kennel, and then hasted to my master, whom I found
feverish, restless, and raving, and yet with an earnestness in his demeanour that stunned and terrified me.
He seized my hand in both his, which were burning
like fire, and gave me such a look of despair as I shall
never forget. 'Johnston, I am ill,' said he, 'grievously ill, and know not what is to become of me. Every
nerve in my body is in a burning heat, and my soul is
as it were torn to fritters with amazement. Johnston,
as sure as you are in the body, something most deplorable hath happened to em.'

" ' Yes, as sure as I am in the body, there has, master,' says I. ' But I'll have you bled and doctored in style ; and you shall soon be as sound as a roach,' says I ; ' for a gentleman must not lose heart altogether for a little fire-raising in his outworks, if it does not reach the citadel,' says I to him. But he cut me short by shaking his head and flinging my hand from him.

" ' A truce with your talking,' says he. ' That which hath befallen me is as much above your comprehension as the sun is above the earth, and never will be comprehended by mortal man ; but I must inform you of it, as I have no other means of gaining the intelligence I yearn for, and which I am incapable of gaining personally. Johnston, there never was a mortal man suffered what I have suffered since midnight. I believe I have had doings with hell ; for I have been disembodied, and embodied again, and the intensity of my tortures has been unparalleled.——I was at home this morning at day-break.'

" ' At home at Cassway !' says I. ' I am sorry to hear you say so, master, because you know, or should know, that the thing is impossible, you being in the ancient town of Shrewsbury on the King's business.'

" ' I was at home in very deed, Andrew,' returned he ; ' but whether in the body, or out of the body, I cannot tell—the Lord only knoweth. But there I was in this guise, and with this heart and all its feelings

within me, where I saw scenes, heard words, and spoke
others, which I will here relate to you.   I had finished my dispatches last night by midnight, and was sitting musing on the hard fate and improvidence of my
sovereign master, when, ere ever I was aware, a neighbour of ours, Mrs Jane Jerdan, of Drumfielding, a
mysterious character, with whom I have had some
strange doings in my time, came suddenly into the
chamber, and stood before me.   I accosted her with
doubt and terror, asking what had brought her so far
from home.'

" ' You are not so far from home as you imagine,'
said she ; ' and it is fortunate for some that it is so.
Your two sons have quarrelled about the possession of
niece Ellen, and though the eldest is blameless of the
quarrel, yet has he been forced into it, and they are engaged to fight at day-break at the Crook of Glen-dearg.
There they will assuredly fall by each other's hands,
if you interpose not ; for there is no other authority now
on earth that can prevent this woful calamity.'

" ' Alas ! how can I interfere,' said I, ' at this distance ?   It is already within a few hours of the meeting, and before I get from among the windings of the
Severn, their swords will be bathed in each other's
blood !   I must trust to the interference of Heaven.'

" ' Is your name and influence, then, to perish for
ever ?' said she. Is it so soon to follow your master's,

the great Maxwell of the Dales, into utter oblivion ? Why not rather rouse into requisition the energies of the spirits that watch over human destinies ? At least step aside with me, that I may disclose the scene to your eyes. You know I can do it ; and you may then act according to your natural impulse.'

" ' Such were the import of the words she spoke to me, if not the very words themselves. I understood them not at the time ; nor do I yet. But when she had done speaking, she took me by the hand, and hurried me towards the door of the apartment, which she opened, and the first step we took over the threshold, we stepped into a void space, and fell downward. I was going to call out, but felt my descent so rapid, that my voice was stifled, and I could not so much as draw my breath. I expected every moment to fall against something, and be dashed to pieces; and I shut my eyes, clenched my teeth, and held by the dame's hand with a frenzied grasp, in expectation of the catastrophe. But down we went—down and down, with a celerity which tongue cannot describe, without light, breath, or any sort of impediment. I now felt assured that we had both at once stepped from off the earth, and were hurled into the immeasurable void. The airs of darkness sung in my ears with a booming din as I rolled down the steeps of everlasting night, an outcast from nature and all its harmonies, and a journeyer into the depths of hell.

" ' I still held my companion's hand, and felt the pressure of hers ; and so long did this our alarming descent continue, that I at length caught myself breathing once more, but as quick as if I had been in the height of a fever. I then tried every effort to speak, but they were all unavailing ; for I could not emit one sound, although my lips and tongue fashioned the words. Think, then, of my astonishment, when my companion sung out the following stanza with the greatest glee :—

> ' Here we roll,
> Body and soul,
> Down to the deeps of the Paynim's goal—
> With speed and with spell,
> With yo and with yell,
> This is the way to the palace of hell—
> Sing Yo! Ho!
> Level and low,
> Down to the Valley of Vision we go !'

" ' Ha, ha, ha ! Tam Beattie,' added she, ' where is a' your courage now ? Cannot ye lift up your voice and sing a stave wi' your auld crony ? And cannot ye lift up your een, and see what region you are in now ?'

" ' I did force open my eyelids, and beheld light, and apparently worlds, or huge lurid substances, gliding by me with speed beyond that of the lightning of heaven. I certainly perceived light, though of a dim uncertain nature ; but so precipitate was my descent, I could not distinguish from whence it proceeded, or of what it consisted, whether of the vapours of chaotic wastes, or the streamers of hell. So I again shut my eyes closer than ever, and waited the event in terror unutterable.

" ' We at length came upon something which interrupted our farther progress. I had no feeling as we fell against it, but merely as if we came in contact with some soft substance that impeded our descent ; and immediately afterwards I perceived that our motion had ceased.

" ' What a terrible tumble we hae gotten, Laird !' said my companion. ' But ye are now in the place where you should be ; and deil speed the coward !'

" ' So saying, she quitted my hand, and I felt as if she were wrested from me by a third object ; but still I durst not open my eyes, being convinced that I was lying in the depths of hell, or some hideous place not to be dreamt of ; so I lay still in despair, not even daring to address a prayer to my Maker. At length I lifted my eyes slowly and fearfully ; but they had no power of distinguishing objects. All that I perceived was a vision of something in nature, with which I had in life been too well acquainted. It was a glimpse of green glens, long withdrawing ridges, and one high hill, with a cairn on its summit. I rubbed my eyes to divest them of the enchantment, but when I opened them again, the illusion was still brighter and more magnificent. Then springing to my feet, I perceived that I

was lying in a little fairy ring, not one hundred yards
from the door of my own hall !

"'I was, as you may well conceive, dazzled with admiration ; still I felt that something was not right with
me, and that I was struggling with an enchantment ;
but recollecting the hideous story told me by the bel-
dame, of the deadly discord between my two sons, I
hasted to watch their motions, for the morning was yet
but dawning.   In a few seconds after recovering my
senses, I perceived my eldest son Thomas leave his
tower armed, and pass on towards the place of appointment.   I waylaid him, and remarked to him that he was
very early astir, and I feared on no good intent.   He
made no answer, but stood like one in a stupor, and
gazed at me.   ' I know your purpose, son Thomas,'
said I ; ' so it is in vain for you to equivocate.   You
have challenged your brother, and are going to meet
him in deadly combat ; but as you value your father's
blessing, and would deprecate his curse—as you value
your hope in heaven, and would escape the punishment
of hell—abandon the hideous and cursed intent, and be
reconciled to your only brother.'

"'On this, my dutiful son Thomas kneeled to me,
and presented his sword, disclaiming, at the same time,
all intentions of taking away his brother's life, and all
animosity for the vengeance sought against himself, and
thanked me in a flood of tears for my interference.   I

then commanded him back to his couch, and taking his cloak and sword, hasted away to the Crook of Glendearg, to wait the arrival of his brother.' "

Here Andrew Johnston's narrative detailed the selfsame circumstances recorded in a former part of this tale, as having passed between the father and his younger son, so that it is needless to recapitulate them ; but beginning where that broke off, he added, in the words of the Old Laird, " ' As soon as my son Francis had left me, in order to be reconciled to his brother, I returned to the fairy knowe and ring where I first found myself seated at daybreak. I know not why I went there, for though I considered with myself, I could discover no motive that I had for doing so, but was led thither by a sort of impulse which I could not resist, and from the same feeling spread my son's mantle on the spot, laid his sword down beside it, and stretched me down to sleep. I remember nothing farther with any degree of accuracy, for I instantly fell into a chaos of suffering, confusion, and racking dismay, from which I was only of late released by awaking from a trance, on the very seat, and in the same guise in which I was the evening before. I am certain I was at home in body or in spirit—saw my sons—spake these words to them, and heard theirs in return. How I returned I know even less, if that is possible, than how I went ; for it seemed to me that the mysterious force that presses us to this sphere, and supports us on it, was in my case withdrawn or subverted, and that I merely fell from one part of the earth's surface and alighted on another. Now I am so ill that I cannot move from this couch; therefore, Andrew, do you mount and ride straight home.   Spare no horse-flesh, by night or by day, to bring me word of my family, for I dread that some evil hath befallen them.   If you find them in life, give them many charges from me of brotherly love and affection; if not—what can I say, but, in the words of the patriarch, If I am bereaved of my children, I am bereaved.' "

· The two brothers, in utter amazement, went together to the green ring on the top of the knoll above the Castle of Cassway, and there found the mantle lying spread, and the sword beside it.   They then, without letting Johnston into the awful secret, mounted straight,.and rode off with him to their father. They found him still in bed, and very ill; and though rejoiced at seeing them, they soon lost hope of his recovery, his spirits being broken and deranged in a wonderful manner.   Their conversations together were of the most solemn nature, the visitation deigned to them having been above their capacity.   On the third or fourth day, their father was removed by death from this terrestrial scene, and the minds of the young men were so much impressed by the whole of the circumstances, that it made a great alteration in their after life. Thomas, as solemnly charged by his father, married Ellen Scott, and Francis was well known afterward as the celebrated Dr Beattie of Amherst. Ellen was mother to twelve sons, and on the night that her seventh son was born, her aunt Jerdan was lost, and never more heard of, either living or dead.

This will be viewed as a most romantic and unnatural story, as without doubt it is ; but I have the strongest reasons for believing that it is founded on a literal fact, of which all the three were sensibly and positively convinced. It was published in England in Dr Beattie's lifetime, and by his acquiescence, and owing to the respectable source from whence it came, it was never disputed in that day that it had its origin in truth. It was again republished, with some miserable alterations, in a London collection of 1770, by J. Smith, at No. 15, Paternoster-Row; and though I have seen none of these accounts, but relate the story wholly from tradition, yet the assurance attained from a friend of their existence, is a curious corroborative circumstance, and proves that, if the story was not true, the parties at least believed it to be so.

CHAPTER VIII.-

TIBBY HYSLOP'S DREAM.

In the year 1807, when on a jaunt through the valleys of Nith and Annan, I learned the following story on the spot where the incidents occurred, and even went and visited all those connected with it, so that there is no doubt with regard to its authenticity.

In a cottage called Knowe-back, on the large farm of Drumlochie, lived Tibby Hyslop, a respectable spinster, about the age of forty I thought when I saw her, but, of course, not so old when the first incidents occurred which this singular tale relates. Tibby was represented to me as being a good Christian, not in name and profession only, but in word and in deed; and I believe I may add, in heart and in soul. Nevertheless, there was something in her manner and deportment different from other people—a sort of innocent simplicity, bordering on silliness, together with an instability of thought, that, in the eyes of many, approached to abstraction.

But then Tibby could repeat the book of the Evangelist Luke by heart, and many favourite chapters both of the Old and New Testaments; while there was scarcely one in the whole country so thoroughly acquainted with those Books from beginning to end ; for, though she had read a portion every day for forty years, she had never perused any other books but the Scriptures. They were her week-day books, and her Sunday books, her books of amusement, and books of devotion. Would to God that all our brethren and sisters of the human race—the poor and comfortless, as well as the great and wise—knew as well how to estimate these books as Tibby Hyslop did !

Tibby's history is shortly this : Her mother married a sergeant of a recruiting party. The year following he was obliged to go to Ireland, and from thence nobody knew whither ; but neither he nor his wife appeared again in Scotland. On their departure, they left Tibby, then a helpless babe, with her grandmother, who lived in a hamlet somewhere about Tinwald ; and with that grandmother was she brought up, and taught to read her Bible, to card, spin, and work at all kinds of country labour to which women are accustomed. Jane Hervey was her grandmother's name, a woman then scarcely past her prime, certainly within forty years of age ; with whom lived her elder sister, named Douglas : and with these two were the early years of

Tibby Hyslop spent, in poverty, contentment, and devotion.

At the age of eighteen, Tibby was hired at the Candlemas fair, for a great wage, to be a byre-woman to Mr Gilbert Forret, then farmer at Drumlochie. Tibby ha then acquired a great deal of her mother's dangerous bloom—dangerous, when attached to poverty and so much simplicity of heart ; and when she came home and told what she had done, her mother and aunt, as she always denominated the two, marvelled much at the extravagant conditions, and began to express some fears regarding her new master's designs, till Tibby put them all to rest by the following piece of simple information :

" Dear, ye ken, ye needna be feared that Mr Forret has ony design o' courting me, for dear, ye ken, he has a wife already, and five bonny bairns ; and he'll never be sae daft as fa' on and court anither ane. I'se warrant he finds ane enow for him, honest man !"

" Oh, then, you are safe enough, since he is a married man, my bairn," said Jane.

The truth was, that Mr Forret was notorious for debauching young and pretty girls, and was known in Dumfries market by the name of Gibby Gledger, from the circumstance of his being always looking slyly after them.   Perceiving Tibby so comely, and at the same time so simple, he hired her at nearly double wages, and moreover gave her a crown as arle-money.

Tibby went home to her service, and being a pliable, diligent creature, she was beloved by all. Her master commended her for her neatness, and whenever a quiet opportunity offered, would pat her rosy cheek, and say kind things. Tibby took all these in good part, judging them tokens of approbation of her good services, and was proud of them ; and if he once or twice whispered a place and an hour of assignation, she took it for a joke, and paid no farther attention to it. A whole year passed over without the worthy farmer having accomplished his cherished purpose regarding poor Tibby. He hired her to remain with him, still on the former high conditions, and moreover he said to her : " I wish your grandmother and grand-aunt would take my pleasant cottage of Knowe-back. They should have it for a mere trifle—a week's shearing or so—so long as you remain in my service ; and as it is likely to be a long while before you and I part, it would be better to have them near you, that you might see them often, and attend to their wants. I could give them plenty of work through the whole year, on the best conditions. What think you of this proposal, Rosy ?"—a familiar name he often called her by.

" O, I'm sure, sir, I think ye are the kindest man that ever existed. ' What a blessing is it when riches

open up the heart to acts of charity and benevolence !
My poor auld mother and aunty will be blythe to grip
at the kind offer ; for they sit under a hard master yonder.   The Almighty will bestow a blessing on you for
this, sir !"

Tibby went immediately with the joyful news to her
poor mother and aunt.   Now, they had of late found
themselves quite easy in their circumstances, owing to
the large wages Tibby received, every farthing of which
was added to the common stock ; and though Tibby
displayed a little more finery at the meeting-house, it
was her grandmother who purchased it for her, without
any consent on her part.   " I am sure," said her grandmother, when Tibby told the story of her master's kindness and attention, " I am sure it was the kindest in-
tervention o' Providence that ever happened to poor
things afore, when ye fell in wi' that kind worthy man,
i' the mids o' a great hiring market, where ye might
just as easily hae met wi' a knave, or a niggard, as wi'
this man o' siccan charity an' mercy."

> " Ay ; the wulcat maun hae his collop,
>   And the raven maun hae his part,
> And the tod will creep through the heather,
>   For the bonny moor-hen's heart,"

said old Douglas Hervey, poking the fire all the while
with the tongs, and speaking only as if speaking to herself—" Hech-wow, and lack-a-day ! but the times are

altered sair since I first saw the sun! Poor, poor Religion, wae's me for her! She was first driven out o' the lord's castle into the baron's ha'; out o' the baron's ha' into the farmer's bien dwelling; and at last out o' that into the poor cauldrife shiel, where there's nae ither comfort but what she brings wi' her."

" What has set ye onna thae reflections the day, aunty?" cried Tibby aloud at her ear; for she was half deaf, and had so many flannel mutches on, besides a blue napkin, which she always wore over them all, that her deafness was nearly completed altogether.

" Oogh! what's the lassie saying?" said she, after listening a good while, till the sounds penetrated to the interior of her ear, " what's the young light-head saying about the defections o' the day? what kens she about them?—oogh! Let me see your face, dame, and find your hand, for I hae neither seen the ane, nor felt the tither, this lang and mony a day." Then taking her grand-niece by the hand, and looking close into her face through the spectacles, she added,—" Ay, it is a weel-faured sonsy face, very like the mother's that bore ye; and hers was as like *her* mother's; and there was never as muckle common sense amang a' the three as to keep a brock out o' the kail-yard. Ye hae an unco good master, I hear—oogh! I'm glad to hear't—hoh-oh-oh-oh!—verra glad. I hope it will lang continue, this kindness. Poor Tibby!—as lang as the heart disna gang wrang, we maun excuse the head, for it'll never since gang right. I hope they were baith made for a better warld, for nane o' them were made for this."

When she got this length, she sat hastily down, and began her daily and hourly task of carding wool for her sister's spinning, abstracting herself from all external considerations.

" I think aunty's unco parabolical the day," said Tibby to her grandmother; " what makes her that gate ?"

" O dear, hinny, she's aye that gate now. She speaks to naebody but hersell," said Jane. " But—lownly be it spoken—I think whiles there's ane speaks till her again that my een canna see."

" The angels often conversed wi' good folks langsyne. I ken o' naething that can hinder them to do sae still, if they're sae disposed," said Tibby ; and so the dialogue closed for the present.

Mr Forret sent his carts at the term, and removed the old people to the cottage of Knowe-back, free of all charge, like a gentleman as he was ; and things went on exceedingly well. Tibby had a sincere regard for her master ; and as he continued to speak to her, when alone, in a kind and playful manner, she had several times ventured to broach religion to him, trying to discover the state of his soul. Then he would shake his head, and look demure in mockery, and repeat some grave, becoming words. Poor Tibby thought he *was* a righteous man.

But in a short time his purposes were divulged in such a manner as to be no more equivocal. That morn- ing immediately preceding the developement of this long-cherished atrocity, Jane Hervey was awaked at an early hour by the following unintelligible dialogue in her elder sister's bed.

" Have ye seen the news o' the day, kerlin?"

" Oogh?"

" Have ye seen the news o' the day?"

" Ay, that I hae, on a braid open book, without clasp or seal. Whether will you or the deil win?"

" That depends on the citadel. If it stand out, a' the powers o' hell winna shake the fortress, nor sap a stane o' its foundation."

" Ah, the fortress is a good ane, and a sound ane; but the poor head captain!—ye ken what a sweet-lip- ped, turnip-headit brosey he is. O, lack-a-day, my poor Tibby Hyslop!—my innocent, kind, thowless Tibby Hyslop!"

Jane was frightened at hearing such a colloquy, but particularly at that part of it where her darling child was mentioned. She sprung from her own bed to that of her sister, and cried in her ear with a loud voice,—

" Sister, sister Douglas, what is that you are saying
about our dear bairn ?"

" Oogh ? I was saying naething about your bairn.
She lies in great jeopardy yonder ; but nane as yet.
Gang away to your bed—wow, but I was sound
asleep."

" There's naebody can make aught out o' her but
nonsense," said Jane.

After the two had risen from their scanty breakfast,
which Douglas had blessed with more fervency than
ordinary, she could not settle at her carding, but always stopped short, and began mumbling and speaking
to herself.   At length, after a long pause, she looked
over her shoulder, and said,—" Jeanie, warna ye speaking o' ganging ower to see our bairn the day ? Haste
thee and gang away, then ; and stay nouther to put on
clean bussing, kirtle, nor barrie, else ye may be an an-
trin meenut or twa ower lang."

Jane made no reply, but, drawing the skirt of her
gown over her shoulders, she set out for Drumlochie,
a distance of nearly a mile ; and as she went by the
corner of the byre, she imagined she heard her grand-
child's voice, in great passion or distress, and ran straight
into the byre, crying, " What's the matter wi' you, Tibby ? what ails you, my bairn ?" but, receiving no answer, she thought the voice must have been somewhere

without, and slid quietly away, looking everywhere, and at length went down to the kitchen.

Mr Forret, *alias* Gledging Gibby, had borne the brunt of incensed kirk-sessions before that time, and also the unlicensed tongues of mothers, roused into vehemence by the degradation of beloved daughters ; but never in his life did he bear such a rebuke as he did that day from the tongue of one he had always viewed as a mere simpleton. It was a lesson—a warning of the most sublime and terrible description, couched in the pure and emphatic language of Scripture. Gibby cared not a doit for these things, but found himself foiled, and exposed to his family, and the whole world, if this fool chose to do it. He was, therefore, glad to act a part of deep hypocrisy, pretending the sincerest contrition, regretting, with tears, his momentary derangement. Poor Tibby readily believed and forgave him ; and thinking it hard to ruin a repentant sinner in his worldly and family concerns, she promised never to divulge what had passed ; and he, knowing well the value of her word, was glad at having so escaped.

Jane found her grand-daughter apparently much disturbed ; but having asked if she was well enough, and receiving an answer in the affirmative, she was satisfied, and only added, " Your crazed aunty wad gar me believe ye war in some jeopardy, and hurried me away to see you, without giving me leave to change a steek."

One may easily conceive Tibby's astonishment at hearing this, considering the moment at which her grandmother arrived. As soon as the latter was gone, she kneeled before her Maker, and poured out her soul in grateful thanksgiving for her deliverance ; and, in particular, for such a manifest interference of some superior intelligence in her behalf.

"How did ye find our poor bairn the day, titty Jean ? Did she no tell ye ony thing ?" asked Douglas, on Jane's return.

"She tauld me naething, but said she was weel."

"She's ae fool, and ye're another ! If I had been her, I wad hae blazed it baith to kirk and council ;—to his wife's ear, and to his minister's ! She's very weel, is she ?—Oogh ! Ay. Hoh—oh—oh—oh !—silly woman—silly woman—Hoh—oh—oh !"

In a few weeks, Mr Forret's behaviour to his simple dairymaid altered very materially. He called her no more by the endearing name of Rosy ; poor idiot was oftener the term ; and finding he was now safe from accusation, his malevolence towards her had scarcely any bounds. She made out her term with difficulty, but he refused to pay the stipulated wage, on pretence of her incapacity ; and as she had by that time profited well at his hand, she took what he offered, thanked him, and said no more about it. She was no more hired as a servant, but having at the first taken a long lease of the cottage, she continued, from year to year, working on the farm by the day, at a very scanty allowance. Old Douglas in a few years grew incapable of any work, through frailty of person, being constantly confined to bed, though in mind as energetic and mysterious as ever. Jane wrought long, till at length a severe illness in 1799 rendered her unfit to do any thing further than occasionally knit a stocking; and Tibby's handywork was all that herself and the two old women had to depend upon. They had brought her up with care and kindness amid the most pinching poverty, and now, indeed, her filial affection was severely put to the proof; but it was genuine, and knew no bounds. Night and day she toiled for her aged and feeble relatives, and a murmur or complaint never was heard from her lips. Many a blessing was bestowed on her as they raised their palsied heads to partake of her hard-earned pittance; and many a fervent prayer was poured out, when no mortal heard it.

Times grew harder and harder. Thousands yet living remember what a period that was for the poor, while meal, for seasons, was from four to five shillings a-stone, and even sometimes as high as seven. Tibby grew fairly incapable of supporting herself and her aged friends. She stinted herself for their sakes, and that made her still more incapable; yet often with tears in her eyes did she feed these frail beings, her heart like to melt because she had no more to give them. There are no poor-rates in that country. Knowe-back is quite retired—nobody went near it, and Tibby complained to none, but wrought on, night and day, in sorrow and anxiety, but still with a humble and thankful heart.

In this great strait, Mrs Forret was the first who began, unsolicited, to take compassion on the destitute group. She could not conceive how they existed on the poor creature's earnings. So she went privately to see them, and when she saw their wretched state, and heard their blessings on their dear child, her heart was moved to pity, and she determined to assist them in secret; for her husband was such a churl, that she durst not venture to do it publicly. Accordingly, whenever she had an opportunity, she made Tibby come into the kitchen, and get a meal for herself; and often the considerate lady slid a small loaf, or a little tea and sugar, into her lap, for the two aged invalids;—for gentle woman is always the first to pity, and the first to relieve.

Poor Tibby! how her heart expanded with gratitude on receiving these little presents! for her love for the two old dependent creatures was of so pure and sacred a sort, as scarcely to retain in it any thing of the common feelings of humanity. There was no selfish principle there—they were to her as a part of her own nature.

Tibby never went into the kitchen unless her mistress desired her, or sent her word by some of the other day-labourers to come in as she went home. One evening, having got word in this last way, she went in, and the lady of the house, with her own hand, presented her with a little bowl of beat potatoes, and some milk. This was all; and one would have thought it was an aliment so humble and plain, that scarcely any person would have grudged it to a hungry dog. It so happened, however, that as Tibby was sitting behind backs enjoying the meal, Mr Forret chanced to come into the kitchen to give some orders; and perceiving Tibby so comfortably engaged, he, without speaking a word, seized her by the neck with one hand, and by the shoulder with the other, and hurrying her out at the back-door into the yard, flung her, with all his might, on a dunghill. "Wha the devil bade you come into my house, and eat up the meat that was made for others?" cried he, in a demoniac voice, choking with rage; and then he swore a terrible oath, which I do not choose to set down, that, "if he found her again at such employment, he would cut her throat, and fling her to the dogs."

Poor Tibby was astounded beyond the power of utterance, or even of rising from the place where he had thrown her down, until lifted by two of the maid-servants, who tried to comfort her as they supported her part of the way home; and bitterly did they blame their master, saying it would have been a shame to any one, who had the feelings of a man, to do such an act; but as for their master, he scarcely had the feelings of a beast. Tibby never opened her mouth, neither to blame, nor complain, but went on her way crying till her heart was like to break.

She had no supper for the old famishing pair that night. They had tasted nothing from the time that she left them in the morning; and as she had accounted herself sure of receiving something from Mrs Forret that night, she had not asked her day's wages from the grieve, glad to let a day run up now and then, when able to procure a meal in any other honest way. She had nothing to give them that night, so what could she do? She was obliged, with a sore heart, to kiss them and tell them so; and then, as was her custom, she said a prayer over their couch, and laid herself down to sleep, drowned in tears.

She had never so much as mentioned Mr Forret's name either to her grandmother or grand-aunt that night, or by the least insinuation given them to understand that he had used her ill; but no sooner were they composed to rest, and all the cottage quiet, than old Douglas began abusing him with great vehemence. Tibby, to her astonishment, heard some of his deeds spoken of with great familiarity, which she was sure never had been whispered to the ear of flesh. But what shocked her most of all, was the following terrible prognostication, which she heard repeated three several times:—— " Na, na, I'll no see it, for I'll never see aught earthly again beyond the wa's o' this cottage; but Tibby will live to see it;—ay, ay, she'll see it." Then a different voice asked—" What will *she* see, kerlin ?"—" She'll see the craws picking his banes at the back o' the dyke."

Tibby's heart grew cold within her when she heard this terrible announcement, because, for many years bygone, she had been convinced, from sensible demonstration, that old Douglas Hervey had commerce with some superior intelligence; and after she had heard the above sentence repeated again and again, she shut her ears, that she might hear no more; committed herself once more to the hands of a watchful Creator, and fell into a troubled sleep.

The elemental spirits that weave the shadowy tapestry of dreams, were busy at their aerial looms that night in the cottage of Knowe-back, bodying forth the destinies of men and women in brilliant and quick succession. One only of these delineations I shall here set down, precisely as it was related to me, by my friend the worthy clergyman of that parish, to whom Tibby told it the very next day. There is no doubt that her grand-aunt's disjointed prophecy formed the groundwork of the picture; but be that as it may, this was her

dream ; and it was for the sake of telling it, and tracing
it to its fulfilment, that I began this story :

Tibby Hyslop dreamed, that on a certain spot which
she had never seen before, between a stone-dyke and
the verge of a woody precipice, a little, sequestered,
inaccessible corner, of a triangular shape,—or, as she
called it to the minister, " a three-neukit crook o' the
linn," she saw Mr Forret lying without his hat, with
his throat slightly wounded, and blood running from
it ; but he neither appeared to be dead, nor yet dying,
but in excellent spirits.   He was clothed in a fine new
black suit, had full boots on, which appeared likewise
to be new, and gilt spurs.   A great number of rooks
and hooded crows were making free with his person ;
—some picking out his eyes, some his tongue, and some
tearing out his bowels.   In place of being distressed by
their voracity, he appeared much delighted, encouraging them all that he could, and there was a perfectly
good understanding between the parties.   In the midst
of this horrible feast, a large raven dashed down from
a dark cloud, and, driving away all the meaner birds,
fell a-feasting himself ;—opened the breast of his victim,
who was still alive, and encouraging him on ; and after
preying on his vitals for some time, at last picked out
his heart, and devoured it ; and then the mangled wretch,
after writhing for a short time in convulsive agonies,
groaned his last.

This was precisely Tibby's dream as it was told to me, first by my friend Mr Cunningham of Dalswinton, and afterwards by the clergyman to whom she herself had related it next day. But there was something in it not so distinctly defined; for though the birds which she saw devouring her master, were rooks, blood-crows, and a raven, still each individual of the number had a likeness, by itself, distinguishing it from all the rest; a certain character, as it were, to support; and these particular likenesses were so engraven on the dreamer's mind, that she never forgot them, and she could not help looking for them both among " birds and bodies," as she expressed it, but never could distinguish any of them again; and the dream, like many other distempered visions, was forgotten, or only remembered now and then with a certain tremor of antecedent knowledge.

Days and seasons passed over, and with them the changes incident to humanity. The virtuous and indefatigable Tibby Hyslop was assisted by the benevolent, who had heard of her exertions and patient sufferings; and the venerable Douglas Hervey had gone in peace to the house appointed for all living, when one evening in June, John Jardine, the cooper, chanced to come to Knowe-back, in the course of his girding and hooping peregrinations. John was a living and walking chronicle of the events of the day, all the way from the head of Glen-Breck to the bridge of Stony-Lee. He knew every man, and every man's affairs—every woman, and every woman's failings; and his intelligence was not like that of many others, for it was generally to be depended on. How he got his information so correctly, was a mystery to many, but whatever John the cooper told as a fact, was never disputed, and any woman, at least, might have ventured to tell it over again.

"These are hard times for poor folks, Tibby. How are you and auld granny coming on?"

"Just fighting on as we hae done for mony a year. She is aye contentit, poor body, and thankfu', whether I hae little to gie her, or muckle. This life's naething but a fight, Johnnie, frae beginning to end."

"It's a' true ye say, Tibby," said the cooper, interrupting her, for he was afraid she was about to enter upon religious topics, a species of conversation that did not accord with John's talents or dispositions; "It's a' true ye say, Tibby; but your master will soon be sic a rich man now, that we'll a' be made up, and you amang the lave will be made a lady."

"If he get his riches honestly, and the blessing o' the Almighty wi' them, John, I shall rejoice in his prosperity; but neither me nor ony ither poor body will ever be muckle the better o' them. What way is he gaun to get siccan great riches? If a' be true that I hear, he is gaun to the wrang part to seek them."

"Aha, lass, that's a' that ye ken about it. Did ye

no hear that he had won the law-plea on his laird, whilk
has been afore the Lords for mair than seven years?
And did ye no hear that he had won ten pleas afore the
courts o' Dumfries, a' rising out o' ane anither, like ash
girderings out o' ae root, and that he's to get, on the
haill, about twenty thousand punds worth o' damages?"

"That's an unco sight o' siller, John. How muckle
is that?"

"Aha, lass, ye hae fixed me now; but they say it
will come to as muckle gowd as six men can carry on
their backs. And we're a' to get twenties, and thirties,
and forties o' punds for bribes, to gar us gie faithfu' and
true evidence at the great concluding trial afore the
Lords; and you are to be bribit amang the rest, to gar
ye tell the haill truth, and nothing but the truth."

"There needs nae waste o' siller to gar me do that.
But, Johnnie, I wad like to ken whether that mode o'
taking oaths,—solemn and saucred oaths,—about the
miserable trash o' this warld, be according to the tenor
o' Gospel revelation, and the third o' the Commands?"

"Aha, lass, ye *hae* fixed me now! That's rather
a kittle point; but I believe it's a' true that ye say.
However, ye'll get the offer of a great bribe in a few
days; and take ye my advice, Tibby—Get haud o' the
bribe afore hand; for if ye lippen to your master's promises, you will never finger a bodle after the job's done."

"I'm but a poor simple body, Johnnie, and canna

manage ony siccan things.   But I shall need nae fee to
gar me tell the truth, and I winna tell an untruth for a'
my master's estate, and his sax backfu's o' gowd into the
bargain.   If the sin o' the soul, Johnnie——"

"Ay, ay, that's very true, Tibby, very true, indeed,
about the sin o' the soul! But as ye were saying about
being a simple body——What wad ye think if I were to
cast up that day Gledging Gibby came here to gie you
your lesson——I could maybe help you on a wee bit——
What wad you gie me if I did?"

"Alack, I hae naething to gie you but my blessing;
but I shall pray for the blessing o' God on ye."

"Ay, ay, as ye say. I daresay there might be waur
things.   But could you think o' naething else to gie a
body wha likes as weel to be paid aff-hand as to gie
credit?   That's the very thing I'm cautioning you
against."

"I dinna expect ony siller frae that fountain-head,
Johnnie: It is a dry ane to the puir and the needy, and
an unco sma' matter wad gar me make over my rights
to a pose that I hae neither faith nor hope in. But ye're
kenn'd for an auld-farrant man; if ye can bring a little
honestly my way, I sall gie you the half o't; for weel
I ken it will never come by ony art or shift o' mine."

"Ay, ay, that's spoken like a sensible and reasonable
woman, Tibby Hyslop, as ye are and hae always been.
But think you that nae way could be contrived"——and

here the cooper gave two winks with his left eye——" by
the whilk ye could gie me it a', and yet no rob yoursell
of a farthing ?"

" Na, na, Johnnie Jardine, that's clean aboon my
comprehension : But ye're a cunning draughty man,
and I leave the haill matter to your guidance."

" Very weel, Tibby, very weel. I'll try to ca' a gayan
substantial gird round your success, if I can hit the
width o' the chance, and the girth o' the gear. Gude
day to you the day ; and think about the plan o' equal-
aqual that I spake o'."

Old maids are in general very easily courted, and
very apt to take a hint. I have, indeed, known a great
many instances in which they took hints very seriously,
before ever they were given. Not so with Tibby Hyslop. So heavy a charge had lain upon her the greater
part of her life, that she had never turned her thoughts
to any earthly thing beside, and she knew no more what
the cooper aimed at, than if the words had not been
spoken. When he went away, her grandmother called
her to the bedside, and asked if the cooper had gone
away. Tibby answered in the affirmative ; on which
granny said, " What has he been havering about sae
lang the day ? I thought I heard him courting ye."

" Courting me ! Dear granny, he was courting nane
o' me ; he was telling me how Mr Forret had won as

muckle siller at the law as sax men can carry on their backs, and how we are a' to get a part of it."

" Dinna believe him, hinny; the man that can win siller at the law, will lose it naewhere. But, Tibby, I heard the cooper courting you, and I thought I heard you gie him your consent to manage the matter as he likit. Now you hae been a great blessing to me. I thought you sent to me in wrath, as a punishment of my sins, but I have found that you were indeed sent to me in love and in kindness. You have been the sole support of my old age, and of hers wha is now in the grave, and it is natural that I should like to see you put up afore I leave you. But, Tibby Hyslop, John Jardine is not the man to lead a Christian life with. He has nae mair religion than the beasts that perish—he shuns it as a body would do a loathsome or poisonous draught: And besides, it is weel kenn'd how sair he neglected his first wife. Hae naething to do wi' him, my dear bairn, but rather live as you are. There is neither sin nor shame in being unwedded; but there may be baith in joining yourself to an unbeliever."

Tibby was somewhat astonished at this piece of information. She had not conceived that the cooper meant any thing in the way of courtship; but found that she rather thought the better of him for what it appeared he had done. Accordingly she made no promises to her grandmother, but only remarked, that " it was a pity no to gie the cooper a chance o' conversion, honest man."

The cooper kept watch about Drumlochie and the hinds' houses, and easily found out all the farmer's movements, and even the exact remuneration he could be prevailed on to give to such as were pleased to remember according to his wishes. Indeed it was believed that the most part of the hinds and labouring people recollected nothing of the matter in dispute farther than he was pleased to inform them, and that in fact they gave evidence to the best of their knowledge or remembrance, although that evidence might be decidedly wrong.

One day Gibby took his gun, and went out towards Knowe-back. The cooper also, guessing what his purpose was, went thither by a circuitous route, in order to come in as it were by chance. Ere he arrived, Mr Forret had begun his queries and instructions to Tibby. —The two could not agree by any means; Tibby either could not recollect the yearly crops on each field on the farm of Drumlochie, or recollected wrong. At length, when the calculations were at the keenest, the cooper came in, and at every turn he took Mr Forret's side, with the most strenuous asseverations, abusing Tibby for her stupidity and want of recollection.

" Hear me speak, Johnnie Jardine, afore ye condemn me aff-loof: Mr Forret says that the Crooked Holm

was pease in the 96, and corn in the 97 ; I say it was
corn baith the years.   How do ye say about that ?"

" Mr Forret's right—perfectly right. It grew pease
in the 96, and aits, good Angus aits, in the 97.   Poor
gowk ! dinna ye think that he has a' thae things merkit
down in black and white ? and what good could it do
to him to mislead you ? Depend on't, he is right there."

" Could ye tak your oath on that, Johnnie Jardine ?"

" Ay, this meenint,—sax times repeated, if it were
necessary."

" Then I yield—I am but a poor silly woman, liable
to mony errors and shortcomings—I maun be wrang,
and I yield that it is sae.   But I am sure, John, you
cannot but remember this sae short while syne,—for ye
shure wi' us that har'st,—Was the lang field niest Robie
Johnston's farm growing corn in the dear year, or no ?
I say it was."

" It was the next year, Tibby," said Mr Forret ; " you
are confounding one year with another again ; and I see
what is the reason.   It was oats in 99, grass in 1800,
and oats again in 1801 ; now you never remember any
of the intermediate years, but only those that you shore
on these fields.   I cannot be mistaken in a rule I never
break."

The cooper had now got his cue. He perceived that
the plea ultimately depended on proof relating to the
proper cropping of the land throughout the lease ; and

he supported the farmer so strenuously, that Tibby, in her simplicity, fairly yielded, although not convinced; but the cooper assured the farmer that he would put all to rights, provided she received a handsome acknowledgment; for there was not the least doubt that Mr Forret was right in every particular.

This speech of the cooper's gratified the farmer exceedingly, as his whole fortune now depended upon the evidence to be elicited in the court at Dumfries, on a day that was fast approaching, and he was willing to give any thing to secure the evidence on his side; so he made a long set speech to Tibby, telling her how necessary it was that she should adhere strictly to the truth——that, as it would be an awful thing to make oath to that which was false, he had merely paid her that visit to instruct her remembrance a little in that which was the truth, it being impossible, on account of his jottings, that he could be mistaken; and finally it was settled, that for thus telling the truth, and nothing but the truth, Tibby Hyslop, a most deserving woman, was to receive a present of £15, as wages for time bygone. This was all managed in a very sly manner by the cooper, who assured Forret that all should go right, as far as related to Tibby Hyslop and himself.

The day of the trial arrived, and counsel attended from Edinburgh for both parties, to take full evidence before the two Circuit Lords and Sheriff. The evidence

was said to have been unsatisfactory to the Judges, but
upon the whole in Mr Forret's favour.   The cooper's
was decidedly so, and the farmer's counsel were crow-
ing and bustling immoderately, when at length Tibby
Hyslop was called to the witnesses' box.   At the first
sight of her master's counsel, and the Dumfries writers
and notaries that were hanging about him, Tibby was
struck dumb with amazement, and almost bereaved of
sense.   She at once recognised them, all and severally,
as the birds that she saw, in her dream, devouring her
master, and picking the flesh from his bones ; while
the great lawyer from Edinburgh was, in feature, eye,
and beak, the identical raven which at last devoured
his vitals and heart.

This singular coincidence brought reminiscences of
such a nature over her spirit, that, on the first questions
being put, she could not answer a word.   She knew
from thenceforward that her master was a ruined man,
and her heart failed, on thinking of her kind mistress
and his family.   The counsel then went, and whispering Mr Forret, inquired what sort of a woman she was,
and if her evidence was likely to be of any avail.   As
the cooper had behaved in a very satisfactory way, and
had answered for Tibby, the farmer was intent on not
losing her evidence, and answered his counsel that she
was a worthy honest woman, who would not swear to
a lie for the king's dominions, and that her evidence

was of much consequence. This intelligence the lawyer announced to the bench with great pomposity, and
the witness was allowed a little time to recover her
spirits.

Isabella Hyslop, spinster, was again called, answered to her name, and took the oath distinctly, and without hesitation, until the official querist came to the
usual question, " Now, has any one instructed you what
to say, or what you are to answer ?" when Tibby replied, with a steady countenance, " Nobody, except my
master." The counsel and client stared at one another,
while the Court could hardly maintain their gravity of
deportment. The querist went on—

" What ? Do you say your master instructed you
what to say ?"

" Yes."

" And did he give, or promise to give you, any reward for what you were to say ?"

" Yes."

" How much did he give, or promise you, for answering as he directed you ?"

" He gave me fifteen pound-notes."

Here Mr Forret and his counsel, losing all patience
at seeing the case take this unexpected turn, interrupted the proceedings, the latter addressing the Judges,
with vehemence, to the following purport :—

" My Lords, in my client's name, and in the names

of justice and reason, I protest against proceeding with this woman's evidence, it being manifest that she is talking through a total derangement of intellect. At first she is dumb, and cannot answer nor speak a word, and now she is answering in total disregard of all truth and propriety. I appeal to your Lordships if such a farrago as this can be at all inferential or relevant?"

" Sir, it was but the other minute," said the junior Judge, " that you announced to us with great importance, that this woman was a person noted for honesty and worth, and one who would not tell a lie for the king's dominions. Why not then hear her evidence to the end? For my own part, I perceive no tokens of discrepancy in it, but rather a scrupulous conscientiousness. Of that, however, we shall be better able to judge when we have heard her out. I conceive that, for the sake of both parties, this woman ought to be strictly examined."

" Proceed with the evidence, Mr Wood," said the senior Lord, bowing to his assistant.

Tibby was reminded that she was on her great oath, and examined over again; but she adhered strictly to her former answers.

" Can you repeat any thing to the Court that he desired you to say?"

" Yes; he desired me, over and over again, to tell the whole truth, and nothing but the truth."

" And, in order that you should do this, he paid you down fifteen pounds sterling ?"

" Yes."

" This is a very singular transaction : I cannot perceive the meaning of it. You certainly must be sensible that you made an advantageous bargain ?"

" Yes."

" But you depone that he charged you to tell only the truth ?"

" Yes, he did, and before witnesses, too."

Here Mr Forret's counsel began to crow amain, as if the victory had been his own ; but the junior Judge again took him short by saying, " Have patience, sir.—My good woman, I esteem your principles and plain simplicity very highly. We want only to ascertain the truth, and you say your master charged you to tell that only. Tell me this, then—did he not inform you what the truth was ?"

" Yes. It was for that purpose he came over to see me, to help my memory to what was the truth, for fear I should hae sworn wrang ; which wad hae been a great sin, ye ken."

" Yes, it would so. I thought that would be the way.—You may now proceed with your questions regularly, Mr Wood."

" Are you quite conscious, now, that those things

L

he brought to your remembrance were actually the truth ?"

" No."

" Are you conscious they were *not* the truth ?"

" Yes ; at least some of them, I am sure, were not."

" Please to condescend on one instance."

" He says he has it markit in his buik, that the Crookit Houm, that lies at the back o' the wood, ye ken, grew pease in the ninety-sax, and corn in the ninety-se'en ; now, it is unco queer that he should hae settin't down wrang, for the Houm was really and truly aits baith the years."

" It is a long time since ; perhaps your memory may be at fault."

" If my master had not chanced to mention it, I could not have been sure, but he set me a-calculating and comparing ; and my mother and me have been consulting about it, and have fairly settled it."

" And are you absolutely positive it was oats both years ?"

" Yes."

" Can you mention any circumstance on which you rest your conclusions ?"

" Yes ; there came a great wind ae Sabbath day, in the ninety-sax, and that raised the shearers' wages, at Dumfries, to three shillings the day. We began to the Crookit Houm on a Monanday's morning, at three

shillings a-day, and that very day twalmonth, we began till't again at tenpence. We had a gude deal o'
speaking about it, and I said to John Edie, 'What need
we grumble? I made sae muckle at shearing, the last
year, that it's no a' done yet.' And he said, 'Ah, Tibby,
Tibby, but wha can hain like you?'"

"Were there any others that you think your master
had marked down wrong?"

"There was ane, at ony rate—the lang field niest
Robie Johnston's march: He says it was clover in the
drouthy dear year, and aits the neist; but that's a year
I canna forget; it was aits baith years. I lost a week's
shearing on it the first year, waiting on my aunty, and
the niest year she was dead; and I shore the lang field
niest Robie Johnston's wi' her sickle-heuk, and black
ribbons on my mutch."

The whole of Tibby's evidence went against Mr
Forret's interest most conclusively, and the Judges at
last dismissed her, with high compliments on her truth
and integrity. The cause was again remitted to the
Court of Session for revisal after this evidence taken;
and the word spread over all the country that Mr Forret had won. Tibby never contradicted this, nor disputed it; but she was thoroughly convinced, that in
place of winning, he would be a ruined man.

About a month after the examination at Dumfries,
he received a letter from his agents in Edinburgh, buoy-

ing him up with hopes of great and instant success, and
urging the utility of his presence in town at the final
decision of the cause on which all the minor ones rest-
ed.   Accordingly he equipped himself, and rode into
Dumfries in the evening, to be ready to proceed by the
mail the following morning, saying to his wife, as he
went away, that he would send home his mare with the
carrier, and that as he could not possibly name the day
on which he would be home, she was to give herself no
uneasiness. The mare was returned the following night,
and put up in her own stall, nobody knew by whom ;
but servants are such sleepy, careless fellows, that few
regarded the circumstance. This was on a Tuesday
night. A whole week passed over, and still Mrs Forret received no news of her husband, which kept her
very uneasy, as their whole fortune, being, and subsist-
ence, now depended on the issue of this great law-suit,
and she suspected that the case still continued dubious,
or was found to be going against him.

A more unhappy result followed than that she anticipated. On the arrival of the Edinburgh papers next
week, the whole case, so important to farmers, was detailed ; and it was there stated, that the great farmer
and improver, Mr Forret of Drumlochie, had not only
forfeited his whole fortune by improper husbandry, and
manifest breaches of the conditions on which he held
his lease, but that criminal letters had been issued

against him for attempts to pervert justice, and rewards offered for his detention or seizure. This was terrible news for the family at Drumlochie; but there were still sanguine hopes entertained that the circumstances were misstated, or, if the worst should prove true, that perhaps the husband and father might make his escape; and as there was no word from him day after day, this latter sentiment began to be cherished by the whole family as their only remaining and forlorn hope.

But one day, as poor Tibby Hyslop was going over to the Cat Linn, to gather a burden of sticks for firewood, she was surprised, on looking over the dike, to see a great body of crows collected, all of which were so intent on their prey, that they seemed scarcely to regard her presence as a sufficient cause for their desisting; she waved her burden-rope at them over the dike, but they refused to move. Her heart nearly failed her, for she remembered of having before seen the same scene, with some fearful concomitants. But pure and unfeigned religion, the first principle of which teaches a firm reliance on divine protection, can give courage to the weakest of human beings. Tibby climbed over the dike, drove the vermin away, and there lay the corpse of her late unfortunate master, wofully mangled by these voracious birds of prey. He had bled himself to death in the jugular vein, was lying without the hat, and clothed in a fine new black suit of clothes, top-boots, which appeared likewise to be new, and gilt spurs; and the place where he lay was a little three-cornered sequestered spot, between the dike and the precipice, and inaccessible by any other way than through the field. It was a spot that Tibby had never seen before.

A letter was found in Mr Forret's pocket, which had blasted all his hopes, and driven him to utter distraction; he had received it at Dumfries, returned home, and put up his mare carefully in the stable, but not having courage to face his ruined family, he had hurried to that sequestered spot, and perpetrated the deed of self-destruction.

The only thing more I have to add is, that the Lord President, having made the remark that he paid more regard to that poor woman, Isabella Hyslop's evidence, than to all the rest elicited at Dumfries, the gainers of the great plea became sensible that it was principally in consequence of her candour and invincible veracity that they were successful, and sent her a present of twenty pounds. She was living comfortably at Knoweback when I saw her, a contented and happy old maiden.

CHAPTER IX.

MARY BURNET.

THE following incidents are related as having occurred at a shepherd's house, not a hundred miles from
St Mary's Loch ; but, as the descendants of one of the
families still reside in the vicinity, I deem it requisite
to use names which cannot be recognised, save by those
who have heard the story.

John Allanson, the farmer's son of Inverlawn, was
a handsome, roving, and incautious young man, enthu-
siastic, amorous, and fond of adventure, and one who
could hardly be said to fear the face of either man, woman, or spirit. Among other love adventures, he fell
a-courting Mary Burnet, of Kirkstyle, a most beautiful
and innocent maiden, and one who had been bred up
in rural simplicity. She loved him, but yet she was
afraid of him ; and though she had no objection to meeting with him among others, yet she carefully avoided
meeting him alone, though often and earnestly urged
to it. One day, the young man, finding an opportuni-

THE SHEPHERD'S CALENDAR.

ty, at Our Lady's Chapel, after mass, urged his suit for a private meeting so ardently, and with so many vows of love and sacred esteem, that Mary was so far won, as to promise, that *perhaps* she would come and meet him.

The trysting place was a little green sequestered spot, on the very verge of the lake, well known to many an angler, and to none better than the writer of this old tale ; and the hour appointed, the time when the King's Elwand (now foolishly termed the Belt of Orion) set his first golden knob above the hill. Allanson came too early ; and he watched the sky with such eagerness and devotion, that he thought every little star that arose in the south-east the top knob of the King's Elwand. At last the Elwand did arise in good earnest, and then the youth, with a heart palpitating with agitation, had nothing for it but to watch the heathery brow by which bonny Mary Burnet was to descend. No Mary Burnet made her appearance, even although the King's Elwand had now measured its own equivocal length five or six times up the lift.

Young Allanson now felt all the most poignant miseries of disappointment ; and, as the story goes, uttered in his heart an unhallowed wish—he wished that some witch or fairy would influence his Mary to come to him in spite of her maidenly scruples. This wish was thrice repeated with all the energy of disappointed love. It was thrice repeated, and no more, when, behold, Mary appeared on the brae, with wild and eccentric motions, speeding to the appointed place. Allanson's excitement seems to have been more than he was able to bear, as he instantly became delirious with joy, and always professed that he could remember nothing of their first meeting, save that Mary remained silent, and spoke not a word, neither good nor bad. In a short time she fell a-sobbing and weeping, refusing to be comforted, and then, uttering a piercing shriek, sprung up, and ran from him with amazing speed.

At this part of the loch, which, as I said, is well known to many, the shore is overhung by a precipitous cliff, of no great height, but still inaccessible, either from above or below. Save in a great drought, the water comes to within a yard of the bottom of this cliff, and the intermediate space is filled with rough unshapely pieces of rock fallen from above. Along this narrow and rude space, hardly passable by the angler at noon, did Mary bound with the swiftness of a kid, although surrounded with darkness. Her lover, pursuing with all his energy, called out, " Mary ! Mary ! my dear Mary, stop and speak with me. I'll conduct you home, or anywhere you please, but do not run from me. Stop, my dearest Mary—stop !"

Mary would not stop ; but ran on, till, coming to a little cliff that jutted into the lake, round which there

was no passage, and, perceiving that her lover would
there overtake her, she uttered another shriek, and
plunged into the lake.   The loud sound of her fall into the still water rung in the young man's ears like the
knell of death; and if before he was crazed with love,
he was now as much so with despair.   He saw her
floating lightly away from the shore towards the deepest part of the loch; but, in a short time, she began to
sink, and gradually disappeared, without uttering a
throb or a cry.   A good while previous to this, Allanson had flung off his bonnet, shoes, and coat, and plunged in.   He swam to the place where Mary disappeared; but there was neither boil nor gurgle on the water,
nor even a bell of departing breath, to mark the place
where his beloved had sunk.   Being strangely impressed,
at that trying moment, with a determination to live or die
with her, he tried to dive, in hopes either to bring her up
or to die in her arms; and he thought of their being so
found on the shore of the lake, with a melancholy satisfaction; but by no effort of his could he reach the
bottom, nor knew he what distance he was still from
it.   With an exhausted frame, and a despairing heart,
he was obliged again to seek the shore, and, dripping
wet as he was, and half naked, he ran to her father's
house with the woful tidings.   Every thing there was
quiet.   The old shepherd's family, of whom Mary was
the youngest, and sole daughter, were all sunk in silent

repose; and oh how the distracted lover wept at the
thoughts of wakening them to hear the doleful tidings!
But waken them he must; so, going to the little window close by the goodman's bed, he called, in a melancholy tone, " Andrew! Andrew Burnet, are you
waking?"

" Troth, man, I think I be : or, at least, I'm half-
and-half. What hast thou to say to auld Andrew Burnet at this time o' night?"

" Are you waking, I say?"

" Gudewife, am I waking? Because if I be, tell that
stravaiger sae. He'll maybe tak your word for it, for
mine he winna tak."

" O Andrew, none of your humour to-night;—I
bring you tidings the most woful, the most dismal, the
most heart-rending, that ever were brought to an honest
man's door."

" To his window, you mean," cried Andrew, bolting
out of bed, and proceeding to the door. " Gude sauff
us, man, come in, whaever you be, and tell us your
tidings face to face; and then we'll can better judge
of the truth of them. If they be in concord wi' your
voice, they are melancholy indeed. Have the reavers
come, and are our kye driven?"

" Oh, alas! waur than that—a thousand times waur
than that! Your daughter—your dear beloved and only daughter, Mary—"

" What of Mary?" cried the goodman.   " What of
Mary?" cried her mother, shuddering and groaning
with terror; and at the same time she kindled a light.

The sight of their neighbour, half-naked, and dripping with wet, and madness and despair in his looks,
sent a chillness to their hearts, that held them in silence,
and they were unable to utter a word, till he went on
thus—" Mary is gone; your darling and mine is lost,
and sleeps this night in a watery grave,—and I have
been her destroyer!"

" Thou art mad, John Allanson," said the old man,
vehemently, " raving mad; at least I hope so. Wicked
as thou art, thou hadst not the heart to kill my dear child,
O yes, you are mad—God be thanked, you are mad. I
see it in your looks and demeanour. Heaven be praised,
you are mad! You *are* mad; but you'll get better again.
But what do I say?" continued he, as recollecting himself,—" We can soon convince our own senses. Wife,
lead the way to our daughter's bed."

With a heart throbbing with terror and dismay, old
Jean Linton led the way to Mary's chamber, followed
by the two men, who were eagerly gazing, one over
each of her shoulders.   Mary's little apartment was in
the farther end of the long narrow cottage; and as soon
as they entered it, they perceived a form lying on the
bed, with the bed-clothes drawn over its head; and
on the lid of Mary's little chest, that stood at the

bedside, her clothes were lying neatly folded, as they
wont to be. Hope seemed to dawn on the faces of
the two old people when they beheld this, but the
lover's heart sunk still deeper in despair. The father
called her name, but the form on the bed returned no
answer; however, they all heard distinctly sobs, as
of one weeping. The old man then ventured to pull
down the clothes from her face; and, strange to say,
there indeed lay Mary Burnet, drowned in tears, yet
apparently nowise surprised at the ghastly appearance
of the three naked figures. Allanson gasped for breath,
for he remained still incredulous. He touched her
clothes—he lifted her robes one by one,—and all of
them were dry, neat, and clean, and had no appearance
of having sunk in the lake.

There can be no doubt that Allanson was confounded by the strange event that had befallen him, and felt
like one struggling with a frightful vision, or some
energy beyond the power of man to comprehend. Nevertheless, the assurance that Mary was there in life,
weeping although she was, put him once more beside
himself with joy; and he kneeled at her bedside, be-
seeching permission but to kiss her hand. She, however, repulsed him with disdain, saying, with great em-
phasis—" You are a bad man, John Allanson, and I
entreat you to go out of my sight. The sufferings that
I have undergone this night, have been beyond the

power of flesh and blood to endure ; and by some cursed
agency of yours have these sufferings been brought
about. I therefore pray you, in His name, whose law
you have transgressed, to depart out of my sight."

Wholly overcome by conflicting passions, by circumstances so contrary to one another, and so discordant
with every thing either in the works of Nature or Providence, the young man could do nothing but stand
like a rigid statue, with his hands lifted up, and his visage like that of a corpse, until led away by the two
old people from their daughter's apartment. They then
lighted up a fire to dry him, and began to question him
with the most intense curiosity ; but they could elicit
nothing from him, but the most disjointed exclamations
—such as, " Lord in Heaven, what can be the meaning of this !" And at other times—" It is all the enchantment of the devil ; the evil spirits have got do-
minion over me !"

Finding they could make nothing of him, they began
to form conjectures of their own. Jean affirmed that
it had been the Mermaid of the loch that had come to
him in Mary's shape, to allure him to his destruction ;
but Andrew Burnet, setting his bonnet to one side, and
raising his left hand to a level with it, so that he might
have full scope to motion and flourish, suiting his action
to his words, thus began, with a face of sapience never
to be excelled :—

"Gudewife, it doth strike me that thou art very wide of the mark. It must have been a spirit of a great deal higher quality than a meer-maiden, who played this extra-õrdinary prank. The meer-maiden is not a spirit, but a beastly sensitive creature, with a malicious spirit within it. Now, what influence could a cauld clatch of a creature like that, wi' a tail like a great saumont-fish, hae ower our bairn, either to make her happy or unhappy? Or where could it borrow her claes, Jean? Tell me that. Na, na, Jean Linton, depend on it, the spirit that courtit wi' poor sinfu' Jock there, has been a fairy; but whether a good ane or an ill ane, it is hard to determine."

Andrew's disquisition was interrupted by the young man falling into a fit of trembling that was fearful to look at, and threatened soon to terminate his existence. Jean ran for the family cordial, observing, by the way, that "though he was a wicked person, he was still a fellow-creature, and might live to repent;" and influenced by this spark of genuine humanity, she made him swallow two horn-spoonfuls of strong aquavitæ. Andrew then put a piece of scarlet thread round each wrist, and taking a strong rowan-tree staff in his hand, he conveyed his trembling and astonished guest home, giving him at parting this sage advice :—

"I'll tell you what it is, Jock Allanson,—ye hae run a near risk o' perdition, and, escaping that for the present, o' losing your right reason. But tak an auld man's advice—never gang again out by night to beguile ony honest man's daughter, lest a worse thing befall thee."

Next morning Mary dressed herself more neatly than usual, but there was manifestly a deep melancholy settled on her lovely face, and at times the unbidden tear would start into her eye. She spoke no word, either good or bad, that ever her mother could recollect, that whole morning; but she once or twice observed her daughter gazing at her, as with an intense and melancholy interest. About nine o'clock in the morning, she took a hay-raik over her shoulder, and went down to a meadow at the east end of the loch, to coil a part of her father's hay, her father and brother engaging to join her about noon, when they came from the sheep-fold. As soon as old Andrew came home, his wife and he, as was natural, instantly began to converse on the events of the preceding night; and in the course of their conversation, Andrew said, " Gudeness be about us, Jean, was not yon an awfu' speech o' our bairn's to young Jock Allanson last night?"

" Ay, it was a downsetter, gudeman, and spoken like a good Christian lass."

" I'm no sae sure o' that, Jean Linton. My good woman, Jean Linton, I'm no sae sure o' that. Yon speech has gi'en me a great deal o' trouble o' heart; for 'ye ken, an take my life,—ay, an take your life, Jean,

—nane o' us can tell whether it was in the Almighty's name, or the devil's, that she discharged her lover."

" O fy, Andrew, how can ye say sae ? How can ye doubt that it was in the Almighty's name ?"

" Couldna she have said sae then, and that wad hae put it beyond a' doubt ? And that wad hae been the natural way too ; but instead of that, she says, ' I pray you, in the name of him whose law you have transgress- ed, to depart out o' my sight.' I confess I'm terrified when I think about yon speech, Jean Linton. Didna she say, too, that ' her sufferings had been beyond what flesh and blood could have endured ?' What was she but flesh and blood ? Didna that remark infer that she was something mair than a mortal creature ? Jean Lin- ton, Jean Linton ! what will you say, if it should turn out that our daughter *is* drowned, and that yon was the fairy we had in the house a' the night and this morn- ing ?"

" O haud your tongue, Andrew Burnet, and dinna make my heart cauld within me. We hae aye trusted in the Lord yet, and he has never forsaken us, nor will he yet gie the Wicked One power ower us or ours."

" Ye say very weel, Jean, and we maun e'en hope for the best," quoth old Andrew ; and away he went, ac- companied by his son Alexander, to assist their beloved Mary on the meadow.

No sooner had Andrew set his head over the bents,

and come in view of the meadow, than he said to his son,
" I wish Jock Allanson maunna hae been east-the-loch
fishing for geds the day, for I think my Mary has made
very little progress in the meadow."

" She's ower muckle ta'en up about other things this
while, to mind her wark," said Alexander: " I wadna
wonder, father, if that lassie gangs a black gate yet."

Andrew uttered a long and a deep sigh, that seemed to
ruffle the very fountains of life, and, without speaking
another word, walked on to the hay field. It was three
hours since Mary had left home, and she ought at least
to have put up a dozen coils of hay each hour. But,
in place of that, she had put up only seven altogether,
and the last was unfinished. Her own hay-raik, that
had an M and a B neatly cut on the head of it, was
leaning on the unfinished coil, and Mary was wanting.
Her brother, thinking she had hid herself from them in
sport, ran from one coil to another, calling her many
bad names, playfully; but, after he had turned them all
up, and several deep swathes besides, she was not to be
found. This young man, who slept in the byre, knew
nothing of the events of the foregoing night, the old
people and Allanson having mutually engaged to keep
them a profound secret, and he had therefore less reason than his father to be seriously alarmed. When they
began to work at the hay, Andrew could work none ;
he looked this way and that way, but in no way could

he see Mary approaching: so he put on his coat, and went away home, to pour his sorrows into the bosom of his wife; and in the meantime, he desired his son to run to all the neighbouring farming-houses and cots, every one, and make inquiries if any body had seen Mary.

When Andrew went home and informed his wife that their darling was missing, the grief and astonishment of the aged couple knew no bounds. They sat down, and wept together, and declared, over and over, that this act of Providence was too strange for them, and too high to be understood. Jean besought her husband to kneel instantly, and pray urgently to God to restore their child to them; but he declined it, on account of the wrong frame of his mind, for he declared, that his rage against John Allanson was so extreme, as to unfit him for approaching the throne of his Maker. "But if the profligate refuses to listen to the entreaties of an injured parent," added he, "he shall feel the weight of an injured father's arm."

Andrew went straight away to Inverlawn, though without the least hope of finding young Allanson at home; but, on reaching the place, to his amazement, he found the young man lying ill of a burning fever, raving incessantly of witches, spirits, and Mary Burnet. To such a height had his frenzy arrived, that when Andrew went there, it required three men to hold him in

the bed. Both his parents testified their opinions openly, that their son was bewitched, or possessed of a de-
mon, and the whole family was thrown into the greatest consternation. The good old shepherd, finding
enough of grief there already, was obliged to confine
his to his own bosom, and return disconsolate to his
little family circle, in which there was a woful blank
that night.

His son returned also from a fruitless search. No
one had seen any traces of his sister, but an old crazy
woman, at a place called Oxcleuch, said that she had
seen her go by in a grand chariot with young Jock Allanson, toward the Birkhill Path, and by that time they
were at the Cross of Dumgree. The young man said,
he asked her what sort of a chariot it was, as there was
never such a thing in that country as a chariot, nor yet
a road for one. But she replied that he was widely
mistaken, for that a great number of chariots sometimes
passed that way, though never any of them returned.
These words appearing to be merely the ravings of
superannuation, they were not regarded; but when no
other traces of Mary could be found, old Andrew went
up to consult this crazy dame once more, but he was
not able to bring any such thing to her recollection.
She spoke only in parables, which to him were incom-
prehensible.

Bonny Mary Burnet was lost. She left her father's

house at nine o'clock on a Wednesday morning, the 17th
of September, neatly dressed in a white jerkin and
green bonnet, with her hay-raik over her shoulder ; and
that was the last sight she was doomed ever to see of
her native cottage. She seemed to have had some pre-
sentiment of this, as appeared from her demeanour that
morning before she left it. Mary Burnet of Kirkstyle
was lost, and great was the sensation produced over
the whole country by the mysterious event. There was
a long ballad extant at one period on the melancholy
catastrophe, which was supposed to have been composed by the chaplain of St Mary's ; but I have only
heard tell of it, without ever hearing it sung or recited.
Many of the verses concluded thus :—

> " But Bonny Mary Burnet
> We will never see again."

The story soon got abroad, with all its horrid circumstances, (and there is little doubt that it was grievously exaggerated,) and there was no obloquy that was
not thrown on the survivor, who certainly in some degree deserved it, for, instead of growing better, he grew
ten times more wicked than he was before. In one
thing the whole country agreed, that it had been the
real Mary Burnet who was drowned in the loch, and
that the being which was found in her bed, lying weeping and complaining of suffering, and which vanished

the next day, had been a fairy, an evil spirit, or a change-
ling of some sort, for that it never spoke save once, and
that in a mysterious manner ; nor did it partake of any
food with the rest of the family. Her father and mother knew not what to say or what to think, but they
wandered through this weary world like people wandering in a dream. Every thing that belonged to Mary
Burnet was kept by her parents as the most sacred re-
lics, and many a tear did her aged mother shed over
them. - Every article of her dress brought the once
comely wearer to mind. Andrew often said, " That
to have lost the darling child of their old age in any
way would have been a great trial, but to lose her in
the way that they had done, was really mair than human frailty could endure."

Many a weary day did he walk by the shores of the
loch, looking eagerly for some vestige of her garments,
and though he trembled at every appearance, yet did
he continue to search on.   He had a number of small
bones collected, that had belonged to lambs and other
minor animals, and, haply, some of them to fishes, from
a fond supposition that they might once have formed
joints of her toes or fingers. These he kept concealed
in a little bag, in order, as he said, " to let the doctors
see them." But no relic, besides these, could he ever
discover of Mary's body.

Young Allanson recovered from his raging fever

scarcely in the manner of other men, for he recovered all at once, after a few days raving and madness. Mary Burnet, it appeared, was by him no more remembered. He grew ten times more wicked than before, and hesitated at no means of accomplishing his unhallowed purposes. The devout shepherds and cottagers around detested him; and, both in their families and in the wild, when there was no ear to hear but that of Heaven, they prayed protection from his devices, as if he had been the Wicked One; and they all prophesied that he would make a bad end.

One fine day about the middle of October, when the days begin to get very short, and the nights long and dark, on a Friday morning, the next year but one after Mary Burnet was lost, a memorable day in the fairy annals, John Allanson, younger of Inverlawn, went to a great hiring fair at a village called Moffat in Annandale, in order to hire a housemaid. His character was so notorious, that not one young woman in the district would serve in his father's house; so away he went to the fair at Moffat, to hire the prettiest and loveliest girl he could there find, with the intention of ruining her as soon as she came home. This is no supposititious accusation, for he acknowledged his plan to Mr David Welch of Cariferan, who rode down to the market with him, and seemed to boast of it, and dwell on it with delight. But the maidens of Annandale had

a guardian angel in the fair that day, of which neither
he nor they were aware.

Allanson looked through the hiring market, and
through the hiring market, and at length fixed on one
young woman, which indeed was not difficult to do, for
there was no such form there for elegance and beauty.
Mr Welch stood still and eyed him. He took the
beauty aside. She was clothed in green, and as lovely
as a new-blown rose.

" Are you to hire, pretty maiden ?"

" Yes, sir."

" Will you hire with me ?"

" I care not though I do. But if I hire with you, it
must be for the long term."

" Certainly. The longer the better. What are your
wages to be ?"

" You know, if I hire, I must be paid in kind.   I
must have the first living creature that I see about Inverlawn to myself."

" I wish it may be me, then.   But what do you know
about Inverlawn ?"

" I think I *should* know about it."

" Bless me ! I know the face as well as I know my
own, and better.   But the name has somehow escaped
me.   Pray, may I ask your name ?"

" Hush ! hush !" said she solemnly, and holding up

6

her hand at the same time; " Hush, hush, you had better say nothing about that here."

" I am in utter amazement!" he exclaimed. " What is the meaning of this? I conjure you to tell me your name?"

" It is Mary Burnet," said she, in a soft whisper; and at the same time she let down a green veil over her face.

If Allanson's death-warrant had been announced to him at that moment, it could not have deprived him so completely of sense and motion. His visage changed into that of a corpse, his jaws fell down, and his eyes became glazed, so as apparently to throw no reflection inwardly. Mr Welch, who had kept his eye steadily on them all the while, perceived his comrade's dilemma, and went up to him. " Allanson?—Mr Allanson? What is the matter with you, man?" said he. " Why, the girl has bewitched you, and turned you into a statue!"

Allanson made some sound in his throat, as if attempting to speak, but his tongue refused its office, and he only jabbered. Mr Welch, conceiving that he was seized with some fit, or about to faint, supported him into the Johnston Arms; but he either could not, or would not, grant him any explanation. Welch being, however, resolved to see the maiden in green once more, persuaded Allanson, after causing him to drink a good deal, to go out into the hiring-market again, in search

of her.   They ranged the market through and through,
but the maiden in green was gone, and not to be found.
She had vanished in the crowd the moment she divulged her name, and even though Welch had his eye fixed
on her, he could not discover which way she went.
Allanson appeared to be in a kind of stupor as well as
terror, but when he found that she had left the market,
he began to recover himself, and to look out again for
the top of the market.

He soon found one more beautiful than the last.
She was like a sylph, clothed in robes of pure snowy
white, with green ribbons.   Again he pointed this new
flower out to Mr David Welch, who declared that such
a perfect model of beauty he had never in his life seen.
Allanson, being resolved to have this one at any wages,
took her aside, and put the usual question : " Do you
wish to hire, pretty maiden ?"

" Yes, sir."

" Will you hire with me ?"

" I care not though I do."

" What, then, are your wages to be ? Come——say ?
And be reasonable ; I am determined not to part with
you for a trifle."

" My wages must be in kind ; I work on no other
conditions.——Pray, how are all the good people about
Inverlawn ?"

Allanson's breath began to cut, and a chillness to

creep through his whole frame, and he answered, with a faltering tongue,—" I thank you,—much in their ordinary way."

" And your aged neighbours," rejoined she, " are they still alive and well?"

" I—I—I think they are," said he, panting for breath. " But I am at a loss to know whom I am indebted to for these kind recollections."

" What," said she, " have you so soon forgot Mary Burnet of Kirkstyle?"

Allanson started as if a bullet had gone through his heart. The lovely sylph-like form glided into the crowd, and left the astounded libertine once more standing like a rigid statue, until aroused by his friend, Mr Welch. He tried a third fair one, and got the same answers, and the same name given. Indeed, the first time ever I heard the tale, it bore that he tried seven, who all turned out to be Mary Burnets of Kirkstyle; but I think it unlikely that he would try so many, as he must long ere that time have been sensible that he laboured under some power of enchantment. However, when nothing else would do, he helped himself to a good proportion of strong drink. While he was thus engaged, a phenomenon of beauty and grandeur came into the fair, that caught the sole attention of all present. This was a lovely dame, riding in a gilded chariot, with two liverymen before, and two behind,

clothed in green and gold; and never sure was there
so splendid a meteor seen in a Moffat fair. The word
instantly circulated in the market, that this was the
Lady Elizabeth Douglas, eldest daughter to the Earl
of Morton, who then sojourned at Auchincastle, in the
vicinity of Moffat, and which lady at that time was
celebrated as a great beauty all over Scotland. She
was afterwards Lady Keith; and the mention of this
name in the tale, as it were by mere accident, fixes
the era of it in the reign of James the Fourth, at the
very time that fairies, brownies, and witches, were at
the rifest in Scotland.

Every one in the market believed the lady to be the
daughter of the Earl of Morton; and when she came
to the Johnston Arms, a gentleman in green came out
bareheaded, and received her out of the carriage. All
the crowd gazed at such unparalleled beauty and grandeur, but none was half so much overcome as Allanson. He had never conceived aught half so lovely
either in earth, or heaven, or fairyland; and while he
stood in a burning fever of admiration, think of his
astonishment, and the astonishment of the countless
crowd that looked on, when this brilliant and match-
less beauty beckoned him towards her! He could not
believe his senses, but looked this way and that to see
how others regarded the affair; but she beckoned him
a second time, with such a winning courtesy and smile

that immediately he pulled off his beaver cap and hasted up to her ; and without more ado she gave him her arm, and the two walked into the hostel.

Allanson conceived that he was thus distinguished by Lady Elizabeth Douglas, the flower of the land, and so did all the people of the market ; and greatly they wondered who the young farmer could be that was thus particularly favoured ; for it ought to have been mentioned that he had not one personal acquaintance in the fair save Mr David Welch of Cariferan. The first thing the lady did was to inquire kindly after his health. Allanson thanked her ladyship with all the courtesy he was master of ; and being by this time persuaded that she was in love with him, he became as light as if treading on the air. She next inquired after his father and mother.——Oho ! thought he to himself, poor creature, she is terribly in for it ! but her love shall not be thrown away upon a backward or ungrateful object.——He answered her with great politeness, and at length began to talk of her noble father and young Lord William, but she cut him short by asking if he did not recognise her.

" Oh, yes ! He knew who her ladyship was, and remembered that he had seen her comely face often before, although he could not, at that particular moment, recall to his memory the precise time or places of their meeting."

She next asked for his old neighbours of Kirkstyle, and if they were still in life and health!

Allanson felt as if his heart were a piece of ice. A chillness spread over his whole frame; he sank back on a seat, and remained motionless; but the beautiful and adorable creature soothed him with kind words, till he again gathered courage to speak.

"What!" said he; "and has it been your own lovely self who has been playing tricks on me this whole day?"

"A first love is not easily extinguished, Mr Allanson," said she. "You may guess from my appearance, that I have been fortunate in life; but, for all that, my first love for you has continued the same, unaltered and unchanged, and you must forgive the little freedoms I used to-day to try your affections, and the effects my appearance would have on you."

"It argues something for my good taste, however, that I never pitched on any face for beauty to-day but your own," said he. "But now that we have met once more, we shall not so easily part again. I will devote the rest of my life to you, only let me know the place of your abode."

"It is hard by," said she, "only a very little space from this; and happy, happy, would I be to see you there to-night, were it proper or convenient. But my lord is at present from home, and in a distant country."

" I should not conceive that any particular hinderance to my visit," said he.

With great apparent reluctance she at length consented to admit of his visit, and offered to leave one of her gentlemen, whom she could trust, to be his conductor; but this he positively refused. It was his desire, he said, that no eye of man should see him enter or leave her happy dwelling. She said he was a self-willed man; but should have his own way; and after giving him such directions as would infallibly lead him to her mansion, she mounted her chariot and was driven away.

Allanson was uplifted above every sublunary concern. Seeking out his friend, David Welch, he imparted to him his extraordinary good fortune, but he did not tell him that she was not the Lady Elizabeth Douglas. Welch insisted on accompanying him on the way, and refused to turn back till he came to the very point of the road next to the lady's splendid mansion; and in spite of all that Allanson could say, Welch remained there till he saw his comrade enter the court gate, which glowed with lights as innumerable as the stars of the firmament.

Allanson had promised to his father and mother to be home on the morning after the fair to breakfast. He came not either that day or the next; and the third day the old man mounted his white pony, and rode away towards Moffat in search of his son. He called at Ca-

riferan on his way, and made inquiries at Mr Welch.
The latter manifested some astonishment that the
young man had not returned; nevertheless he assured
his father of his safety, and desired him to return home;
and then with reluctance confessed that the young man
was engaged in an amour with the Earl of Morton's
beautiful daughter; that he had gone to the castle by
appointment, and that he, David Welch, had accompanied him to the gate, and seen him enter, and it was
apparent that his reception had been a kind one, since
he had tarried so long.

. Mr Welch, seeing the old man greatly distressed, was
persuaded to accompany him on his journey, as the last
who had seen his son, and seen him enter the castle. On
reaching Moffat they found his steed standing at the
hostel, whither it had returned on the night of the fair,
before the company broke up; but the owner had not
been heard of since seen in company with Lady Elizabeth Douglas. The old man set out for Auchincastle,
taking Mr David Welch along with him; but long ere
they reached the place, Mr Welch assured him he
would not find his son there, as it was nearly in a different direction that they rode on the evening of the fair.
However, to the castle they went, and were admitted
to the Earl, who, after hearing the old man's tale, seemed to consider him in a state of derangement. He sent
for his daughter Elizabeth, and questioned her concern-

ing her meeting with the son of the old respectable
countryman—of her appointment with him on the night
of the preceding Friday, and concluded by saying he
hoped she had him still in some safe concealment about
the castle.

The lady, hearing her father talk in this manner, and
seeing the serious and dejected looks of the old man,
knew not what to say, and asked an explanation. But
Mr Welch put a stop to it by declaring to old Allanson that the Lady Elizabeth was not the lady with
whom his son made the appointment, for he had seen
her, and would engage to know her again among ten
thousand; nor was that the castle towards which he had
accompanied his son, nor any thing like it. "But go with
me," continued he, "and, though I am a stranger in this
district, I think I can take you to the very place."

They set out again; and Mr Welch traced the road
from Moffat, by which young Allanson and he had
gone, until, after travelling several miles, they came to
a place where a road struck off to the right at an angle.
"Now I know we are right," said Welch; "for here
we stopped, and your son intreated me to return, which
I refused, and accompanied him to yon large tree, and
a little way beyond it, from whence I saw him received
in at the splendid gate. We shall be in sight of the
mansion in three minutes."

They passed on to the tree, and a space beyond it;
M 2

but then Mr Welch lost the use of his speech, as he perceived that there was neither palace nor gate there, but a tremendous gulf, fifty fathoms deep, and a dark stream foaming and boiling below.

"How is this?" said old Allanson. "There is neither mansion nor habitation of man here!"

Welch's tongue for a long time refused its office, and he stood like a statue, gazing on the altered and awful scene. "He only, who made the spirits of men," said he, at last, "and all the spirits that sojourn in the earth and air, can tell how this is. We are wandering in a world of enchantment, and have been influenced by some agencies above human nature, or without its pale; for here of a certainty did I take leave of your son—and there, in that direction, and apparently either on the verge of that gulf, or the space above it, did I see him received in at the court gate of a mansion, splendid beyond all conception. How can human comprehension make any thing of this?"

They went forward to the verge, Mr Welch leading the way to the very spot on which he saw the gate opened, and there they found marks where a horse had been plunging. Its feet had been over the brink, but it seemed to have recovered itself, and deep, deep down, and far within, lay the mangled corpse of John Allanson; and in this manner, mysterious beyond all example, terminated the career of that wicked and flagitious young man.—What a beautiful moral may be extracted from this fairy tale!

But among all these turnings and windings, there is no account given, you will say, of the fate of Mary Burnet; for this last appearance of hers at Moffat seems to have been altogether a phantom or illusion. Gentle and kind reader, I can give you no account of the fate of that maiden; for though the ancient fairy tale proceeds, it seems to me to involve her fate in ten times more mystery than what we have hitherto seen of it.

The yearly return of the day on which Mary was lost, was observed as a day of mourning by her aged and disconsolate parents,—a day of sorrow, of fasting, and humiliation. Seven years came and passed away, and the seventh returning day of fasting and prayer was at hand. On the evening previous to it, old Andrew was moving along the sands of the loch, still looking for some relic of his beloved Mary, when he was aware of a little shrivelled old man, who came posting towards him. The creature was not above five spans in height, and had a face scarcely like that of a human creature; but he was, nevertheless, civil in his deportment, and sensible in speech. He bade Andrew a good evening, and asked him what he was looking for. Andrew answered, that he was looking for that which he should never find.

"Pray, what is your name, ancient shepherd?" said

the stranger; "for methinks I should know something of you, and perhaps have a commission to you."

"Alas! why should you ask after my name?" said Andrew. "My name is now nothing to any one."

"Had not you once a beautiful daughter, named Mary?" said the stranger.

"It is a heart-rending question, man," said Andrew; "but certes, I had once a beloved daughter named Mary."

"What became of her?" asked the stranger.

Andrew shook his head, turned round, and began to move away; it was a theme that his heart could not brook. He sauntered along the loch sands, his dim eye scanning every white pebble as he passed along. There was a hopelessness in his stooping form, his gait, his eye, his features,—in every step that he took there was a hopeless apathy. The dwarf followed him, and began to expostulate with him. "Old man, I see you are pining under some real or fancied affliction," said he. "But in continuing to do so, you are neither acting according to the dictates of reason nor true religion. What is man that he should fret, or the son of man that he should repine, under the chastening hand of his Maker?"

"I am far frae justifying mysell," returned Andrew, surveying his shrivelled monitor with some degree of astonishment. "But there are some feelings that nei-

ther reason nor religion can o'ermaster; and there are
some that a parent may cherish without sin."

"I deny the position," said the stranger, "taken either absolutely or relatively. All repining under the
Supreme decree is leavened with unrighteousness. But,
subtleties aside, I ask you, as I did before, What became of your daughter?"

"Ask the Father of her spirit, and the framer of her
body," said Andrew, solemnly; "ask Him into whose
hands I committed her from childhood. He alone
knows what became of her, but I do not."

"How long is it since you lost her?"

"It is seven years to-morrow."

"Ay! you remember the time well. And have you
mourned for her all that while?"

"Yes; and I will go down to the grave mourning for
my only daughter, the child of my age, and of all my
affection. O, thou unearthly-looking monitor, knowest
thou aught of my darling child? for if thou doest, thou
wilt know that she was not like other women. There
was a simplicity and a purity about my Mary, that was
hardly consistent with our frail nature."

"Wouldst thou like to see her again?" said the
dwarf.

Andrew turned round, his whole frame shaking as
with a palsy, and gazed on the audacious imp. "See

her again, creature!" cried he vehemently—"Would I
like to see her again, say'st thou?"

"I said so," said the dwarf, "and I say farther, Dost
thou know this token? Look, and see if thou dost?"

Andrew took the token, and looked at it, then at the
shrivelled stranger, and then at the token again; and at
length he burst into tears, and wept aloud; but they
were tears of joy, and his weeping seemed to have some
breathings of laughter intermingled in it. And still as
he kissed the token, he called out in broken and convulsive sentences,—"Yes, auld body, I *do* know it!—I *do*
know it!—I *do* know it! It is indeed the same golden
Edward, with three holes in it, with which I presented
my Mary on her birth-day, in her eighteenth year, to
buy a new suit for the holidays. But when she took it
she said—ay, I mind weel what my benny woman said,
—'It is sae benny and sae kenspeckle,' said she, 'that
I think I'll keep it for the sake of the giver.' O dear,
dear!—Blessed little creature, tell me how she is, and
where she is? Is she living, or is she dead?"

"She is living, and in good health," said the dwarf;
"and better, and braver, and happier, and lovelier than
ever; and if you make haste, you will see her and her
family at Moffat to-morrow afternoon. They are to
pass there on a journey, but it is an express one, and I
am sent to you with that token, to inform you of the
circumstance, that you may have it in your power to

see and embrace your beloved daughter once before
you die."

" And am I to meet my Mary at Moffat? Come
away, little, dear, welcome body, thou blessed of heaven, come away, and taste of an auld shepherd's best
cheer, and I'll gang foot for foot with you to Moffat,
and my auld wife shall gang foot for foot with us too.
I tell you, little, blessed, and welcome crile, come along
with me."

" I may not tarry to enter your house, or taste of
your cheer, good shepherd," said the being. " May
plenty still be within your walls, and a thankful heart
to enjoy it ! But my directions are neither to taste
meat nor drink in this country, but to haste back to her
that sent me. Go—haste, and make ready, for you
have no time to lose."

" At what time will she be there ?" cried Andrew,
flinging the plaid from him to run home with the tidings.

" Precisely when the shadow of the Holy Cross falls
due east," cried the dwarf; and turning round, he hasted on his way.

When old Jean Linton saw her husband coming hob-
bling and running home without his plaid, and having
his doublet flying wide open, she had no doubt that he
had lost his wits ; and, full of anxiety, she met him at
the side of the kail-yard. " Gudeness preserve us a'

in our right senses, Andrew Burnet, what's the matter
wi' you, Andrew Burnet?"

"Stand out o' my gate, wife, for, d'ye see, I'm rather in a haste, Jean Linton."

"I see that indeed, gudeman; but stand still, and
tell me what has putten you in sic a haste. Ir ye dementit?"

"Na, na; gudewife, Jean Linton, I'm no dementit
—I'm only gaun away till Moffat."

"O, gudeness pity the poor auld body! How can
ye gang to Moffat, man? Or what have ye to do at
Moffat? Dinna ye mind that the morn is the day o'
our solemnity?"

"Haud out o' my gate, auld wife, and dinna speak
o' solemnities to me. I'll keep it at Moffat the morn.
Ay, gudewife, and ye shall keep it at Moffat, too. What
d'ye think o' that, woman? Too-whoo! ye dinna ken
the metal that's in an auld body till it be tried."

"Andrew—Andrew Burnet!"

"Get away wi' your frightened looks, woman; and
haste ye, gang and fling me out my Sabbath-day claes.
And, Jean Linton, my woman, d'ye hear, gang and pit
on your bridal gown; and your silk hood, for ye maun
be at Moffat the morn too; and it is mair nor time we
were away. Dinna look sae surprised, woman, till I
tell ye, that our ain Mary is to meet us at Moffat the
morn."

" O, Andrew ! dinna sport wi' the feelings of an auld forsaken heart !"

" Gude forbid, my auld wife, that I should ever sport wi' feeling o' yours," cried Andrew, bursting into tears ; " they are a' as saacred to me as breathings frae the Throne o' Grace. But it is true that I tell ye ; our dear bairn is to meet us at Moffat the morn, wi' a son in every hand ; and we maun e'en gang and see her since again, and kiss her and bless her afore we dee."

The tears now rushed from the old woman's eyes like fountains, and dropped from her sorrow-worn cheeks to the earth, and then, as with a spontaneous movement, she threw her skirt over her head, kneeled down at her husband's feet, and poured out her soul in thanksgiving to her Maker. She then rose up, quite deprived of her senses through joy, and ran crouching away on the road towards Moffat, as if hasting beyond her power to be at it. But Andrew brought her back ; and they prepared themselves for their journey.

Kirkstyle being twenty miles from Moffat, they set out on the afternoon of Tuesday, the 16th of September ; slept that night at a place called Turnberry Sheil, and were in Moffat next day by noon. Wearisome was the remainder of the day to that aged couple ; they wandered about conjecturing by what road their daughter would come, and how she would come attended.

"I have made up my mind on baith these matters," said Andrew; "at first I thought it was likely that she would come out of the east, because a' our blessings come frae that airt; but finding now that would be o'er near to the very road we hae come oursells, I now take it for granted she'll come frae the south; and I just think I see her leading a bonny boy in every hand, and a servant lass carrying a bit bundle ahint her."

The two now walked out on all the southern roads, in hopes to meet their Mary, but always returned to watch the shadow of the Holy Cross; and, by the time it fell due east, they could do nothing but stand in the middle of the street, and look round them in all directions. At length, about half a mile out on the Dumfries road, they perceived a poor beggar woman approaching with two children following close to her, and another beggar a good way behind. Their eyes were instantly riveted on these objects; for Andrew thought he perceived his friend the dwarf in the one that was behind; and now all other earthly objects were to them nothing, save these approaching beggars. At that moment a gilded chariot entered the village from the south, and drove by them at full speed, having two livery-men before, and two behind, clothed in green and gold. "Ach-wow! the vanity of worldly grandeur!" ejaculated Andrew, as the splendid vehicle went thundering by; but neither he nor his wife deigned to look at it farther, their whole attention being fixed on the group of beggars. "Ay, it is just my woman," said Andrew, "it is just hersell; I ken her gang yet, sair pressed down wi' poortith although she be. But I dinna care how poor she be, for baith her and hers sall be welcome to my fireside as lang as I hae ane."

While their eyes were thus strained, and their hearts melting with tenderness and pity, Andrew felt something embracing his knees, and, on looking down, there was his Mary, blooming in splendour and beauty, kneeling at his feet. Andrew uttered a loud hysterical scream of joy, and clasped her to his bosom; and old Jean Linton stood trembling, with her arms spread, but durst not close them on so splendid a creature, till her daughter first enfolded her in a fond embrace, and then she hung upon her and wept. It was a wonderful event—a restoration without a parallel. They indeed beheld their Mary, their long-lost darling; they held her in their embraces, believed in her identity, and were satisfied. Satisfied, did I say? They were happy beyond the lot of mortals. She had just alighted from her chariot; and, perceiving her aged parents standing together, she ran and kneeled at their feet. They now retired into the hostel, where Mary presented her two sons to her father and mother. They spent the evening in every social endearment; and

Mary loaded the good old couple with rich presents, watched over them till midnight, when they both fell into a deep and happy sleep, and then she remounted her chariot, and was driven away. If she was any more seen in Scotland, I never heard of it ; but her parents rejoiced in the thoughts of her happiness till the day of their death.

CHAPTER X.

THE BROWNIE OF THE BLACK HAGGS.

WHEN the Sprots were Lairds of Wheelhope, which is now a long time ago, there was one of the ladies who was very badly spoken of in the country. People did not just openly assert that Lady Wheelhope (for every landward laird's wife was then styled Lady) was a witch, but every one had an aversion even at hearing her named; and when by chance she happened to be mentioned, old men would shake their heads and say, " Ah! let us alane o' her! The less ye meddle wi' her the better." Old wives would give over spinning, and, as a pretence for hearing what might be said about her, poke in the fire with the tongs, cocking up their ears all the while; and then, after some meaning coughs, hems, and baws, would haply say, " Hech-wow, sirs! An a' be true that's said!" or something equally wise and decisive.

In short, Lady Wheelhope was accounted a very bad woman. She was an inexorable tyrant in her family, quarrelled with her servants, often cursing them, striking them, and turning them away; especially if they were religious, for she could not endure people of that character, but charged them with every thing bad. Whenever she found out that any of the servant men of the Laird's establishment were religious, she gave them up to the military, and got them shot; and several girls that were regular in their devotions, she was supposed to have got rid of by poison. She was certainly a wicked woman, else many good people were mistaken in her character; and the poor persecuted Covenanters were obliged to unite in their prayers against her.

As for the Laird, he was a big, dun-faced, pluffy body, that cared neither for good nor evil, and did not well know the one from the other. He laughed at his lady's tantrums and barley-hoods; and the greater the rage that she got into, the Laird thought it the better sport. One day, when two maid-servants came running to him, in great agitation, and told him that his lady had felled one of their companions, the Laird laughed heartily, and said he did not doubt it.

"Why, sir, how can you laugh?" said they. "The poor girl is killed."

"Very likely, very likely," said the Laird. "Well, it will teach her to take care who she angers again."

"And, sir, your lady will be hanged."

" Very likely; well, it will teach her how to strike so rashly again—Ha, ha, ha ! Will it not, Jessy?"

But when this same Jessy died suddenly one morning, the Laird was greatly confounded, and seemed dimly to comprehend that there had been unfair play going.   There was little doubt that she was taken off by poison ; but whether the Lady did it through jealousy or not, was never divulged ; but it greatly bamboozled and astonished the poor Laird, for his nerves failed him, and his whole frame became paralytic. He seems to have been exactly in the same state of mind with a colley that I once had. He was extremely fond of the gun as long as I did not kill any thing with it, (there being no game laws in Ettrick Forest in those days,) and he got a grand chase after the hares when I missed them.   But there was one day that I chanced for a marvel to shoot one dead, a few paces before his nose.   I'll never forget the astonishment that the poor beast manifested.   He stared one while at the gun, and another while at the dead hare, and seemed to be drawing the conclusion, that if the case stood thus, there was no creature sure of its life.   Finally, he took his tail between his legs, and ran away home, and never would face a gun all his life again.

So was it precisely with Laird Sprot of Wheelhope. As long as his lady's wrath produced only noise and uproar among the servants, he thought it fine sport ; but

when he saw what he believed the dreadful effects of
it, he became like a barrel organ out of tune, and could
only discourse one note, which he did to every one he
met.   " I wish she mayna hae gotten something she
had been the waur of."   This note he repeated early
and late, night and day, sleeping and waking, alone and
in company, from the moment that Jessy died till she
was buried ; and on going to the churchyard as chief
mourner, he whispered it to her relatives by the way.
When they came to the grave, he took his stand at the
head, nor would he give place to the girl's father ; but
there he stood, like a huge post, as though he neither
saw nor heard ; and when he had lowered her head into
the grave, and dropped the cord, he slowly lifted his hat
with one hand, wiped his dim eyes with the back of the
other, and said, in a deep tremulous tone, " Poor lassie !
I wish she didna get something she had been the waur
of."

This death made a great noise among the common
people ; but there was little protection for the life of
the subject in those days ; and provided a man or woman was a real Anti-Covenanter, they might kill a good
many without being quarrelled for it. So there was no
one to take cognizance of the circumstances relating to
the death of poor Jessy.

After this, the Lady walked softly for the space of
two or three years. She saw that she had rendered her-

self odious, and had entirely lost her husband's countenance, which she liked worst of all. But the evil propensity could not be overcome; and a poor boy, whom the Laird, out of sheer compassion, had taken into his service, being found dead one morning, the country people could no longer be restrained; so they went in a body to the Sheriff, and insisted on an investigation. It was proved that she detested the boy, had often threatened him, and had given him brose and butter the afternoon before he died; but notwithstanding of all this, the cause was ultimately dismissed, and the pursuers fined.

No one can tell to what height of wickedness she might now have proceeded, had not a check of a very singular kind been laid upon her. Among the servants that came home at the next term, was one who called himself Merodach; and a strange person he was. He had the form of a boy, but the features of one a hundred years old, save that his eyes had a brilliancy and restlessness, which were very extraordinary, bearing a strong resemblance to the eyes of a well-known species of monkey. He was froward and perverse, and disregarded the pleasure or displeasure of any person; but he performed his work well, and with apparent ease. From the moment he entered the house, the Lady conceived a mortal antipathy against him, and besought the Laird to turn him away. But the Laird would not con-

sent; he never turned away any servant, and moreover
he had hired this fellow for a trivial wage, and he neither wanted activity nor perseverance.   The natural
consequence of this refusal was, that the Lady instantly set herself to embitter Merodach's life as much as
possible, in order to get early quit of a domestic every
way so disagreeable.   Her hatred of him was not like a
common antipathy entertained by one human being
against another,——she hated him as one might hate a
toad or an adder ; and his occupation of jotteryman (as
the Laird termed his servant of all work) keeping him
always about her hand, it must have proved highly an-
noying.

She scolded him, she raged at him ; but he only
mocked her wrath, and giggled and laughed at her, with
the most provoking derision.   She tried to fell him again
and again, but never, with all her address, could she hit
him ; and never did she make a blow at him, that she
did not repent it.   She was heavy and unwieldy, and
he as quick in his motions as a monkey ; besides, he generally contrived that she should be in such an ungovernable rage, that when she flew at him, she hardly
knew what she was doing.   At one time she guided
her blow towards him, and he at the same instant avoided it with such dexterity, that she knocked down the
chief hind, or foresman ; and then Merodach giggled so
heartily, that, lifting the kitchen poker, she threw it at

him with a full design of knocking out his brains; but the missile only broke every article of crockery on the kitchen dresser.

She then hasted to the Laird, crying bitterly, and telling him she would not suffer that wretch Merodach, as she called him, to stay another night in the family.

" Why, then, put him away, and trouble me no more about him," said the Laird.

. " Put him away!" exclaimed she; " I have already ordered him away a hundred times, and charged him never to let me see his horrible face again; but he only grins, and answers with some intolerable piece of impertinence."

The pertinacity of the fellow amused the Laird; his dim eyes turned upwards into his head with delight; he then looked two ways at once, turned round his back, and laughed till the tears ran down his dun cheeks; but he could only articulate, " You're fitted now."

The Lady's agony of rage still increasing from this derision, she upbraided the Laird bitterly, and said he was not worthy the name of man, if he did not turn away that pestilence, after the way he had abused her.

. " Why, Shusy, my dear, what has he done to you?"

" What done to me! has he not caused me to knock down John Thomson? and I do not know if ever he will come to life again!"

" Have you felled your favourite John Thomson?"

said the Laird, laughing more heartily than before;
" you might have done a worse deed than that."

" And has he not broke every plate and dish on the
whole dresser?" continued the Lady ; " and for all this
devastation, he only mocks at my displeasure,—absolutely mocks me,—and if you do not have him turned
away, and hanged or shot for his deeds, you are not
worthy the name of man."

" O alack ! What a devastation among the cheena
metal !" said the Laird ; and calling on Merodach, he
said, " Tell me, thou evil Merodach of Babylon, how
thou dared'st knock down thy Lady's favourite servant,
John Thomson ?"

" Not I, your honour. It was my Lady herself, who
got into such a furious rage at me, that she mistook
her man, and felled Mr Thomson ; and the good man's
skull is fractured."

" That was very odd," said the Laird, chuckling ;
" I do not comprehend it. But then, what set you on
smashing all my Lady's delft and cheena ware ?——That
was a most infamous and provoking action."

" It was she herself, your honour. Sorry would I
be to break one dish belonging to the house. I take
all the house servants to witness, that my Lady smashed all the dishes with a poker ; and now lays the blame
on me !"

The Laird turned his dim eyes on his lady, who was

crying with vexation and rage, and seemed meditating
another personal attack on the culprit, which he did
not at all appear to shun, but rather to court.   She,
however, vented her wrath in threatenings of the most
deep and desperate revenge, the creature all the while
assuring her that she would be foiled, and that in all
her encounters and contests with him, she would uni-
formly come to the worst ; he was resolved to do his
duty, and there before his master he defied her.

The Laird thought more than he considered it prudent to reveal ; he had little doubt that his wife would
find some means of wreaking her vengeance on the object of her displeasure ; and he shuddered when he recollected one who had taken " something that she had
been the waur of."

In a word, the Lady of Wheelhope's inveterate ma-
lignity against this one object, was like the rod of Mo-
ses, that swallowed up the rest of the serpents.   All
her wicked and evil propensities seemed to be super-
seded, if not utterly absorbed by it.   The rest of the
family now lived in comparative peace and quietness ;
for early and late her malevolence was venting itself
against the jotteryman, and against him alone.   It was
a delirium of hatred and vengeance, on which the whole
bent and bias of her inclination was set.   She could
not stay from the creature's presence, or, in the inter-
vals when absent from him, she spent her breath in

curses and execrations; and then, not able to rest, she ran again to seek him, her eyes gleaming with the anticipated delights of vengeance, while, ever and anon, all the ridicule and the harm redounded on herself.

Was it not strange that she could not get quit of this sole annoyance of her life? One would have thought she easily might. But by this time there was nothing farther from her wishes; she wanted vengeance, full, adequate, and delicious vengeance, on her audacious opponent. But he was a strange and terrible creature, and the means of retaliation constantly came, as it were, to his hand.

Bread and sweet milk was the only fare that Merodach cared for, and having bargained for that, he would not want it, though he often got it with a curse and with ill will. The Lady having, upon one occasion, intentionally kept back his wonted allowance for some days, on the Sabbath morning following, she set him down a bowl of rich sweet milk, well drugged with a deadly poison; and then she lingered in a little anteroom to watch the success of her grand plot, and prevent any other creature from tasting of the potion. Merodach came in, and the house-maid said to him, "There is your breakfast, creature."

"Oho! my Lady has been liberal this morning," said he; "but I am beforehand with her.——Here, little Missie, you seem very hungry to-day—take you my break-

fast." And with that he set the beverage down to the
Lady's little favourite spaniel. It so happened that
the Lady's only son came at that instant into the anteroom seeking her, and teasing his mamma about something, which withdrew her attention from the hall-table
for a space. When she looked again, and saw Missie lap-
ping up the sweet milk, she burst from her hiding-place
like a fury, screaming as if her head had been on fire,
kicked the remainder of its contents against the wall,
and lifting Missie in her bosom, retreated hastily, crying all the way.

"Ha, ha, ha—I have you now!" cried Merodach,
as she vanished from the hall.

Poor Missie died immediately, and very privately;
indeed, she would have died and been buried, and never
one have seen her, save her mistress, had not Merodach, by a luck that never failed him, looked over
the wall of the flower garden, just as his lady was laying her favourite in a grave of her own digging. She,
not perceiving her tormentor, plied on at her task,
apostrophizing the insensate little carcass,—"Ah! poor
dear little creature, thou hast had a hard fortune, and
hast drank of the bitter potion that was not intended
for thee; but he shall drink it three times double for
thy sake!"

"Is that little Missie?" said the eldrich voice of the
jotteryman, close at the Lady's ear. She uttered a loud

scream, and sunk down on the bank. "Alack for poor Missie!" continued the creature in a tone of mockery, "my heart is sorry for Missie. What has befallen her—whose breakfast cup did she drink?"

"Hence with thee, fiend!" cried the Lady; "what right hast thou to intrude on thy mistress's privacy? Thy turn is coming yet; or may the nature of woman change within me!"

"It is changed already," said the creature, grinning with delight; "I have thee now, I have thee now! And were it not to show my superiority over thee, which I do every hour, I should soon see thee strapped like a mad cat, or a worrying bratch. What wilt thou try next?"

"I will cut thy throat, and if I die for it, will rejoice in the deed; a deed of charity to all that dwell on the face of the earth."

"I have warned thee before, dame, and I now warn thee again, that all thy mischief meditated against me will fall double on thine own head."

"I want none of your warning, fiendish cur. Hence with your elvish face, and take care of yourself."

It would be too disgusting and horrible to relate or read all the incidents that fell out between this unaccountable couple. Their enmity against each other had no end, and no mitigation; and scarcely a single day passed over on which the Lady's acts of malevolent ingenuity did not terminate fatally for some favourite thing of her own.   Scarcely was there a thing, animate or inanimate, on which she set a value, left to her, that was not destroyed ; and yet scarcely one hour or minute could she remain absent from her tormentor, and all the while, it seems, solely for the purpose of tormenting him.   While all the rest of the establishment enjoyed peace and quietness from the fury of their termagant dame, matters still grew worse and worse between the fascinated pair.   The Lady haunted the menial, in the same manner as the raven haunts the eagle,—for a perpetual quarrel, though the former knows that in every encounter she is to come off the loser. Noises were heard on the stairs by night, and it was whispered among the servants, that the Lady had been seeking Merodach's chamber, on some horrible intent. Several of them would have sworn that they had seen her passing and repassing on the stair after midnight, when all was quiet ; but then it was likewise well known, that Merodach slept with well-fastened doors, and a companion in another bed in the same room, whose bed, too, was nearest the door.   Nobody cared much what became of the jotteryman, for he was an unsocial and disagreeable person ; but some one told him what they had seen, and hinted a suspicion of the Lady's intent.   But the creature only bit his upper lip,

N 2

winked with his eyes, and said, " She had better let that alone ; she will be the first to rue that."

Not long after this, to the horror of the family and the whole country side, the Laird's only son was found murdered in his bed one morning, under circumstances that manifested the most fiendish cruelty and inveteracy on the part of his destroyer. As soon as the atrocious act was divulged, the Lady fell into convulsions, and lost her reason ; and happy had it been for her had she never recovered the use of it, for there was blood upon her hand, which she took no care to conceal, and there was little doubt that it was the blood of her own innocent and beloved boy, the sole heir and hope of the family.

This blow deprived the Laird of all power of action ; but the Lady had a brother, a man of the law, who came and instantly proceeded to an investigation of this unaccountable murder. Before the Sheriff arrived, the housekeeper took the Lady's brother aside, and told him he had better not go on with the scrutiny, for she was sure the crime would be brought home to her unfortunate mistress ; and after examining into several corroborative circumstances, and viewing the state of the raving maniac, with the blood on her hand and arm, he made the investigation a very short one, declaring the domestics all exculpated.

The Laird attended his boy's funeral, and laid his

head in the grave, but appeared exactly like a man walking in a trance, an automaton, without feelings or sensations, oftentimes gazing at the funeral procession, as on something he could not comprehend.   And when the death-bell of the parish church fell a-tolling, as the corpse approached the kirk-stile, he cast a dim eye up towards the belfry, and said hastily, "What, what's that ? Och ay, we're just in time, just in time."   And often was he hammering over the name of " Evil Merodach, King of Babylon," to himself.   He seemed to have some far-fetched conception that his unaccountable jotteryman was in some way connected with the death of his only son, and other lesser calamities, although the evidence in favour of Merodach's innocence was as usual quite decisive.

This grievous mistake of Lady Wheelhope can only be accounted for, by supposing her in a state of derangement, or rather under some evil influence, over which she had no control ; and to a person in such a state, the mistake was not so very unnatural.   The mansion-house of Wheelhope was old and irregular. The stair had four acute turns, and four landing-places, all the same.   In the uppermost chamber slept the two domestics,——Merodach in the bed farthest in, and in the chamber immediately below that, which was exactly similar, slept the Young Laird and his tutor, the former in the bed farthest in ; and thus, in the turmoil of her wild and raging passions, her own hand made herself childless.

Merodach was expelled the family forthwith, but refused to accept of his wages, which the man of law pressed upon him, for fear of farther mischief; but he went away in apparent sullenness and discontent, no one knowing whither.

When his dismissal was announced to the Lady, who was watched day and night in her chamber, the news had such an effect on her, that her whole frame seemed electrified; the horrors of remorse vanished; and another passion, which I neither can comprehend nor define, took the sole possession of her distempered spirit. "He *must* not go!—He *shall* not go!" she exclaimed. "No, no, no—he shall not—he shall not—he shall not!" and then she instantly set herself about making ready to follow him, uttering all the while the most diabolical expressions, indicative of anticipated vengeance.—"Oh, could I but snap his nerves one by one, and birl among his vitals! Could I but slice his heart off piecemeal in small messes, and see his blood lopper, and bubble, and spin away in purple slays; and then to see him grin, and grin, and grin, and grin! Oh—oh—oh—How beautiful and grand a sight it would be to see him grin, and grin, and grin!" And in such a style would she run on for hours together.

She thought of nothing, she spake of nothing, but

the discarded jotteryman, whom most people now began to regard as a creature that was "not canny." They had seen him eat, and drink, and work, like other people; still he had that about him that was not like other men.   He was a boy in form, and an antediluvian in feature.   Some thought he was a mongrel, between a Jew and an ape; some a wizard, some a kelpie, or a fairy, but most of all, that he was really and truly a Brownie.   What he was I do not know, and therefore will not pretend to say; but be that as it may, in spite of locks and keys, watching and waking, the Lady of Wheelhope soon made her escape, and eloped after him.   The attendants, indeed, would have made oath that she was carried away by some invisible hand, for it was impossible, they said, that she could have escaped on foot like other people; and this edition of the story took in the country; but sensible people viewed the matter in another light.

As for instance, when Wattie Blythe, the Laird's old shepherd, came in from the hill one morning, his wife Bessie thus accosted him.——"His presence be about us, Wattie Blythe! have ye heard what has happened at the ha'?   Things are aye turning waur and waur there, and it looks like as if Providence had gi'en up our Laird's house to destruction.   This grand estate maun now gang frae the Sprots; for it has finished them."

" Na, na, Bessie, it isna the estate that has finished the Sprots, but the Sprots that hae finished the estate, and themsells into the boot. They hae been a wicked and degenerate race, and aye the langer the waur, till they hae reached the utmost bounds o' earthly wickedness ; and it's time the deil were looking after his ain."

" Ah, Wattie Blythe, ye never said a truer say. And that's just the very point where your story ends, and mine begins ; for hasna the deil, or the fairies, or the brownies, ta'en away our Leddy bodily ! and the haill country is running and riding in search o' her ; and there is twenty hunder merks offered to the first that can find her, and bring her safe back. They hae ta'en her away, skin and bane, body and soul, and a', Wattie !"

" Hech-wow ! but that is awsome ! And where is it thought they have ta'en her to, Bessie ?"

" O, they hae some guess at that frae her ain hints afore. It is thought they hae carried her after that Satan of a creature, wha wrought sae muckle wae about the house. It is for him they are a' looking, for they ken weel, that where they get the tane they will get the tither."

" Whew ! Is that the gate o't, Bessie ? Why, then, the awfu' story is nouther mair nor less than this, that the Leddy has made a 'lopement, as they ca't, and run away after a blackguard jotteryman. Hech-wow ! wae's

me for human frailty ! But that's just the gate ! When
since the deil gets in the point o' his finger, he will
soon have in his haill hand. Ay, he wants but a hair
to make a tether of, ony day ! I hae seen her a braw
sonsy lass ; but even then I feared she was devoted to
destruction, for she aye mockit at religion, Bessie, and
that's no a good mark of a young body. And she
made a' its servants her enemies ; and think you these
good men's prayers were a' to blaw away i' the wind,
and be nae mair regarded ? Na, na, Bessie, my woman, take ye this mark baith o' our ain bairns and
ither folk's——If ever ye see a young body that disre-
gards the Sabbath, and makes a mock at the ordinances
o' religion, ye will never see that body come to muckle
good.——A braw hand our Leddy has made o' her gibes
and jeers at religion, and her mockeries o' the poor persecuted hill-folk !——sunk down by degrees into the very
dregs o' sin and misery ! run away after a scullion !"

" Fy, fy, Wattie, how can ye say sae ? It was weel
kenn'd that she hatit him wi' a perfect and mortal
hatred, and tried to make away wi' him mae ways nor
ane."

" Aha, Bessie ; but nipping and scarting is Scots
folk's wooing ; and though it is but right that we sus-
pend our judgments, there will naebody persuade me
if she be found alang wi' the creature, but that she has

run away after him in the natural way, on her twa shanks, without help either frae fairy or brownie."

" I'll never believe sic a thing of ony woman born, let be a leddy weel up in years."

" Od help ye, Bessie ! ye dinna ken the stretch o' corrupt nature.   The best o' us, when left to oursells, are nae better than strayed sheep, that will never find the way back to their ain pastures ; and of a' things made o' mortal flesh, a wicked woman is the warst."

" Alack-a-day ! we get the blame o' muckle that we little deserve. But, Wattie, keep ye a geyan sharp look-out about the cleuchs and the caves o' our hope ; for the Leddy kens them a' geyan weel ; and gin the twenty hunder merks wad come our way, it might gang a waur gate.   It wad tocher a' our bonny lasses."

" Ay, weel I wat, Bessie, that's nae lee.   And now, when ye bring me amind o't, I'm sair mista'en if I didna hear a creature up in the Brockholes this morning, skirling as if something war cutting its throat. It gars a' the hairs stand on my head when I think it may hae been our Leddy, and the droich of a creature murdering her.   I took it for a battle of wulcats, and wished they might pu' out ane anither's thrapples ; but when I think on it again, they war unco like some o' our Leddy's unearthly screams."

" His presence be about us, Wattie ! Haste ye—pit

on your bonnet—tak' your staff in your hand, and gang and see what it is."

" Shame fa' me, if I daur gang, Bessie."

" Hout, Wattie, trust in the Lord."

" Aweel, sae I do. But ane's no to throw himsell ower a linn, and trust that the Lord will kep him in a blanket. And it's nae muckle safer for an auld stiff man like me to gang away out to a wild remote place, where there is ae body murdering another.—What is that I hear, Bessie ? Haud the lang tongue o' you, and rin to the door, and see what noise that is."

Bessie ran to the door, but soon returned, with her mouth wide open, and her eyes set in her head.

" It is them, Wattie ! it is them ! His presence be about us ! What will we do ?"

" Them ? whaten them ?"

" Why, that blackguard creature, coming here, leading our Leddy by the hair o' the head, and yerking her wi' a stick. I am terrified out o' my wits. What will we do ?"

" We'll *see* what they *say*," said Wattie, manifestly in as great terror as his wife ; and by a natural impulse, or as a last resource, he opened the Bible, not knowing what he did, and then hurried on his spectacles ; but before he got two leaves turned over, the two entered,—a frightful-looking couple indeed. Mero-dach, with his old withered face, and ferret eyes, leading the Lady of Wheelhope by the long hair, which was mixed with grey, and whose face was all bloated with wounds and bruises, and having stripes of blood on her garments.

" How's this!—How's this, sirs?" said Wattie Blythe.

" Close that book, and I will tell you, goodman," said Merodach.

" I can hear what you hae to say wi' the beuk open, sir," said Wattie, turning over the leaves, pretending to look for some particular passage, but apparently not knowing what he was doing. " It is a shamefu' business this; but some will hae to answer for't. My Leddy, I am unco grieved to see you in sic a plight. Ye hae surely been dooms sair left to yoursell."

The Lady shook her head, uttered a feeble hollow laugh, and fixed her eyes on Merodach. But such a look! It almost frightened the simple aged couple out of their senses. It was not a look of love nor of hatred exclusively; neither was it of desire or disgust, but it was a combination of them all. It was such a look as one fiend would cast on another, in whose everlasting destruction he rejoiced. Wattie was glad to take his eyes from such countenances, and look into the Bible, that firm foundation of all his hopes and all his joy.

" I request that you will shut that book, sir," said the horrible creature; " or if you do not, I will shut it for you with a vengeance ;" and with that he seized it, and flung it against the wall. Bessie uttered a scream, and Wattie was quite paralysed ; and although he seemed disposed to run after his best friend, as he called it, the hellish looks of the Brownie interposed, and glued him to his seat.

" Hear what I have to say first," said the creature, " and then pore your fill on that precious book of yours. One concern at a time is enough. I came to do you a service. Here, take this cursed, wretched woman, whom you style your Lady, and deliver her up to the lawful authorities, to be restored to her husband and her place in society. She has followed one that hates her, and never said one kind word to her in his life ; and though I have beat her like a dog, still she clings to me, and will not depart, so enchanted is she with the laudable purpose of cutting my throat. Tell your master and her brother, that I am not to be burdened with their maniac. I have scourged—I have spurned and kicked her, afflicting her night and day, and yet from my side she will not depart. Take her. Claim the reward in full, and your fortune is made ; and so farewell !"

The creature went away, and the moment his back was turned, the Lady fell a-screaming and struggling, like one in an agony, and, in spite of all the old couple's exertions, she forced herself out of their hands, and ran after the retreating Merodach. When he saw better would not be, he turned upon her, and, by one blow with his stick, struck her down; and, not content with that, continued to maltreat her in such a manner, as to all appearance would have killed twenty ordinary persons. The poor devoted dame could do nothing, but now and then utter a squeak like a half-worried cat, and writhe and grovel on the sward, till Wattie and his wife came up, and withheld her tormentor from further violence. He then bound her hands behind her back with a strong cord, and delivered her once more to the charge of the old couple, who contrived to hold her by that means, and take her home.

Wattie was ashamed to take her into the hall, but led her into one of the out-houses, whither he brought her brother to receive her. The man of the law was manifestly vexed at her reappearance, and scrupled not to testify his dissatisfaction; for when Wattie told him how the wretch had abused his sister, and that, had it not been for Bessie's interference and his own, the Lady would have been killed outright, he said, " Why, Walter, it is a great pity that he did *not* kill her outright. What good can her life now do to her, or of what value is her life to any creature living ? After one has lived to disgrace all connected with them, the sooner they are taken off the better."

The man, however, paid old Walter down his two

thousand merks, a great fortune for one like him in those days; and not to dwell longer on this unnatural story, I shall only add, very shortly, that the Lady of Wheelhope soon made her escape once more, and flew, as if drawn by an irresistible charm, to her tormentor. Her friends looked no more after her; and the last time she was seen alive, it was following the uncouth creature up the water of Daur, weary, wounded, and lame, while he was all the way beating her, as a piece of excellent amusement. A few days after that, her body was found among some wild haggs, in a place called Crook-burn, by a party of the persecuted Covenanters that were in hiding there, some of the very men whom she had exerted herself to destroy, and who had been driven, like David of old, to pray for a curse and earthly punishment upon her. They buried her like a dog at the Yetts of Keppel, and rolled three huge stones upon her grave, which are lying there to this day. When they found her corpse, it was mangled and wounded in a most shocking manner, the fiendish creature having manifestly tormented her to death. He was never more seen or heard of in this kingdom, though all that country-side was kept in terror for him many years afterwards; and to this day, they will tell you of THE BROWNIE OF THE BLACK HAGGS, which title he seems to have acquired after his disappearance.

This story was told to me by an old man named

Adam Halliday, whose great-grandfather, Thomas Halliday, was one of those that found the body and buried it. It is many years since I heard it; but, however ridiculous it may appear, I remember it made a dreadful impression on my young mind. I never heard any story like it, save one of an old fox-hound that pursued a fox through the Grampians for a fortnight, and when at last discovered by the Duke of Athole's people, neither of them could run, but the hound was still continuing to walk after the fox, and when the latter lay down, the other lay down beside him, and looked at him steadily all the while, though unable to do him the least harm. The passion of inveterate malice seems to have influenced these two exactly alike. But, upon the whole, I scarcely believe the tale can be true.

CHAPTER XI.

THE LAIRD OF WINEHOLM.

" HAVE you heard any thing of the apparition which has been seen about Wineholm Place ?" said the Dominie.

" Na, I never heard o' sic a thing as yet," quoth the smith ; " but I wadna wonder muckle that the news should turn out to be true."

The Dominie shook his head, and uttered a long " h'm-h'm-h'm," as if he knew more than he was at liberty to tell.

" Weel, that beats the world," said the smith, as he gave over blowing the bellows, and looked anxiously in the Dominie's face.

The Dominie shook 'his head again.

The smith was now in the most ticklish quandary ; eager to learn particulars, that he might spread the astounding news through the whole village, and the rest of the parish to boot, but yet afraid to press the inquiry, for fear the cautious Dominie should take the alarm of being reported as a tattler, and keep all to himself.   So the smith, after waiting till the wind-pipe of the great bellows ceased its rushing noise, covered the gloss neatly up with a mixture of small coals, culm, and cinders ; and then, perceiving that nothing more was forthcoming from the Dominie, he began blowing again with more energy than before—changed his hand —put the other sooty one in his breeches-pocket— leaned to the horn—looked in a careless manner to the window, or rather gazed on vacancy, and always now and then stole a sly look at the Dominie's face. It was quite immovable.   His cheek was leaned on his open hand, and his eyes fixed on the glowing fire.   It was very teasing this for poor Clinkum the smith.   But what could he do ? He took out his glowing iron, and made a shower of fire sweep through the whole smithy, whereof a good part, as intended, sputtered upon the Dominie ; but that imperturbable person only shielded his face with his elbow, turned his shoulder half round, and held his peace.   Thump, thump ! clink, clink ? went the hammer for a space ; and then when the iron was returned to the fire, " Weel, that beats the world !" quoth the smith.

" What is this that beats the world, Mr Clinkum ?" asked the Dominie, with the most cool and provoking indifference.

" This story about the apparition," quoth the smith.
4

" What story ?" said the Dominie.

Now really this perversity was hardly to be endured, even in a learned Dominie, who, with all his cold indifference of feeling, was sitting toasting himself at a good smithy fire. The smith felt this, (for he was a man of acute feeling,) and therefore he spit upon his hand and fell a-clinking and pelting at the stithy with both spirit and resignation, saying within himself, " These dominie bodies just beat the world !"

" What story ?" reiterated the Dominie. " For my part, I related no story, nor have ever given assent to a belief in such a story that any man has heard. Nevertheless, from the results of ratiocination, conclusions may be formed, though not algebraically, yet corporately, by constituting a quantity, which shall be equivalent to the difference, subtracting the less from the greater, and striking a balance in order to get rid of any ambiguity or paradox."

At the long adverb, *nevertheless,* the smith gave over blowing, and pricked up his ears ; but the definition went beyond his comprehension.

" Ye ken, that just beats the whole world for deepness," said the smith ; and again began blowing the bellows.

" You know, Mr Clinkum," continued the Dominie, " that a proposition is an assertion of some distinct truth, which only becomes manifest by demonstration.

A corollary is an obvious, or easily inferred consequence *of* a proposition ; while an hypothesis is a *supposition*, or concession made, during the process of demonstration.   Now, do you take me along with you ? Because, if you do not, it is needless to proceed."

" Yes, yes, I understand you middling weel ; but I wad like better to hear what other folks say about it than you."

" And why so ?   Wherefore would you rather hear another man's demonstration than mine ?" said the Dominie, sternly.

" Because, ye ken, ye just beat the whole world for words," quoth the smith.

" Ay, ay ! that is to say, words without wisdom," said the Dominie, rising and stepping away.   " Well, well, every man to his sphere, and the smith to the bellows."

" Ye're quite mistaen, master," cried the smith after him ; " it isna the want o' wisdom in you that plagues me, it is the owerplush o't."

This soothed the Dominie, who returned, and said, mildly—" By the by, Clinkum, I want a leister of your making ; for I see there is no other tradesman makes them so well.   A five-grained one make it ; at your own price."

" Very weel, sir.   When will you be needing it ?"

" Not till the end of close-time."

THE LAIRD OF WINEHOLM.

"Ay, ye may gar the three auld anes do till then."

"What do you wish to insinuate, sir? Would you infer, because I have three leisters, that therefore I am a breaker of the laws? That I, who am placed here as a pattern and monitor of the young and rising generation, should be the first to set them an example of insubordination?"

"Na, but, ye ken, that just beats the world for words! but we ken what we ken, for a' that, master."

"You had better take a little care what you say, Mr Clinkum; just a little care. I do not request you to take particular care, for of that your tongue is incapable, but a very little is necessary. And mark you——don't go to say that I said this or that about a ghost, or mentioned such a ridiculous story."

"The crabbitness o' that body beats the world!" said the smith to himself, as the Dominie went halting homeward.

The very next man that entered the smithy door was no other than John Broadcast, the new Laird's hind, who had also been hind to the late laird for many years, and who had no sooner said his errand than the smith addressed him thus :——"Have *you* ever seen this ghost that there is such a noise about?"

"Ghost! Na, goodness be thankit, I never saw a ghost in my life, save since a wraith. What ghost do you mean?"

" So you never saw nor heard tell of any apparition about Winebolm Place, lately ?"

" No, I hae reason to be thankfu' I have not."

" Weel, that beats the world ! Whow, man, but ye are sair in the dark ! Do you no think there are sic-can things in nature, as folk no coming fairly to their ends, John ?"

" Goodness be wi' us ! Ye gar a' the hairs o' my head creep, man. What's that you're saying ?"

" Had ye never ony suspicions o' that kind, John ?"

" No ; I canna say that I had."

" None in the least ? Weel, that beats the world !"

" O, haud your tongue, haud your tongue ! We hae great reason to be thankfu' that we are as we are !"

" How as we are ?"

" That we arena stocks or stones, or brute beasts, as the Minister o' Traquair says. But I hope in God there is nae siccan a thing about my master's place as an unearthly visitor."

The smith shook his head, and uttered a long hem, hem, hem ! He had felt the powerful effect of that himself, and wished to make the same appeal to the feelings and longings after information of John Broad-cast. The bait took ; for the latent spark of supersti-tion, not to say any thing about curiosity, was kindled in the heart of honest John, and there being no wit in the head to counteract it, the portentous hint had its full away. John's eyes stelled in his head, and his visage grew long, assuming something of the hue of dried clay in winter. " Hech, man, but that's an awsome story!" exclaimed he. " Folks hae great reason to be thankfu' that they are as they are. It is truly an awsome story."

" Ye ken, it just beats the world for that," quoth the smith.

" And is it really thought that this Laird made away wi' our auld master?" said John.

The smith shook his head again, and gave a strait wink with his eyes.

" Weel, I hae great reason to be thankfu' that I never heard siccan a story as that!" said John. " Wha was it tauld you a' about it?"

" It was nae less a man than our mathewmatical Dominie," said the smith; " he that kens a' things, and can prove a proposition to the nineteenth part of a hair. But he is terrified the tale should spread; and therefore ye maunna say a word about it."

" Na, na; I hae great reason to be thankfu' I can keep a secret as weel as the maist feck o' men, and better than the maist feck o' women. What did he say? Tell us a' that he said."

" It is not so easy to repeat what he says, for he has sae mony lang-nebbit words, which just beat the world. But he said, though it was only a supposition, yet it was easily made manifest by positive demonstration."

"Did you ever hear the like o' that! Now, havena we reason to be thankfu' that we are as we are? Did he say that it was by poison that he was taken off, or that he was strangled?"

"Na; I thought he said it was by a collar, or a collary, or something to that purpose."

"Then, it wad appear there is no doubt of it? I think, the Doctor has reason to be thankfu' that he's no taken up. Is not that strange?"

"O, ye ken, it just beats the world!"

"He deserves to be torn at young horses' tails," said the ploughman.

"Ay, or nippit to death with red-hot pinchers," quoth the smith.

"Or harrowed to death, like the children of Ammon," continued the ploughman.

"Na, I'll tell you what should be done wi' him— he should just be docked and fired like a farcied horse," quoth the smith. "Od help ye, man, I could beat the world for laying on a proper poonishment."

John Broadcast went home full of terror and dismay. He told his wife the story in a secret—she told the dairymaid with a tenfold degree of secrecy; and so ere long it reached the ears of Dr Davington himself, the New Laird, as he was called. He was unusually affected, at hearing such a terrible accusation against himself; and the Dominie being mentioned as the propagator of the report, a message was forthwith dispatched to desire him to come up to the Place, and speak with the Laird. The Dominie suspected there was bad blood a-brewing against him; and as he had too much self-importance to think of succumbing to any man alive, he sent an impertinent answer to the Laird's message, bearing, that if Dr Davington had any business with him, he would be so good as attend at his class-room when he dismissed his scholars.

When this message was delivered, the Doctor, being almost beside himself with rage, instantly dispatched two village constables with a warrant to seize the Dominie, and bring him before him; for the Doctor was a justice of the peace. Accordingly, the poor Dominie was seized at the head of his pupils, and dragged away, crutch and all, up before the new Laird, to answer for such an abominable slander. The Dominie denied every thing concerning it, as indeed he might, save having asked the smith the simple question, "if he had heard ought of a ghost at the Place?" But he refused to tell why he asked that question. He had his own reasons for it, he said, and reasons that to him were quite sufficient; but as he was not obliged to disclose them, neither would he.

The smith was then sent for, who declared that the

Dominie had told him of the ghost being seen, and a murder committed, which he called a *rash assassination*, and said it was obvious, and easily inferred that it was done by a collar.

How the Dominie did storm! He even twice threatened to knock down the smith with his crutch; not for the slander,—he cared not for that nor the Doctor a pin,—but for the total subversion of his grand illustration from geometry; and he therefore denominated the smith's head *the logarithm to number one*, a reproach of which I do not understand the gist, but the appropriation of it pleased the Dominie exceedingly, made him chuckle, and put him in better humour for a good while. It was in vain that he tried to prove that his words applied only to the definition of a problem in geometry,—he could not make himself understood; and the smith maintaining his point firmly, and apparently with conscientious truth, appearances were greatly against the Dominie, and the Doctor pronounced him a malevolent and dangerous person.

"O, ye ken, he just beats the world for that," quoth the smith.

"I a malevolent and dangerous person, sir!" said the Dominie, fiercely, and altering his crutch from one place to another of the floor, as if he could not get a place to set it on. "Dost thou call me a malevolent and dangerous person, sir? What then art thou? If

thou knowest not I will tell thee. Add a cipher to a
ninth figure, and what does that make? Ninety you
will say. Ay, but then put a cipher *above* a nine, and
what does that make? ha—ha—ha—I have you there.
Your case exactly in higher geometry! for say the
chord of sixty degrees is radius, then the sine of ninety
degrees is equal to the radius, so the secant of 0, that
is nickle-nothing, as the boys call it, is radius, and so
is the co-sine of 0. The versed sine of 90 degrees is
radius, (that is nine with a cipher added, you know,)
and the versed sine of 180 degrees is the diameter;
then of course the sine increases from 0 (that is cipher
or nothing) till it becomes radius, and then it de-
creases till it becomes nothing. After this you note it
lies on the *contrary* side of the diameter, and consequently, if positive before, is negative now, so that it
must end in 0, or a cipher above a nine at most."

" This unintelligible jargon is out of place here, Mr
Dominie ; and if you can show no better reasons for
raising such an abominable falsehood, in representing
me as an incendiary and murderer, I shall procure you
a lodging in the house of correction."

" Why, sir, the long and short of the matter is this
—I only asked at that fellow there, that logarithm of
stupidity ! if he had heard aught of a ghost having been
seen about Wineholm Place. I added nothing farther,

either positive or negative. Now, do you insist on my reasons for asking such a question?"

"I insist on having them."

"Then what will you say, sir, when I inform you, and declare my readiness to depone to the truth of it, that I saw the ghost myself?—yes, sir—that I saw the ghost of your late worthy father-in-law myself, sir; and though I said no such thing to that decimal fraction, yet it told me, sir—yes, the spirit of your father-in-law told me, sir, that you are a murderer."

"Lord, now, what think ye o' that?" quoth the smith. "Ye had better hae letten him alane; for od, ye ken, he's the deevil of a body that ever was made! He just beats the world!"

The Doctor grew as pale as death, but whether from fear or rage, it was hard to say. "Why, sir, you are mad! stark, raving mad," said the Doctor; "therefore for your own credit, and for the peace and comfort of my wife and myself, and our credit among our retainers, you must unsay every word that you have now said."

"I'll just as soon say that the parabola and the ellipsis are the same," said the Dominie; "or that the diameter is not the longest line that can be drawn in the circle. And now, sir, since you have forced me to divulge what I was much in doubt about, I have a great mind to have the old Laird's grave opened to-night, and have the body inspected before witnesses."

"If you dare disturb the sanctuary of the grave," said the Doctor vehemently, "or with your unhallowed hands touch the remains of my venerable and revered predecessor, it had been better for you, and all who make the attempt, that you never had been born. If not then for my sake, for the sake of my wife, the sole daughter of the man to whom you have all been obliged; let this abominable and malicious calumny go no farther, but put it down; I pray of you to put it down, as you would value your own advantage."

"I have seen him, and spoke with him—that I aver," said the Dominie. "And shall I tell you what he said to me?"

"No, no! I'll hear no more of such absolute and disgusting nonsense," said the Laird.

"Then, since it hath come to this, I will declare it in the face of the whole world, and pursue it to the last," said the Dominie, "ridiculous as it is, and I confess that it is even so. I have seen your father-in-law within the last twenty hours; at least a being in his form and habiliments, and having his aspect and voice. And he told me, that he believed you were a very great scoundrel, and that you had helped him off the stage of time in a great haste, for fear of the operation of a will, which he had just executed, very much to your prejudice. I

was somewhat aghast, but ventured to remark, that he
must surely have been sensible whether you murdered
him or not, and in what way. He replied, that he was
not absolutely certain, for at the time you put him
down, he was much in his customary way of nights,—
very drunk; but that he greatly suspected you had
hanged him, for, ever since he had died, he had been
troubled with a severe criek in his neck. Having seen
my late worthy patron's body deposited in the coffin,
and afterwards consigned to the grave, these things
overcame me, and a kind of mist came over my senses;
but I heard him saying as he withdrew, what a pity it
was that my nerves could not stand this disclosure.
Now, for my own satisfaction, I am resolved that to-
morrow, I shall raise the village, with the two ministers
at the head of the multitude, and have the body, and
particularly the neck of the deceased, minutely inspected."

"If you do so, I shall make one of the number,"
said the Doctor. "But I am resolved that in the first
place every mean shall be tried to prevent a scene of
madness and absurdity so disgraceful to a well-regu-
lated village, and a sober community."

"There is but one direct line that can be followed,
and any other would either form an acute or obtuse
angle," said the Dominie; "therefore I am resolved to
proceed right forward, on mathematical principles;" and

away he went, skipping on his crutch, to arouse the villagers to the scrutiny.

The smith remained behind, concerting with the Doctor, how to controvert the Dominie's profound scheme of unshrouding the dead; and certainly the smith's plan, viewed professionally, was not amiss. " O, ye ken, sir, we maun just gie him another heat, and try to saften him to reason, for he's just as stubborn as Muirkirk ir'n. He beats the world for that."

While the two were in confabulation, Johnston, the old house-servant, came in and said to the Doctor— " Sir, your servants are going to leave the house, every one, this night, if you cannot fall on some means to divert them from it. The old Laird is, it seems, risen again, and come back among them, and they are all in the utmost consternation. Indeed, they are quite out of their reason. He appeared in the stable to Broadcast, who has been these two hours dead with terror, but is now recovered, and telling such a tale down stairs, as never was heard from the mouth of man."

" Send him up here," said the Doctor. " I will silence him. What does the ignorant clown mean by joining in this unnatural clamour?"

John came up, with his broad bonnet in his hand, shut the door with hesitation, and then felt twice with his hand if it really was shut. " Well, John," said the Doctor, " what absurd lie is this that you are vending

among your fellow servants, of having seen a ghost?"
John picked some odds and ends of threads out of his
bonnet, and said nothing. "You are an old superstitious dreaming detard," continued the Doctor; "but if
you propose in future to manufacture such stories, you
must, from this instant, do it somewhere else than in
my service, and among my domestics. What have you
to say for yourself?"

"Indeed, sir, I hae naething to say but this, that we
hae a' muckle reason to be thankfu' that we are as we
are."

"And whereon does that wise saw bear? What relation has that to the seeing of a ghost? Confess then
this instant, that you have forged and vended a deliberate lie."

"Indeed, sir, I hae muckle reason to be thankfu' "——
"For what?"

"That I never tauld a deliberate lee in my life. My
late master came and spake to me in the stable; but
whether it was his ghaist or himsell—a good angel or
a bad ane, I hae reason to be thankfu' I never said; for
I *do—not—ken.*"

"Now, pray let us hear from that sage tongue of
yours, so full of sublime adages, what this doubtful being said to you?"

"I wad rather be excused, an it were your honour's
will, and wad hae reason to be thankfu'."

" And why should you decline telling this ?"

" Because I ken ye wadna believe a word o't, it is siccan a strange story. O sirs, but folks hae muckle reason to be thankfu' that they are as they are !"

" Well, out with this strange story of yours. I do not promise to credit it, but shall give it a patient hearing, provided you swear that there is no forgery in it."

" Weel, as I was suppering the horses the night, I was dressing my late kind master's favourite mare, and I was just thinking to mysell, An he had been leeving, I wadna hae been my lane the night, for he wad hae been standing over me cracking his jokes, and swearing at me in his good-natured hamely way. Aye, but he's gane to his lang account, thinks I, and we poor frail dying creatures that are left ahind hae muckle reason to be thankfu' that we are as we are ; when I looks up, and behold there's my auld master standing leaning against the trivage, as he used to do, and looking at me. I canna but say my heart was a little astoundit, and maybe lap up through my midriff into my breath-bellows—I couldna say ; but in the strength o' the Lord I was enabled to retain my senses for a good while. ' John Broadcast,' said he, with a deep and angry tone,—' John Broadcast, what the d——l are you thinking about ? You are not currying that mare half. What a d——d lubberly way of dressing a horse is that ?'

" 'L—d make us thankfu', master !' says I, 'are you there ?'

" 'Where else would you have me to be at this hour of the night, old blockhead ?' says he.

" 'In another hame than this, master,' says I ; 'but I fear me it is nae good ane, that ye are sae soon tired o't.'

" 'A d—d bad one, I assure you,' says he.

" 'Ay, but, master,' says I, ' ye hae muckle reason to be thankfu' that ye are as ye are.'

" 'In what respects, dotard ?' says he.

" 'That ye hae liberty to come out o't a start now and then to get the air,' says I ; and oh, my heart was sair for him when I thought o' his state ! and though I was thankfu' that I was as I was, my heart and flesh began to fail me, at thinking of my being speaking face to face wi' a being frae the unhappy place.   But out he briks again wi' a grit round o' swearing about the mare being ill keepit ; and he ordered me to cast my coat and curry her weel, for that he had a lang journey to take on her the morn.

" 'You take a journey on her !' says I, ' I fear my new master will dispute that privilege with you, for he rides her himsell the morn.'

" 'He ride her !' cried the angry spirit ; and then it burst out into a lang string of imprecations, fearsome to hear, against you, sir ; and then added, ' Soon soon shall he be levelled with the dust ! The dog ! the parricide ! first to betray my child, and then to put down myself ! ——But he shall not escape ! he shall not escape !' cried he with such a hellish growl, that I fainted, and heard no more."

" Weel, that beats the world !" quoth the smith ; " I wad hae thought the mare wad hae luppen ower yird and stane, or fa'en down dead wi' fright."

" Na, na," said John, " in place o' that, whenever she heard him fa' a-swearing, she was sae glad that she fell a-nickering."

" Na, but that beats the haill world a'thegither !" quoth the smith. " Then it has been nae ghaist ava, ye may depend on that."

" I little wat what it was," said John, " but it was a being in nae good or happy state o' mind, and is a warning to us a' how muckle reason we hae to be thankfu' that we are as we are."

The Doctor pretended to laugh at the absurdity of John's narrative, but it was with a ghastly and doubtful expression of countenance, as though he thought the story far too ridiculous for any clodpole to have contrived out of his own head ; and forthwith he dismissed the two dealers in the marvellous, with very little ceremony, the one protesting that the thing beat the world, and the other that they had both reason to be thankfu' that they were as they were.

The next morning the villagers, small and great, were assembled at an early hour to witness the lifting of the body of their late laird, and headed by the established and dissenting clergymen, and two surgeons, they proceeded to the tomb, and soon extracted the splendid coffin, which they opened with all due caution and ceremony. But instead of the murdered body of their late benefactor, which they expected in good earnest to find, there was nothing in the coffin but a layer of gravel, of about the weight of a corpulent man!

The clamour against the new laird then rose all at once into a tumult that it was impossible to check, every one declaring aloud that he had not only murdered their benefactor, but, for fear of the discovery, had raised the body, and given, or rather sold it, for dissection. The thing was not to be tolerated! so the mob proceeded in a body up to Wineholm Place, to take out their poor deluded lady, and burn the Doctor and his basely acquired habitation to ashes. It was not till the multitude had surrounded the house, that the ministers and two or three other gentlemen could stay them, which they only did by assuring the mob that they would bring out the Doctor before their eyes, and deliver him up to justice. This pacified the throng; but on inquiry at the hall, it was found that the Doctor had gone off early that morning, so that nothing further could be done for the present. But the coffin, filled with gravel, was laid up in the aisle, and kept open for inspection.

Nothing could now exceed the consternation of the simple villagers of Wineholm at these dark and mysterious events. Business, labour, and employment of every sort, were at a stand, and the people hurried about to one another's houses, and mingled their conjectures together in one heterogeneous mass. The smith put his hand to the bellows, but forgot to blow till the fire went out; the weaver leaned on his beam, and listened to the legends of the ghastly tailor. The team stood in mid furrow, and the thrasher agaping over his flail; and even the Dominie was heard to declare that the geometrical series of events was increasing by no common measure, and therefore ought to be calculated rather arithmetically than by logarithms; and John Broadcast saw more and more reason for being thankful that he was as he was, and neither a stock nor a stone, nor a brute beast.

Every new thing that happened was more extraordinary than the last; and the most puzzling of all was the circumstance of the late Laird's mare, saddle, bridle, and all, being off before day the next morning; so that Dr Davington was obliged to have recourse to his own, on which he was seen posting away on the road towards Edinburgh. It was thus but too obvious that the ghost of the late Laird had ridden off on his favourite mare,

the Lord only knew whither! for as to that point none
of the sages of Wineholm could divine. But their souls
grew chill as an iceberg, and their very frames rigid, at
the thoughts of a spirit riding away on a brute beast to
the place appointed for wicked men. And had not John
Broadcast reason to be thankful that he was as he was?

However, the outcry of the community became so
outrageous, of murder, and foul play in so many ways,
that the officers of justice were compelled to take note
of it; and accordingly the Sheriff-substitute, the Sheriff-clerk, the Fiscal, and two assistants, came in two
chaises to Wineholm to take a precognition; and there
a court was held which lasted the whole day, at which,
Mrs Davington, the late Laird's only daughter, all the
servants, and a great number of the villagers, were examined on oath. It appeared from the evidence that
Dr Davington had come to the village and set up as
a surgeon—that he had used every endeavour to be
employed in the Laird's family in vain, as the latter detested him. That he, however, found means of inducing his only daughter to elope with him, which
put the Laird quite beside himself, and from thenceforward he became drowned in dissipation. That such,
however, was his affection for his daughter, that he
caused her to live with him, but would never suffer
the Doctor to enter his door—that it was nevertheless
quite customary for the Doctor to be sent for to his

lady's chamber, particularly when her father was in his
cups ; and that on a certain night, when the Laird had
had company, and was so overcome that he could not
rise from his chair, he had died suddenly of apoplexy ;
and that no other skill was sent for, or near him, but
this his detested son-in-law, whom he had by will dis-
inherited, though the legal term for rendering that will
competent had not expired. The body was coffined
the second day after death, and locked up in a low
room in one of the wings of the building ; and nothing
farther could be elicited. The Doctor was missing,
and it was whispered that he had absconded ; indeed
it was evident, and the Sheriff acknowledged, that according to the evidence taken, the matter had a very
suspicious aspect, although there was no direct proof
against the Doctor. It was proved that he had attempted to bleed the patient, but had not succeeded,
and that at that time the old Laird was black in the
face.

When it began to wear nigh night, and nothing farther could be learned, the Sheriff-clerk, a quiet considerate gentleman, asked why they had not examined
the wright who made the coffin, and also placed the
body in it ? The thing had not been thought of ; but
he was found in court, and instantly put into the witness's box, and examined on oath. His name was
James Sanderson, a stout-made, little, shrewd-looking

man, with a very peculiar squint.   He was examined
thus by the Procurator-fiscal.

" Were you long acquainted with the late Laird of
Wineholm, James ?"

" Yes, ever since I left my apprenticeship ; for I
suppose about nineteen years."

" Was he very much given to drinking of late ?"

" I could not say.   He took his glass geyan heartily."

" Did you ever drink with him ?"

" O yes, mony a time."

" You must have seen him very drunk then ?   Did
you ever see him so drunk that he could not rise, for
instance ?"

" O never ! for, lang afore that, I could not have
kenn'd whether he was sitting or standing."

" Were you present at the corpse-chesting ?"

" Yes, I was."

" And were you certain the body was then deposited in the coffin ?"

" Yes ; quite certain."

" Did you screw down the coffin-lid firmly then, as
you do others of the same make ?"

" No, I did not."

" What were your reasons for that ?"

" They were no reasons of mine—I did what I was
ordered.   There were private reasons, which I then

wist not of. But, gentlemen, there are some things connected with this affair, which I am bound in honour not to reveal—I hope you will not compel me to divulge them at present."

" You are bound by a solemn oath, James, which is the highest of all obligations; and for the sake of justice, you must tell every thing you know; and it would be better if you would just tell your tale straight forward, without the interruption of question and answer."

" Well, then, since it must be so : That day, at the chesting, the Doctor took me aside, and says to me, ' James Sanderson, it will be necessary that something be put into the coffin to prevent any unpleasant flavour before the funeral ; for, owing to the corpulence, and inflamed state of the body by apoplexy, there will be great danger of this.'

" ' Very well, sir,' says I—' what shall I bring ?'

" ' You had better only screw down the lid lightly at present, then,' said he, ' and if you could bring a bucketful of quicklime, a little while hence, and pour it over the body, especially over the face, it is a very good thing, an excellent thing for preventing any deleterious effluvia from escaping.'

" ' Very well, sir,' says I ; and so I followed his directions. I procured the lime ; and as I was to come privately in the evening to deposit it in the coffin, in

company with the Doctor alone, I was putting off the
time in my workshop, polishing some trifle, and thinking to myself that I could not find in my heart to choke
up my old friend with quicklime, even after he was
dead, when, to my unspeakable horror, who should
enter my workshop but the identical Laird himself,
dressed in his dead-clothes in the very same manner
in which I had seen him laid in the coffin, but apparently all streaming in blood to the feet. I fell back
over against a cart-wheel, and was going to call out,
but could not ; and as he stood straight in the door,
there was no means of escape. At length the apparition spoke to me in a hoarse trembling voice, enough
to have frightened a whole conclave of bishops out of
their senses ; and it says to me, ' Jamie Sanderson !
O, Jamie Sanderson ! I have been forced to appear to
you in a d——d frightful guise !' These were the very
first words it spoke,—and they were far frae being a
lie ; but I hafflins thought to mysell, that a being in
such circumstances might have spoke with a little more
caution and decency. I could make no answer, for my
tongue refused all attempts at articulation, and my lips
would not come together ; and all that I could do, was
to lie back against my new cart-wheel, and hold up my
hands as a kind of defence. The ghastly and blood-
stained apparition, advancing a step or two, held up

both its hands, flying with dead ruffles, and cried to me in a still more frightful voice, ' O, my faithful old friend ! I have been murdered ! I am a murdered man, Jamie Sanderson ! and if you do not assist me in bringing upon the wretch due retribution, you will be d—d to hell, sir.' "

" This is sheer raving, James," said the Sheriff, interrupting him. " These words can be nothing but the ravings of a disturbed and heated imagination. I entreat you to recollect, that you have appealed to the great Judge of heaven and earth for the truth of what you assert here, and to answer accordingly."

" I know what I am saying, my Lord Sheriff," said Sanderson ; " and am telling naething but the plain truth, as nearly as my state of mind at the time permits me to recollect. The appalling figure approached still nearer and nearer to me, breathing threatenings if I would not rise and fly to its assistance, and swearing like a sergeant of dragoons at both the Doctor and myself. At length it came so close on me, that I had no other shift but to hold up both feet and hands to shield me, as I had seen herons do when knocked down by a goshawk, and I cried out ; but even my voice failed, so that I only cried like one through his sleep.

" ' What the devil are you lying gaping and braying at there ?' said he, seizing me by the wrists, and

VOL. I.   P.

dragging me after him.   ' Do you not see the plight
I am in, and why won't you fly to succour me ?'

"I now felt to my great relief, that this terrific apparition was a being of flesh, blood, and bones, like
myself ; that, in short, it was indeed my kind old
friend the Laird popped out of his open coffin, and
come over to pay me an evening visit, but certainly
in such a guise as earthly visit was never paid. I soon
gathered up my scattered senses, took my old friend
into my room, bathed him all over, and washed him
well in lukewarm water ; then put him into a warm
bed, gave him a glass or two of warm punch, and he
came round amazingly. He caused me to survey his
neck a hundred times I am sure ; and I had no doubt
he had been strangled, for there was a purple ring
round it, which in some places was black, and a little
swollen ; his voice creaked like a door hinge, and his
features were still distorted. He swore terribly at
both the Doctor and myself ; but nothing put him
half so mad as the idea of the quicklime being poured
over him, and particularly over his face. I am mistaken if that experiment does not serve him for a
theme of execration as long as he lives."

"So he is then alive, you say ?" asked the Fiscal.

"O yes, sir ! alive and tolerably well, considering.
We two have had several bottles together in my quiet
room ; for I have still kept him concealed, to see what

the Doctor would do next. He is in terror for him somehow, until sixty days be over from some date that he talks of, and seems assured that that dog will have his life by hook or crook, unless he can bring him to the gallows betimes, and he is absent on that business to-day. One night lately, when fully half-seas over, he set off to the schoolhouse, and frighten-ed the Dominie; and last night he went up to the stable, and gave old Broadcast a hearing for not keep-ing his mare well enough.

" It appeared that some shaking motion in the cof-fining of him had brought him to himself, after bleed-ing abundantly both at mouth and nose; that he was on his feet ere ever he knew how he had been dispo-sed of, and was quite shocked at seeing the open coffin on the bed, and himself dressed in his grave-clothes, and all in one bath of blood. He flew to the door, but it was locked outside; he rapped furiously for something to drink; but the room was far removed from any inhabited part of the house, and none re-garded. So he had nothing for it but to open the window, and come through the garden and the back loaning to my workshop. And as I had got orders to bring a bucketful of quicklime, I went over in the forenight with a bucketful of heavy gravel, as much as I could carry, and a little white lime sprinkled on the top of it; and being let in by the Doctor, I de-

posited that in the coffin, screwed down the lid, and
left it, and the funeral followed in due course, the
whole of which the Laird viewed from my window,
and gave the Doctor a hearty day's cursing for daring
to support his head and lay it in the grave.——And this,
gentlemen, is the substance of what I know concerning this enormous deed, which is, I think, quite sufficient.   The Laird bound me to secrecy until such
time as he could bring matters to a proper bearing
for securing of the Doctor ; but as you have forced it
from me, you must stand my surety, and answer the
charges against me."

The Laird arrived that night with proper authority,
and a number of officers, to have the Doctor, his son-
in-law, taken into custody ; but the bird had flown ;
and from that day forth he was never seen, so as to be
recognised, in Scotland. The Laird lived many years
after that ; and though the thoughts of the quicklime made him drink a great deal, yet from that time
he never suffered himself to get *quite* drunk, lest some
one might have taken it into his head to hang him,
and he not know any thing about it.   The Dominie
acknowledged that it was as impracticable to calculate what might happen in human affairs as to square
the circle, which could only be effected by knowing
the ratio of the circumference to the radius.   For
shoeing horses, vending news, and awarding proper

punishments, the smith to this day just beats the world. And old John Broadcast is as thankful to Heaven as ever that things are as they are.

END OF THE FIRST VOLUME.

EDINBURGH
PRINTED BY BALLANTYNE AND COMPANY,
PAUL'S WORK, CANONGATE.

RETURN TO the circulation desk of any

University of California Library

or to the

NORTHERN REGIONAL LIBRARY FACILITY
Bldg. 400, Richmond Field Station
University of California
Richmond, CA 94804-4698

ALL BOOKS MAY BE RECALLED AFTER 7 DAYS
2-month loans may be renewed by calling
    (510) 642-6753
1-year loans may be recharged by bringing books
    to NRLF
Renewals and recharges may be made 4 days
    prior to due date

DUE AS STAMPED BELOW

SEP 7 1996